MISSISSIPPIANS IN THE GREAT WAR

MISSISSIPPIANS IN THE GREAT WAR

Selected Letters

COMPILED AND EDITED BY
ANNE L. WEBSTER

UNIVERSITY PRESS OF MISSISSIPPI ❧ JACKSON

www.upress.state.ms.us

Designed by Peter D. Halverson

The University Press of Mississippi is a member of the Association of American University Presses.

Copyright © 2015 by University Press of Mississippi
All rights reserved
Manufactured in the United States of America

First printing 2015

∞

Library of Congress Cataloging-in-Publication Data

Webster, Anne L. (Anne Lipscomb)
Mississippians in the Great War : selected letters / compiled and edited by Anne L. Webster.
pages cm
Includes bibliographical references and index.
ISBN 978-1-4968-0279-8 (cloth : alk. paper) — ISBN 978-1-4968-0280-4 (ebook) 1. World War, 1914–1918—Mississippi. 2. World War, 1914–1918—Personal narratives, American. 3. Mississippi—History, Military—20th century. 4. Soldiers—Mississippi—Correspondence. 5. Soldiers—United States—Correspondence. I. Title.
D570.85.M7W43 2015
940.4'12762—dc23

2015008903

British Library Cataloging-in-Publication Data available

TO SIGRID AND DONNA, WHO ARE FIGHTING THE BIGGEST BATTLE OF ALL

One day... people will have forgotten any of this happened. This war, these deaths, this demolition. Oh, not for some time, but eventually it will fade. Take its place amongst the layers of the past. Its savagery and horrors replaced in popular imagination by others still to come.

—KATE MORTON, *THE HOUSE AT RIVERTON*

CONTENTS

ACKNOWLEDGMENTS { XI }

EDITORIAL NOTE { XIII }

WORLD WAR I TERMINOLOGY { XV }

INTRODUCTION { 3 }

1. AMERICANS ENTER THE WAR { 11 }

2. CROSSING THE POND AND GETTING READY { 69 }

3. OVER THE TOP AND INTO BATTLE { 117 }

4. ALL QUIET ON THE WESTERN FRONT { 205 }

EPILOGUE { 219 }

BIBLIOGRAPHY { 221 }

INDEX { 227 }

ACKNOWLEDGMENTS

SOME YEARS AGO, MY HUSBAND, HAROLD, AND I VISITED GREAT BRITAIN during the month of November. We were both struck by the World War I memorials and poppy decorations commemorating the lives lost. To this day, the British people stop whatever they are doing at the eleventh hour of the eleventh day of the eleventh month and pay silent homage to the men and women who served during that time. Their quiet, dignified observance was a wake-up call to me about how little we Mississippians (Americans) do to honor and commemorate the sacrifice of our servicemen and -women. I salute all of you.

Professor Bill Storey of Millsaps College has no idea that he planted a seed for this project when he came to the state archives about five years ago and asked what resources we might have on World War I for a class project. At the time of his visit, the archives had only a few related manuscript collections and scattered material in the Works Projects Administration county files. His inquiry led me to search for more.

Appreciation also goes to several former colleagues at the Mississippi archives, Mike Allard, Clinton Bagley, Jeff Giambrone, and Grady Howell, who suggested newspapers to examine and offered information regarding military terms and unit designations. Chad Daniels, director of the Armed Forces Museum at Camp Shelby, also gave assistance.

Thanks also to the librarians at Eudora Welty Library (Jackson) and Quisenberry Library (Clinton) for their patience as I checked and rechecked World War I books from their holdings. The library staff at Mississippi College were kind to let me use their facility as a quiet space to compile and reflect.

Craig Gill, Anne Stascavage, and Courtney McCreary at the University Press of Mississippi have been very patient and encouraging, offering suggestions at each step along the way. Special mention goes to copyeditor Ellen Goldlust, who went to great lengths to make this a better book.

A final note of appreciation goes to friends and family who quietly supported the project and offered encouraging words when my energies waned.

EDITORIAL NOTE

MANY OF THE LETTERS REPRODUCED HERE ARE TAKEN FROM PUBLISHED sources such as newspapers, which frequently printed correspondence from local men and women—soldiers, aviators, sailors, and YMCA and Red Cross workers. Other letters have been transcribed from originals found in collections at the Mississippi Department of Archives and History, Jackson. Some of the writers were barely literate, while others went on to become published authors and journalists. The letters are generally reproduced as they appeared in the published versions or as they were written, although spelling and occasionally punctuation have been regularized, and obvious typographical errors have been corrected. Editorial additions appear in brackets; [?] indicates a missing or illegible word.

Letter writers have been identified as much as possible. The information used comes primarily from draft registration cards, census returns, city directories, and other resources accessible through ancestry.com, findagrave.com, and www.geni.com. Additional information has been taken from US Selective Service System, *World War I Draft Registration Cards*; Mississippi, Veterans Affairs Board, World War One Statement of Service Cards; Mississippi State Board of Health, Death Certificates; Social Security Death Records, Mississippi Department of Archives and History subject files, and the American Battle Monuments Commission (www.abmc.org). All other sources are cited individually.

Even though some of the writers included have only tenuous connections to Mississippi, the fact that their letters appeared in the state's newspapers means that their experiences affected Mississippians who read those letters.

WORLD WAR I TERMINOLOGY

AEF	American Expeditionary Force, the US armed forces in Europe
BOCHE/BOSCH/BOSCHE	a German, especially a soldier
BULLY BEEF	corned beef
CANTONMENT	a temporary military camp
DOUGHBOY	a US infantryman
FRITZ	a German soldier; more commonly used by British soldiers than Americans
HUN	a German soldier
JERRY	a German soldier; a jerry was a chamber pot, which German helmets were thought to resemble
NO MAN'S LAND	the strip of ground between the lines of trenches on the front, occupied by neither side but sometimes the scene of skirmishes and hand-to-hand combat
OVER THE TOP	over the bank of a military trench
OVER THERE	in Europe as a member of the American Expeditionary Force
SAMMIE	an American soldier; used on government posters and patriotic advertisements
SLACKER	a person who evades military service
SOS	Services of Supply, the unit of the US Army responsible for logistical support of the fighting men; also can refer to Save Our Ship, a distress call
TOMMY	a British soldier

MISSISSIPPIANS IN THE GREAT WAR

INTRODUCTION

BETWEEN APRIL 2, 1917, AND OCTOBER 31, 1918, 56,740 MISSISSIPPIANS left their homes and families to serve in what was called the Great War.[1] Their reasons varied and overlapped: to escape poverty, small-town living, the endless toil of sharecropping; to see the world; patriotism; because they were drafted and had no choice.

 The Great War, the first truly global conflict, began in 1914 and ultimately involved twenty-three Allied countries against the forces of the Central Powers (Germany, Austria-Hungary, and Turkey) before hostilities came to a close on November 11, 1918.[2] By the end of 1914, the war on the Western Front had become a war of position, confined largely to trench warfare. It was said that the spade had become as important a weapon of war as the rifle: everywhere along the line, men were digging for their lives.[3] All but a small tip of Belgium was occupied by German troops, who also controlled about one-tenth of France's territory, including many of the country's coal mines and industrial areas. Over the next three years, the front line did not vary by more than ten miles, and the fighting devastated both France and Belgium.[4] This book presents Mississippians' story of the Great War, using their own words to describe their part in it.

Americans were stunned and bewildered, though not completely surprised, when war broke out in Europe in the summer of 1914 and almost overnight most of the continent was drawn into an upheaval of massive proportions. Europe had not seen a major war since 1815, and neither leaders nor the soldiers who waged the twentieth-century battles had fully absorbed the technological advances that had changed the nature of war over the preceding century. The Industrial Revolution, with its new weapons (for example, artillery and machine guns) and methods of transportation, as well as advances in communication and ways of preserving and handling food profoundly affected the conduct of war. Barbed wire, for example, was originally designed to control cattle but became a strangely vital part of the World War I fighting.[5]

On August 19, 1914, US president Woodrow Wilson issued a proclamation of neutrality. Many new Americans had fled Europe to escape conflict there and had no desire to fight against family and friends in the Old Country. At heart, however, Wilson was pro-Ally, as were most Americans, many of whom could trace their lineage back to Anglo-Saxon lines, and those sympathies grew as wartime propaganda reached American ears. Large numbers of Americans began to question how their country could remain neutral and out of the war. Moreover, the United States had endured a recession in 1913 and 1914, and British and French orders for war materials spurred the US economy, further reducing public sentiment in favor of neutrality.[6] And as the war effort improved the economic situation in the North, poor Mississippians, both black and white, began to leave behind their sharecropper existence in favor of jobs in cities such as Chicago, Detroit, and New York.

When war broke out, both Germany and Britain possessed major fleets concentrated in the North Sea. Germany initially did little to interfere with the British naval forces but gradually imposed blockades and declared a submarine war zone around the British Isles. Any vessel entering the zone ran the risk of attack by a German U-boat, a clear threat to US shipping. Between February and May 1915, U-boats sank about ninety vessels of various kinds, including the England-bound *Lusitania*, a passenger ship also carrying munitions that was torpedoed without warning off the coast of Ireland; 128 of the 1,198 persons lost were Americans.[7]

The incident led President Wilson reluctantly to conclude that the US military had to move toward active preparedness. Still desperately striving to maintain peaceful coexistence, however, Wilson now undertook the role of world mediator, thinking that the surest way to keep his country out of war was to bring the conflict to an end before the United States could be dragged in. In January 1917, the president declared before the US Senate that the war needed to end with "a peace without victory." His comments dismayed the Allies but did not satisfy the Germans, who responded by reopening unrestricted submarine warfare: all merchant ships in the war zone would be sunk.[8]

The same month, British intelligence intercepted a telegram from German officials instructing the country's ambassador to Mexico to propose an alliance between the two countries. In exchange for helping the German war effort, Mexico would receive territory—Texas, New Mexico, and Arizona—that it had previously held but had lost to the United States. The British did not share the contents of the telegram with President Wilson until February 24, and the American press published it on March 1, inflaming public opinion in favor of war.[9] Nevertheless, President Wilson remained hesitant.

In March, German U-boats sank four unarmed and clearly marked American merchant ships, killing thirty-six. On April 1, the US ambassador in Paris, William Sharp, submitted a report to his superiors, including Wilson, vividly describing the horrors suffered by the people of France at the hands of German forces:

> Accepting an invitation, kindly extended to me several days ago, I yesterday visited many of the French towns recently retaken in the invaded territory, making the trip in a military automobile. I was accompanied by military attaché [Carl] Boyd.
>
> I regret to say that I found the various reports in circulation in, and doubtless forwarded to American newspapers, of the deplorable conditions in those towns are in no way exaggerated. With very few exceptions the places visited by me, though few in comparison, numbering upwards of thirty, had been quite destroyed by the Germans before evacuating them.
>
> The destruction wrought in the larger towns of Roye, Ham, and particularly the once thriving and attractive city Chauny, was complete. In many of the other smaller villages scarcely a house remains with its roof intact. A scene of desolation reigns everywhere over the reconquered territory.
>
> This is true not alone where the possibly excusable military operations carried out by the Germans protected their retreat, by the blowing up of all the bridges and the destruction of the means of telegraphic and telephonic connections, including portions of railway lines, and the blocking of highways by the felling of many trees, but also where, as far as the eye could see, nearly all the fruit trees had either been cut down or exploded so as to completely ruin them.
>
> Not only were the towns destroyed for no seeming military reason, but every private house along the country highways, including some of the most beautiful chateaux of great value, had been completely gutted by explosives or by fires systematically planned.

> *I am told that before the retreat commenced the agricultural implements found on the farms were also destroyed. Blackened walls of what must have been extensive manufacturing establishments were to be seen in many places, the salvage of which, including likewise that of most of all the other structures destroyed, would scarcely pay for the removal of the debris.*
>
> *The churches and cathedrals in some of the towns had been reduced to a mass of ruins by the Germans either by heavy charges of explosives or by fires.*
>
> *At Ham I was told by the mother of six children that her husband and two daughters, one of the age of fifteen and the other eighteen, had been carried away by the Germans at the time of their evacuating the town, and upon her remonstrating she had been told that as an alternative, she might find their bodies in the canal in the rear of her home.*
>
> *The same woman informed me that out of that town's total population several hundred people had been compelled to accompany the Germans, nearly half of whom were women and girls above fifteen years of age.*
>
> *There is the belief that a large number of French people in the evacuated towns and surrounding country were forced by the Germans to go with them in their retreat, from the fact that so comparatively few are now to be found.*
>
> *After traversing a distance of more than one hundred miles in this invaded territory, I left with the conviction that history records no parallel in the thoroughness of destruction wrought either by a victorious or a vanquished army.*[10]

With Sharp's report in hand and American casualties escalating, Wilson hesitated no more. On April 2, 1917, he appeared before a joint session of Congress and called for a declaration of a state of war with Germany, and four days later, Congress passed the measure. The first American war casualties occurred on April 28, 1917, when a U-boat torpedoed and sank an armed US steamship, the *Vacuum*, about 120 miles west of Scotland's Hebrides Islands, killing twenty-four.[11]

On May 23, Major General John J. Pershing, head of the American Expeditionary Force (AEF) in France, boarded the British ship *Baltic* in New York Harbor to sail for Liverpool. He and the 187 officers, enlisted men, and civilians who accompanied him onboard comprised the entirety of the AEF. While they were still at sea, a Mississippian, Lieutenant Colonel Fox Conner,

When General John J. Pershing and his small officer crew landed, they were the AEF. (Quekemeyer Papers, Box 6, Folder 8)

began working to plan the artillery needs for what was anticipated to be a force of half a million men. Ultimately, Conner served as Pershing's "right-hand man in building the American Expeditionary Force."[12]

The United States was essentially unprepared to support the declaration of war and had never before attempted military operations against an overseas nation on such an enormous scale, and US land, sea, and air forces were totally inadequate to the task. The army had a grand total of 208,034 men, while the Aviation Section of the Signal Corps had only 130 pilots and 55 planes; the navy had just 197 ships. The government requisitioned all available American ships, arranged with foreign governments to receive as many ships as could be spared, and seized ninety-one German-owned vessels in American ports.[13]

On May 18, 1917, Congress passed the Selective Service Act, which drafted more than two million men into service in three branches of the army, the Regular Army, the National Guard, and the National Army, though the distinctions among them soon became blurred. Another two million volunteered. The act required all males between the ages of eighteen and forty-five to register for the draft and did not permit men to purchase exemptions or hire substitutes, as had been the case during the Civil War. The government would "select" draftees for duty where they would be most useful. As a result, many men received exemptions to work in key industries such as shipbuilding and agriculture. Local draft boards were established for each county and for each city with a population over thirty thousand. While men from all racial groups were subject to the draft, blacks and Native Americans remained segregated within the military and were employed primarily in noncombat roles.[14]

Thirty-two large camps in the South and "cantonments" (mostly in the North) were rapidly constructed for the training of the new recruits, and schools were established or enlarged for the training of specialists. The amount of training received by the troops varied. The average new division received six months' training in the United States, two months' training in France, and one month in a quiet sector before engaging the enemy. However, in the final phases of the war, when heavy losses required replacements to be rushed to the front, some individuals went into battle with very little training.[15]

Mississippians answered the draft notice calls and registered in large numbers—344,724 by September 12, 1918. According to the *Biennial Report of the Adjutant General of the State of Mississippi, 1918–1919*, 173,082 African Americans registered in the state, while 171,424 whites did so. Nearly 60,000 Mississippians served.[16]

American forces were slow to reach Europe and did not arrive in large numbers until 1918. When they finally got there, they were welcomed not only by the exhausted Allied troops, who had already suffered hundreds of thousands of casualties, but also by the civilian population. In France, the young Yanks found primarily women dressed in black, old men, children, and wounded soldiers. Despite their sense of total desperation, they were overjoyed by the new arrivals.[17]

Even with the US entry into the war, Germany appeared to hold the upper hand. The United States was far away and unprepared, and German leaders believed that their U-boats would prevent American forces from arriving quickly enough and in numbers enough to influence the outcome of the conflict. In addition, the collapse of Russia in early 1918 meant that Germany could transfer fifty divisions and five thousand guns from the Eastern Front to France, resulting, German leaders hoped, in a speedy victory. With numerical superiority on the Western Front for the first time in the war, the German commander, Erich Ludendorff, began to prepare for a major advance in the West.[18]

The book is divided into four thematic chapters, each of which describes one aspect of American activity in the war. Within each chapter, letters are presented in chronological order. When appropriate, annotation has been provided to explain terminology and events for readers.

NOTES

1. *Biennial Report*, 76.
2. *Who Declared War and When*.
3. Stokesbury, *Short History*, 16.
4. Thoumin, *First World War*, 116.
5. Stokesbury, *Short History*, 13–14, 15.
6. Welsh, *USA in World War I*, 6; Bailey, *American Pageant*, 710–11.
7. *War to End Wars*, 83; Bailey, *American Pageant*, 715–16.
8. Bailey, *American Pageant*, 721, 722.
9. Stokesbury, *Short History*, 221; *Teaching with Documents*.
10. *William Sharp on the German Retreat*.
11. Bailey, *American Pageant*, 723–24; Biggs, "Review," 3.
12. Brown, "Fox Conner," 207; Brown and Skates, "Fox Conner."
13. Stamps and Esposito, *Short Military History*, 298; "Transporting the Troops"; Biggs, "Review," 3; Horne, *Source Records*, 172; *This Fabulous Century*, 208.
14. Welsh, *USA in World War I*, 12, 13; Bailey, *American Pageant*, 740.
15. Stamps and Esposito, *Short Military History*, 300.
16. *Biennial Report*, 50, 62, 76.
17. Hallas, *Doughboy War*, 17.
18. Thoumin, *First World War*, 343; Stamps and Esposito, *Short Military History*, 205–6.

He was just a long, lean country gink
From 'way out West where th' Hop-toads wink,
He was six feet two in his stockin' feet,
An' kept gittin' thinner th' more he'd eat.
But he was as brave as he was thin,
When th' war broke out he got right in.
Un-hitch'd his plow, put th' mule away,
Then th' old folks heard him say:
Good-by Ma! Good-by Pa!
Good-by Mule, with yer old hee-haw!
I may not know what th' war's about,
But you bet, by gosh, I'll soon find out.
An', O my sweetheart, don't you fear,
I'll bring you a King fer a souvenir;
I'll git you a Turk an' a Kaiser, too,
An' that's about all one feller could do!

—WILLIAM HERSCHELL, "LONG BOY," 1917

- 1 -

AMERICANS ENTER THE WAR

WHILE THOUSANDS OF MISSISSIPPI MEN STEPPED UP AND VOLUNTEERED their services, the state did have to deal with shirkers who sought to avoid their duty.

J. W. GEORGE, US ATTORNEY, TO WILLIAM J. BUCK, PRIVATE SECRETARY TO GOVERNOR THEODORE BILBO, JUNE 20, 1917 (MISSISSIPPI, GOVERNOR, [1916–1920: BILBO], WORLD WAR I CORRESPONDENCE AND PAPERS, SERIES 878, BOX 1321)

Dear Will:
In compliance with your request in regard to the prosecution of slackers, I would state the following:
Except in the case of emergency, and this is rare, all slackers must be arrested upon complaint and warrant. Such complaint will be made by this office upon the following information: reliable witnesses as to the age of the alleged slackers, and as to the precinct at which they should have registered. The chief service which the local officers render is in the verifying of the two items of precinct-residence and age, and they should furnish you this advice with the names of some witnesses as to each of these.
Very truly yours,

J. W. George

DOUGAL KITTERMASTER, E BATTERY, CANADIAN ANTI-AIRCRAFT, FRANCE, TO PARENTS, JULY 11, 1917 (*NATCHEZ DEMOCRAT*, AUGUST 19, 1917)

Canada native Dougal Kittermaster (1894–1973) moved to Chicago as a young boy and was a student at the University of Illinois when war broke out. He officially joined the Canadian Expeditionary Force in May 1917 and was promoted to captain prior to sailing for Europe the following month (*Chicago Examiner*, June 7, 1917). His uncle, Natchez resident George E. Gurd, shared this letter with the newspaper.

Dear Mother and Dad:
I mailed you a note yesterday morn telling you I was all OK, as I haven't had time to write a letter since arriving in France, but will do so now.
There are a number of large Canadian hospitals there, each one capable of taking care of twenty-five hundred cases, you will see that there are plenty of nurses. Friday morn we had to censor mail all morn, but before lunch we set out for a very fashionable watering place about five miles from camp. Street cars run there every half hour, so we got there in time to have a swim before lunch; that night after we got back we were issued with our gas helmets and went through the lachrymatory gas chamber to make sure that the helmets were all in efficient working order. The following day we had to march a party of men to the gas school about five miles away, where we all received instructions on gas, lectures on how it is used, and finally we had to go through the chlorine gas chamber as a final test for the helmets.[1] *We got back to camp that night about five P.M. and found that we were to leave the following morn to come here.*
Our train left at eight A.M. Sunday and we got to our destination about two P.M., a point about [censored] miles behind the line. From there we phoned to the battery who sent back a car for us and we finally got up to the battery headquarters at seven P.M. Found that "Viv" Bishop, who was one of my seniors at RMC and who is the Canadian Permanent Force, is the major commanding the battery, and the acting captain (he is still a subaltern) is a fellow named McLelland, who I came over with from Canada on the old Hesperian in June 1915. The only other officer I knew before is Geoff Hale, who was at UCC when I was there.
Monday morn Mack and I were posted to our sections and we came up the same afternoon. I am with the left of most northern section and our position is about [censored] yards behind the front line. That is about [censored] miles you see, so we are out of range of all but the

longest range guns that Fritz has, and he doesn't bother using them back this far. Of course, we are farther back than a section usually is, but for tactical reasons, which I cannot mention, we have to stay here. The other officer with this section is a fellow called MacNaughton, from Toronto, and seems to be a very decent chap.

Yesterday I started my duties as a section officer. As it rained during the morning there was no flying so we did not go out until three P.M., when it had cleared up. We then waited all afternoon and never saw a Hun plane until eight P.M., when one came within extreme range. I took my first shot then and let him have it. To all appearances my twelfth round seemed to get him as he fluttered down about five hundred feet, but he then got control and ran for his own lines. He was about four miles away when I fired, so I was rather pleased having at least taken a few feathers out of him on my first shoot.

Today is my long duty day, which means that I got up at 3 A.M. this morn, took the guns into action at 3:30 (just before dawn) and stayed there until 10 A.M. when I was relieved by MacNaughton. I came back here and had breakfast and am now writing this (11:30 A.M.) I have lunch at 12:30 and go back to the guns at 1:30 and stay there till dark (now about 9:30), when I come back and have dinner. Tomorrow I am only on from 10:00 to 1:30, when I relieve MacNaughton, and I have the rest of the day to myself. This morn we only saw about four Hun planes and none of them came within fifteen thousand yards of us, so we had no shooting at all. Of course, the Hun isn't usually as inactive as this, but I think it is because he is very active on some other part of the front as announced in this morn's Official Communique.

Will tell you about the country, etc., in my next.

All my love, as ever,

Your loving son,

Dougal

PS Don't forget to send the parcels out each month as I asked you to in my last letter from England. My address is simply, "E" Battery, Canadian Anti-Aircraft, BEF France. If you see Char tell her that I haven't had a moment to write her yet but will try to do so today.

1. Gas was used as a weapon in warfare for the first time on August 22, 1915, when German forces deployed chlorine gas against French troops during the Second Battle of Ypres. For the remainder of the war, both the Allies and the Central Powers used gas against

their enemies. Soldiers in the trenches hated it, and its unpredictable nature, especially if the wind shifted, made it as potentially dangerous to the sender as well as to the intended target (Welsh, *USA in World War I*, 21).

F. R. PRICE, COMPANY C, 8TH US ENGINEERS, FORT BLISS, TEXAS, TO A. F. HERMAN, EDITOR, *PONTOTOC SENTINEL*, AUGUST 5, 1917 (*PONTOTOC SENTINEL*, AUGUST 16, 1917)

My dear Mr. Herman:
Please change the address on my Sentinel *to Frank R. Price, Co. "C," 8th US Engineers, mounted, Camp Stewart, Fort Bliss, Texas.*

Our battalion name has been changed to the 8th regiment of US Engineers Mounted, and mail must be addressed that way to insure prompt delivery.

I haven't gotten my copy of The Sentinel for the last week in July and I don't want to miss any more for I want to keep up with the Pontotoc happenings as closely as possible.

We are still camped near El Paso but are expecting to be moved to some other camp some time soon. There is no timber here and as we use round timber for building military bridges we have no material handy for use in engineer drills. For that reason we need to be moved to some place where we can get to growing timber. We are getting accustomed to the sand and heat now though and don't mind that so much. We are all ready for a move however, we want to see some trees and grass again for the desert grows nothing but sage and mesquite brush besides, of course, the cactus. We are not bothered with centipedes or tarantulas for we are not in a new camp and they don't come into camp very often. I'm glad of it, for they make rather disagreeable "pets."

I have been to the Masonic temple in El Paso several times now and enjoy my visits there very much, they have a fine library with a writing room attached, then there are game tables of all kinds that are free to visiting brothers. It is surely a privilege to be able to go in and use the library and writing rooms and I go in every time I am in town. I haven't attended any of the meetings yet but expect to go in for some of them as soon as we get through on the target range. Our regiment started shooting this morning and we won't be allowed to go to town until we get through with target practice. Will be on the range for at least three weeks and I'm going to be good and ready for something to break the monotony of camp life before our time is up.

As Frank Price writes, engineers had to use round timber for bridge-building drills because no other material was available in the vicinity. (Camp Shelby Photograph Collection, Box 22, Folder 52, No. 3)

Quite a number of us are taking lessons in French now so as to be able to talk to the girls when we get to France. There is no telling when that will be though we hope it will be some time soon for we are all tired of the monotony of camp life and want to see some excitement. We have quite a job cut out for us when we get there though. We are to take charge of the railroads, mines, power houses, water plants and the engineering work of every class and there'll be enough to keep us all busy. There'll always be military engineering work such as laying out trenches, building barbed wire entanglements, bridges, roads and electric lines also. We will be busy enough to keep out of mischief alright. The regulars don't get into much mischief though. It's the militia that set the civilians against the soldiers nearly every time. The bunch down here last year so worked on the feelings of the El Paso people that they will never have any use for a soldier again. They like the soldier only as long as his money lasts and the men are all pretty well disgusted with the El Paso people over it.

We had a big review and parade in honor of a Russian count who is over here in the interest of the Russian government last Tuesday and it was quite an affair. Every soldier in the El Paso district was in it and as there are about twenty thousand of us here there was quite an imposing *parade. I wish the people back home could have seen it for it was a pretty parade.*

Please change the address to the one I have given and keep The Sentinel *coming.*
With best regards, I am
Yours truly,

F. R. Price

❧

THE WAR EFFORT INVOLVED MORE THAN JUST MEN VOLUNTEERING TO fight: the folks at home were encouraged to get involved in some way. Everyone was challenged to "Do Something," as in this 1917 song by Edward Laska:

Everybody isn't built to go and fight;
But we always want to do the thing that's right.
Trenches need brave men of health,
And war loans need the people's wealth,
But ev'ry Yankee Doodle can do something to help.
For when we hear our duty call us, we never lag.
All that Uncle Sam must do is just wave the flag;
And every mother's son or daughter
Tries to help on land or water,
Someway, it doesn't matter how.
Just go and do something, do something do what you can,
It's up to you, every woman or man,
If you can fight, then go do your share,
Or do something here that will help them out there,
A thousand jobs now have to be done;
And if we do them, the war will be won,
So go and do something, do something,
Do what you can, for dear old Uncle Sam.
Just go and do something, do something do what you can.

W. J. LEPPERT, GULF DIVISION DIRECTOR, AMERICAN RED CROSS, NEW ORLEANS, TO DR. J. Q. FOUNTAIN, BAY ST. LOUIS RED CROSS CHAIR, AUGUST 15, 1917 (BAY ST. LOUIS SEA COAST ECHO, AUGUST 25, 1917)

Red Cross has urgent call from Maj. Grayson Murphy[1] for an enormous quantity knitted woolen articles. Here is a cablegram from Major Murphy:

Last winter broke records for cold and misery among people here. Dread coming winter; finds us without supplies to meet situation. Urge on behalf of our soldiers and those of our allies who will suffer from frozen trenches, and also thousands of French and Belgian refugees and repatriates being returned through Switzerland. Everyone here looks to America to begin shipping at once 1,500,000 each of warm knitted woolen articles already requested. They must come before cold weather, and, in view of shortage of fuel and other discomforts they will be of incredible value both in military and civilian work.

We ask the Bay St. Louis Chapter to furnish a definite number of the requirements. Your allotment is Three Hundred Sweaters, Three Hundred Mufflers, Three Hundred Pairs Wristlets, Three Hundred Pairs Socks. Full instructions will follow in two days. Ask your members to furnish [finish?] all knitting work now on hand and clear the deck for action. We want every chapter to have its chance to do its part in making good on this call for help from France. You are urged to place copy of foregoing part of this message, including cablegram from Major Murphy, in the hands of all newspapers with request to give full publicity to this call. Then get knitting committee together and have them lined up for rush job.

W. J. Leppert

1. Grayson M.-P. Murphy (1878–1937) was an American banker and businessman who served as head of the American Red Cross Commission in Europe.

ANOTHER IMPORTANT PART OF THE WAR EFFORT WAS KEEPING UP MOrale, an effort embraced by those in the entertainment field. Among the songs that sought to encourage America's young men was "We're Going Over," by Andrew B. Sterling, Bernie Grossman, and Arthur Lange:

> *The Major wrote the chorus but he fell down on the verse*
> *The Colonel tried to write it but he only made it worse*
> *They called in Captain Cuttle but he missed it by a mile*
> *So they left it to the Sergeant of the file*
> *Said he, we need no verse at all to this here little thing,*
> *So they went and taught the Sammies how to sing.*
> *We're going over, we're going over,*
> *They want to settle up that fuss, and they put it up to us,*
> *So what do we care, So what do we care,*
> *We'll go sailing cross the foam*
> *And we'll show them what the Yankee doodle boys can do*
> *Then we'll all come marching home.*

....

CHRIS H. COOPER, 43RD SQUADRON, KELLY FIELD, SOUTH SAN ANTONIO, TEXAS, TO EDITOR, *BRANDON NEWS*, AUGUST 17, 1917 (*BRANDON NEWS*, AUGUST 23, 1917, WORLD WAR I SUBJECT FILE)

Chris H. Cooper (1895–1954) from Rankin, Mississippi, served overseas from February 26, 1918, to January 30, 1919, with various aviation units.

> *Editor News:*
> *Would you allow me a little space in your paper to tell of the army aviation corps?[1] We are out from town about six miles and are equipped with cars to and from.*
>
> *We use an immense territory of prairie land for field flying practice.*
>
> *A large number of citizens from the country surrounding flock here to view the machines as they sail upward.*
>
> *There are as many as a dozen in the air at once.*
>
> *The boys work on machines and are taught to fly them. Mornings, the boys drill from 7:30 until 11:30; afternoons they are given passes to visit town if desired.*
>
> *At supper time they march in a single file, and are seated at long tables, which are supplied with meats, stew, watermelon, peaches and coffee or tea with puddings and pies with jelly. We are well fed and the food well prepared.*

After supper roll is called and the boys make for the musical instruments to pass away the lonely afternoons and forget for the moment the good homes they left. When the music starts there is singing and rejoicing, because the men feel like life is worth living to serve Uncle Sam.

We have good preaching on Sundays, also a nice YMCA that uplifts the men in a religious way.

The boys that compose my squadron are half from New Orleans and nearby towns, while the other boys are from the east and west. We have learned to like each other, and are willing to fight side by side for our country's cause.

Look out for the boys from old Rankin; you will hear from them later on in the conflict.

Best wishes to you and all my friends,
Sincerely,

Chris. H. Cooper

1. Soon after the conflict broke out, it became clear that airplanes would play a significant role. The United States quickly established flying schools and by the end of the war had trained more than eleven thousand fliers (Stamps and Esposito, *Short Military History*, 298).

༄༅

FIGHTING IN THE AIR BECAME VERY HEAVY DURING JULY 1917. BY THE end of the month, however, the Allies had secured relative mastery of the sky after undertaking an air offensive with five hundred British and two hundred French planes (Thoumin, *First World War*, 400).

....

RALPH PRICE, HEADQUARTERS, 127TH AERO SUPPLY SQUADRON, KELLY FIELD, SAN ANTONIO, TEXAS, TO FATHER, AUGUST 1917 (GILL-PRICE FAMILY PAPERS, BOX 4)

Dearest Papa:
Well I have been here exactly two weeks now. But it does not seem that long. I guess the reason for it is that I have been working all the time.

There are about seven squadrons leaving today. Where? Nobody knows. More than apt they are headed for New York, and from there to France. Everything out here will be moved away by the 1st of the month, except the flying school, and that seems to be growing larger all the time. Only last week they received a train load of machines. Papa it sure is fascinating to watch them way up in the air doing all kinds of circles, spiral twists, loop the loop, and such stunts as that. They have some very good aviators here to be so young in the game.

We are not very much longer to stay here. Just as soon as the squadrons get organized they are shipped out to some other place to begin work. As we have about reached that stage, we will be moving before long. There is one consolation, if we do have to go to France we won't be in such close proximity to the firing line. You see as I have an office job, I will not be exposed as much as I would be if I were in the field. I am certainly glad that I did not take that Sergeant position in the National Army, for I like this work much better.

Papa if our squadron is ordered to France, you must help mother not to worry so much, I know it will be lots harder on you all than it will be me. I don't mind going now nearly as much as I did at first. I have learned more about this war and then if I do have to go I will not be in the trenches. That is the thing that has worried me all the time. Devotedly,

Ralph

THE US NAVY WAS AN ALL-VOLUNTEER SERVICE. ALTHOUGH NAVY SHIPS were the first US forces to enter the war, they did not see battle but were used in convoy duty, mine laying, and troop transport. Early in May 1917, six destroyers arrived in Ireland for urgently needed antisubmarine operations (Bailey, *American Pageant*, 738).

EARL DOUGLAS COTTON, 13TH COMPANY, NAVAL RESERVE RADIO SCHOOL, CAMBRIDGE, MASSACHUSETTS, TO ANNIE L. COTTON, AUGUST 29, 1917 (EARL DOUGLAS COTTON PAPERS, FOLDER 1)

Earl Douglas Cotton (1899–1918) was a native of New Orleans who moved to Jackson before the war.

Dear Mother:
We arrived here all OK and after taking a shower bath, without towels, we reported and after our life history, or something on that order, and physical examination we were assigned to the 13th company, until we can be reassigned. Already I have met quite a few boys from home, Kinberger and a few others; they are going to try to have me transferred to their company. I hope so. There are just fourteen hundred of us here—that's all—a few—with plenty more coming. We have not been to class yet—I suppose that they are giving us time to rest up. As today is our whole first day here it was wash day and believe me, some washing was done. I must have washed a ton of stuff. Believe me we are treated great, our feed this morning for instance was "shredded wheat," pineapple slices and coffee and fish & milk for our wheat—no effects so far—fish & milk. For dinner—pudding, soup, tea, hash, carrots and some other articles, some days we get chicken, cake—etc. Ice cream five cents extra. We feed like the gentlemen of the Navy should.

How did you like the pictures? They seemed pretty good—they should be—I paid enough for them. Tell "bur" when pay day comes I'm going to ship him a Harvard Radio School USN band we wear on our blue hats.

Tell 'em all hello for me and not to worry as I will be here only until the end of December—the course lasts sixteen weeks, then we will be shipped home to wait our call to service, active.

You can make me a "comfort-kit" bag. I have the articles to put in the spaces. Look in one of the windows downtown, they're on exhibition. Your son,

Earl

UNDER THE SELECTIVE SERVICE ACT OF 1917, EACH CITY OR COUNTY WAS required to furnish a certain number of men for military service, with that number determined based on population. Though both white and black men were required to register and were subject to the draft, military units and transportation arrangements remained strictly segregated. Instructions from Washington required that the first contingent of draftees include only whites, since these men would form the nucleus of the army (Biennial

Report, 6–14). Some Mississippi counties, however, had majority-black populations, and officials in those counties had difficulty filling their quotas for white men. The clerk of the Columbus draft board apparently wrote to Governor Bilbo suggesting that Lowndes County could make up the deficit with African Americans.

WILLIAM J. BUCK, PRIVATE SECRETARY TO GOVERNOR THEODORE BILBO, TO J. R. RANDLE, COLUMBUS BOARD CLERK, SEPTEMBER 26, 1917 (MISSISSIPPI, GOVERNOR, [1916–1920: BILBO], WORLD WAR I CORRESPONDENCE AND PAPERS, SERIES 878, BOX 1322)

My dear Mr. Randle:
Your letter of the 25th Inst. Received.
   In instructions to send 16 per cent of your county's quota in negroes was sent under the authority of the War Department. The governor has no authority in the world to authorize a decrease or increase of this number. If your quota based on 16 per cent, in negroes is twenty-four, then you can only send twenty-four. The 40 per cent quota you speak of, to be made up of whites, has nothing in the world to do with the 16 per cent of negroes, and it cannot be filled up by sending negroes in addition to 16 per cent of the net quota your county was instructed to furnish. I want to repeat that this entrainment of negroes in no way or manner can be counted as against 40 per cent you speak of. If the District Board has not certified back a sufficient number of whites to make 40 per cent, why then of course you cannot furnish that. However your Board and all others were instructed to send additional whites as rapidly as certified back, and that no special traffic arrangements were necessary for this, and none are contemplated for the whites. However, special traffic arrangements are to be made for the negroes, beginning on the 3rd. and the American Association of Railways, under the direction of the War Department, are now making up the schedule showing the date on which the several boards shall entrain their negro quota, the route they are to take, etc. Now this schedule will be sent to your board and all others the moment it is received from the War Department and the information as to the exact date cannot be given you or any other board until we receive this. Now please send the quota in negroes on the date to be specified in the schedule to be sent you. This will reach you in ample time. You understand instructions can only go from his office

as they come from the War Department. A number of local boards entrained on dates different from those provided in the schedule formerly sent out and this has caused much confusion, correspondence with the railroads and dissatisfaction.
Yours very truly

Private Secretary

PS I do not wire you because the War Department has requested that no wires be sent to or received from local boards unless absolutely necessary.

F. R. PRICE, COMPANY F, 314TH US ENGINEERS, CAMP FUNSTON, KANSAS, TO A. F. HERMAN, EDITOR, *PONTOTOC SENTINEL*, SEPTEMBER 28, 1917 (*PONTOTOC SENTINEL*, OCTOBER 4, 1917)

My dear Mr. Herman:
You will no doubt be surprised to know that I am away from Texas but I'm glad to be able to say that such is the case and that there is no more Texas sand for me, I hope.

I'm now in the National Army[1] with the rank of sergeant. Twenty-six men from the 8th Regiment of engineers with I were transferred up here to instruct the drafted men. All of us were made sergeants immediately on arrival though we knew that would be done before we left El Paso. The best men in the regiment were suggested to send, but evidently there was a mistake in my case for I wasn't even a first-class private before I left El Paso. From "buck" private to First Sergeant was some promotion, too.

I am at present on duty as company supply sergeant and handle all clothing and equipment used by the company. It's a good job, ordinarily but has been a fright for work in these new companies. I've been busy all day and until late at night issuing and fitting clothing. We have 165 men in the company at present and they each have two complete outfits of clothing. A little later on the company will be filled up to 250 men but I won't mind that for it will be much easier to get clothing for the men then. At present uniforms are hard to get and about half of this company is wearing blue denim overalls and jackets in place of the regulation olive drab uniform.

I'm glad indeed that I was given a chance to come up here for if I make good here I'll stand a chance of going on up higher. But believe me I want to get to drilling, I want to break in a new man and turn the store room over to him as I can get out and show some of these men how a regular army man can get about on the parade ground. We have only two drill sergeants in the company at present and I am needed on the drill ground badly. I suppose I'll get out some next week, though.

This camp is quite an improvement over the one we had at Camp Stewart. We have two-story frame barracks buildings that are built to stand the winter.

They are electrically lighted and will be heated by steam radiators, I understand, and it's already cold in this country. We have had several heavy frosts and of course are getting ready for lots more of them. I issued overcoats to the men tonight. They'll come in handy these mornings too.

The fare in the National Army is about the same as the Regular Army gets and that's pretty good as long as we are in the barracks. I've no kick against the Regular Army but I'm glad I was transferred into the National Army. And the drafted men are learning the drills fast. They are becoming soldiers right along. They've quite a bit to learn in a short time too. They won't have much time for loafing.

I'd certainly like a furlough home for a few days but there's not a chance now. I won't be able to get one before Christmas at least and maybe not then. But I'm going to try to get back then for a few days.

Please send my Sentinel *to the address given below for I have missed the two copies that were sent to El Paso since I have been up here. I left El Paso on the 14th and got here on the night of the 16th but have been too busy to write to any one. There seems to always [be] something for the supply sergeant to do and if I didn't have a good supply of patience, along with the other supplies, I'd just about be driven crazy. Every man thinks he ought to have just a little better fit than any one else has and they always run to me to try to get it.*

I must stop now for its long past "taps" and good soldiers are supposed to be in bed at taps.

Give my regards to the Pontotoc people and please hurry The *Your friend,*
F. R. Price

1. In August 1918, the Regular Army, the National Guard, and the National Army merged to become the US Army (Stamps and Esposito, *Short Military History*, 298).

NOLAN STEWART, CAMP PIKE, ARKANSAS, TO WILLIAM HENRY FITZ-HUGH, MEMBER OF THE VICTORY FUND COMMITTEE FOR THE SALE OF WAR BONDS, NOVEMBER 17, 1917, GREENVILLE DAILY DEMOCRAT-TIMES, NOVEMBER 24, 1917)

Born in Jackson, Mississippi, Nolan Stewart (1863–1926) studied medicine at the University of Nashville Medical Department and Vanderbilt University School of Medicine, graduating in 1888. He practiced medicine in Jackson and served as the head of the State Insane Asylum before serving in the war. He subsequently returned to Jackson and resumed his private practice.

My dear Mr. Fitz-Hugh:
I am writing to advise you of our progress, for I fully appreciate the great interest you feel in what we are doing.
All of our equipment has arrived except the extra parts body for the ambulance equipment and the motorcycles.[1] *All this equipment should arrive within the next few days, and when received we will have the full quota of motor equipment. I know you will take pardonable pride in the statement that, when the missing equipment arrives, we will be the only company at Camp Pike to be fully equipped. None others will be fully equipped this side of the sea. We assembled the ambulances ourselves and while it was a big job, we succeeded admirably and I advised the Division Surgeon that the ambulances were ready for service. In recognition of that fact the Division Surgeon ordered me, from December 1, to do the ambulance service for the entire cantonment. When you come to think that we will have forty-two thousand men, that the cantonment covers three thousand acres, you will readily appreciate that it will be a big undertaking, but, if you will pardon a slang expression, "we will be there with the goods."*
I will keep you advised from time to time of our progress. We are working and working hard, in fact, I have never worked as hard in my life, and I think we are making good headway. It is my ambition to have a company of which Mississippi may be proud and the men I brought with me feel the same way about it.
Sincerely yours,

Nolan Stewart

1. Washington, Warren, and Hinds Counties supplied the Red Cross with ambulance units costing nearly forty thousand dollars (*Greenville Daily Democrat-Times*, November 24, 1917, 6).

PHILIP WOLFSON, CASUALTY COMPANY 4, CAMP PIKE, ARKANSAS, TO A. F. HERMAN, EDITOR, *PONTOTOC SENTINEL*, DECEMBER 10, 1917 (*PONTOTOC SENTINEL*, DECEMBER 13, 1917)

New York City native Philip Wolfson (1896–1932) was living in Pontotoc, Mississippi, and working as a merchant when he registered for the Selective Service in June 1917. He was inducted into the army on November 20, 1917, and served as a medical clerk at Camp Pike, Arkansas, until his discharge on March 15, 1919. After the war, he worked as a clerk in a department store in Reading, Pennsylvania.

> Dear Friend Herman:
> "In the streets of by and by one arrives at the house of never!" I must plead guilty to traveling through said streets, but I haven't quite reached the house of "never." That long delayed letter is now a realization.
> All of the fellows who were in the crowd that left on Nov. 20 are still together, and with exception of a few colds, are getting along as well as could be expected. One man, Casey Hall, a Pontotocian was discharged the other day, due to the fact that he had weak lungs, and his back was injured in some manner.
> We have just had our third and last anti-typhoid injection, and take it from me, the boys are mighty glad it's over. It is not very painful, but it gives a fellow quite a bit of annoyance for a couple of days.
> The vaccinations are generally successful, but I received two inoculations, both of which failed to "take." When two fail, they never try a third time.
> Most of the boys have received some "good eats" from home, but there are quite a number who seem to have been forgotten by their folks. Would suggest that the folks include some butter, sweet potatoes, a jar of preserves, and some biscuits and corn bread, as the boys don't get these foods here. And don't forget candies. In the cold weather, prevalent here now, a fellow appreciates sweets.
> We've been here nineteen days today, and are still under quarantine. There are nearly two hundred men in the barrack, three states being represented—Alabama, Mississippi and Louisiana, and every other day or so, a case of measles will pop out, and the regulations seem to be, that ten days additional quarantine is "clapped on" for every new

contagious case. At that rate, the conclusion is inevitable, that we are in for a perpetual quarantine. In fact, I have met three or four fellows who have been under quarantine for thirty days and more.

Our bunch is still casuals—that is, we haven't been assigned to a regular company or branch of service, like the field artillery, or machine gun battalion, etc. Each company has a lieutenant as commanding officer, and our lieutenant, Russell Ballard, is a mighty nice fellow, well liked by all the boys. Below the lieutenant are the sergeants, who attend to the drilling, and enforcing of the lieutenant's commands and orders and there are two corporals beneath the sergeants.

The weather, since our stay at this camp, has, on the whole, been very satisfactory. Like the South in general, we've been blessed recently with four or five inch snow, and a thermometer reading of ten to twenty degrees above and haven't done a thing in the last three days but eat, sleep and stand around the stove.

Last Thursday evening the boys received a pleasant surprise by having uniforms issued them. The outfit consists of a hat, hat cord, flannel top shirt, coat, breeches, leggings, and a pair of good army shoes, which the majority of the fellows needed badly. Yarn hose and underwear as yet been issued. Also coat and breeches are khaki instead of O.D's. [olive drabs], which are regulation winter wear. In the army, however, a fellow can get along much better by eliminating "why" from his vocabulary.

Another praise-worthy feature of the army is the regulation that no man can draw pay, who is unable to sign his name to the pay roll. No cross marks go here. And the result of this is that a number of fellows are forced to attend night school here in the barracks, where two or three fellows with some teaching experience work with these men to get them to write their names. And these fellows go to it, because they know that to get money on pay day it is positively necessary that the pay roll be signed in person.

I received quite a surprise the other day when I bumped into Joe McCutcheon drilling a bunch of "rookies." We had quite a chat, discussing the Pontotoc boys, the work he was doing, etc. His company had left him for Louisiana, due to the fact that he was laid up in the base hospital with a case of mumps.

Was very glad to read in the Commercial Appeal a week or two ago that Pontotoc was fortunate to secure Mr. Young as pastor, again, for the Methodist church.

You Pontotocians will have an opportunity of seeing a soldier boy when Preston Wells gets home within a day or two. A furlough is being *fixed for him on account of serious illness of his brother. He lives two miles below Algoma.*

Well, Mr. Herman, I've written enough for the "nonce," I am sure, and will close with best wishes to yourself, "Bill T." and Wayne. Kindly remember me to Mrs. Herman, and here's hoping this finds her in good health.

I'd like to take this opportunity of expressing through your paper my best regards to all my Pontotoc friends. Only regret that it is impossible to correspond with as many as I'd like to.

As I've just received a package of "good eats" from my folks in Louisville, Ky., and am just "itching" to investigate same, will have to close now.
Your friend,

Phil Wolfson

1. "By the streets of 'By and By' one arrives at the house of 'Never'" is a saying about procrastination attributed to Miguel de Cervantes.

....

FREDERICK W. PERRIE, AT SEA ABOARD THE USS *VULCAN*, TO "FREDDYE AND FAMILY," DECEMBER 21, 1917 (*NATCHEZ DEMOCRAT*, DECEMBER 30, 1917)

"Natchez boy" Frederick W. Perrie (1891–1961) moved to Massachusetts after the war and worked as an engineer. The *Vulcan* was a coal carrier commissioned in 1909. It was deactivated in 1912 but put back into service on February 25, 1914. During the war, it carried coal, supplies, and ordnance for the Atlantic Fleet Cruiser Squadron (*Dictionary of American Naval Fighting Ships*, 7:565).

Dear Freddye and Family:
How I wish I could call back a year ago today—I was coming home to spend a very happy Christmas, but this year I am flying around dodging the waves for Uncle Sam, but thank goodness it is nothing harder than waves.

On Dec. 2 we were laying in Boston harbor, at the Charlestown Navy Yard, and a SOS call came in that a British steamer was in distress and, of course, they had to pick out us, and we got orders to proceed at once to the rescue, and for a while we all wondered who was coming to our rescue. Well, we got under way in a few hours and hit the troubled sea looking for the lost ship, but did not find her until Friday, the 7th, but the storm was so bad we could not help her, so we lost her until Sunday, the 9th, then we tried to help her in to port, but the storm again drove us away, so Sunday evening we started trying to save the crew, but it took until Monday morning about eleven o'clock to do that, on account of the rough sea, and on Monday evening at three o'clock she went to her watery grave, carrying with her—counting ship and cargo—$6,250,000; a nice pile of money to stand by and see the water close up over, wasn't it? But, wait a minute, look at ourselves here: we were expecting to follow her at any time—seven hundred miles from where the Titanic went down—so we had to get busy to save our own lives; and we managed to get within fifty miles of Boston by Thursday at midnight, and Friday morning at three o'clock another storm—the worst we had experienced—hit us, and when we came to ourselves, we were one hundred miles back at sea, with very little coal and food, and two crews of men to feed, but the wind settled enough so that, by Saturday evening, we made port again, but both ships and crew were a sick looking lot, but we got food, coal, and water; and here we are out at sea again, but if another such storm hits us in the fix we are in now, good night nurse. We are on our way now somewhere for repairs.

After we got back from our exciting trip, we, of course, wanted mail, and when it came aboard Saturday evening, we were all very happy to think we were able to receive and read it again.

I got my box with the pecans and cake in it, and, dear, I could never tell you, if I tried a lifetime, how good that cake tasted, because it was too rough at sea to cook, and we had been eating hard-tack and canned goods.

There were ten men in the room when I opened that box, so I got the bread knife and cut ten slices out of it, and if you [could] have heard them and seen their faces, you would have felt well repaid for all the work and trouble it was to make it for it was certainly good.

I hope you have all had a very merry Christmas and wish you a happy new year, because I know it will all be over when I get a chance to mail this, and before it gets to you, but you will know I was thinking of everyone of you, and that I love all of you, but Uncle Sammie and the war don't care if it is Christmas or Sunday—you must get along the best you can.

Maybe some day I can spend another happy Christmas with you, as the last one was.

Thanking you again for the cake and pecans, and wishing for you and every one in the house a happy New Year. I am as ever, lovingly, Your sailor boy somewhere at sea,

Frederick

....

FINLEY WATSON TINNIN, CAMP BEAUREGARD, LOUISIANA, TO *NATCHEZ DEMOCRAT*, DECEMBER 24, 1917 (*NATCHEZ DEMOCRAT*, DECEMBER 27, 1917)

The Reverend Finley Watson Tinnin (1887–1962) served as pastor of Natchez's First Baptist Church before resigning to enter YMCA work during the war. Tinnin subsequently became a pastor in Shreveport, Louisiana, and held the post of editor of the *Louisiana Baptist Message*.

Dear Democrat:
Many of my friends in Natchez asked that I let them hear from me when I was located in the camp. However, as I am kept rather busy selling stamps, giving out stationery to the boys who want to write home, wrapping Xmas packages that will bring happiness to fathers, mothers and sweethearts back home; preaching, and a thousand and one other things, I don't have time to write many letters.

It is Christmas-time in Camp Beauregard. The boys all feel it, too. They were badly disappointed a few days ago, when the government shut down on their furlough, and instead of letting 50 per cent go home, made it 5 per cent, and later cut out the 5 per cent.

The people back home can hardly imagine what "Christmas-at-home" means to a bunch of fellows who are experiencing their first Xmas away from home; how Christmas around the old family hearth-stone takes on a golden halo to the American soldier.

But while the fellows are disappointed, still they are brave and courageous. I have been among a great many of them, and have still to hear the first one of them whining or complaining.

Yesterday was my first religious service in the camp. I preached to a fine crowd of Red Cross nurses and doctors at the base hospital. They worship in a YMCA hut adjoining the hospital. I have never addressed a more attentive and appreciative audience. I told them that at that hour (eleven A.M.) the Christian people all over America were assembling in their several churches and were remembering in their prayers, in a special way, their boys and girls, in the army and the Red Cross. It would have filled your heart to overflowing to have seen how the eyes of the nurses and doctors filled with tears when I mentioned home.

Sunday night I preached to the boys in my hut. We had a fine bunch. Most of our fellows are in the 114th engineers, made up of Louisiana, Arkansas and Mississippi boys. And, believe me, they are a fine lot of fellows. Any state would be proud of them.

Have seen quite a number of Natchez boys. They all look fine and are in good spirit—even though most of them will spend Xmas away from home.

Excuse the rambling, disjointed letter, please; I write "between the acts," of selling stamps and wrapping up Xmas packages for the boys.

Good-bye for this time.
As ever,

Finley W. Tinnin
Religious Secretary, Hut No. 4, Camp Beauregard

PS Send us some new magazines and novels. Many of our boys are quarantined, and they need something to read.

WILLIAM MAURY FERRELL TO FRANK FERRELL, JANUARY 1918 (FERRELL FAMILY PAPERS, BOX 2)

Ashland, Mississippi, native William Maury Ferrell (1892–1971) was a laborer on his family's farm prior to the war. He subsequently returned to his hometown and became a salesman.

Dear Frank:
I enclose a PO money order for ten dollars in payment for that which I got from you when I was at home. We had a pay day about ten days ago, but I haven't had a chance to go to the PO to get money order until today.

We have been having some rough winter here lately. It seems to be pretty general. I noticed that it snowed in New Orleans.

The health of this camp is fairly good now. We still have some mumps cases. Have had a few cases of pneumonia. Had one death from pneumonia.

The personnel of our medical staff is pretty good. About two of them I think, had no practice in civil life and broke into the Army to get jobs.

The diagnoses used in army are pretty complete and thorough, but the treatment is rotten.

Nobody seems to know when we make a move from here. When we do move I guess we will go to Fort Logan at Houston, Texas. We are in the 5th Division, and their headquarters are at Houston.

Some British army officers and non-coms, are here giving instructions in the uses of gas and gas masks. Tests with real gas were given today. No one was overcome by gas, but it is pretty severe on eyes, when mask is off. The mask is put on in five seconds. The mask itself consists of a rubberized airtight cloth covering for face with goggles for the eyes, and has a rubber tube about 1¾ inches in diameter and 10 inches long, with a metal container about 3 × 6 inches attached on end, for a secret preparation. The British officer in demonstrating it said, it was nobody's business what the metal container held. The upper end of the rubber tube has a mouthpiece that is held to the mouth by the teeth, and you breathe into tube through mouth. Attached on tube near mouthpiece is a small para rubber exhaust pouch. Air can go out of this pouch, but it has a valve preventing air from coming in from outside. The mask can be kept on for five hours.

Am writing mamma tonight, too.

Am well.

Love to all,
Your brother,

Maury

....

ROBERT E. ROSENBERGER, CAMP SHELBY, HATTIESBURG, MISSISSIPPI, TO EDITOR, *BAY ST. LOUIS SEA COAST ECHO*, JANUARY 14, 1918 (*BAY ST. LOUIS SEA COAST ECHO*, JANUARY 26, 1918)

Indiana native Robert E. Rosenberger (1869–) lived in Wisconsin and Louisiana before moving to Mississippi sometime after 1910 and going to work as a clerk/bookkeeper in a shipyard. He later returned to Louisiana and became a land agent for a sawmill.

Dear Editor Echo:
When I entrained, so to speak, at Bay St. Louis for Hattiesburg on July 31st last, I had high hopes of gaining admission to the second officers' training camp, which for Mississippians was to be held at Leon Springs,

Texas. I had worked and worried for weeks in preparing to face the examining board and as a consequence was apprehensive that I might be found lacking in avoirdupois. It did not reassure me any to glance at the plump figure of my fellow candidate, Robert Taylor, as he sat opposite me in the coach, but his ready-flow of cheerful conversation dispelled any system of gloom which might threaten to gather and allowed small chance for my thoughts to dwell for any appreciable time of my possible infirmities. When the hour arrived I appeared before the board and in short order was found to be deficient in the matter of physical requirements. I was pronounced just sixteen ounces underweight, but the principal obstacle which barred my further progress was my teeth or rather my lack of them. I was bitterly disappointed and did not fail in my first letter home to admonish my growing sons and daughters to profit from my experience and diligently and daily cleanse and care for their own good grinders against a possibly similar time of trial. When I left home at Waveland I cast an anchor to windward by taking with me my chest of carpenters tools so that in case I was denied the opportunity to prove myself a good soldier I might find an opportunity of enlisting in the industrial army that was then mobilizing for the great purpose of constructing a great camp for the training of soldiers on a range of hills near Hattiesburg.

Upon my arrival at the camp site seeking employment I was very much impressed by the feverish activity displayed by the crowds of men who were moving about in a ceaseless effort to align themselves with some foreman who might possess the willingness and necessary authority to have their names duly engrossed on the pay roll.

The contractors on their part through their managers and superintendents, seemed quite as anxious to avail themselves of the services of all able bodied applicants, and after viewing the spectacle for a time I felt positive that if they who control the destiny of the Central Empires would have witnessed the determination and enthusiasm displayed by all concerned they would have hastened to request their Uncle Sam to recall the dogs of war, ere they [?] their teeth firmly set in the Teuton trousers. I was not long in realizing however that this was but a beginning and that the crowds of workmen would be multiplied many times both in numbers and enthusiasm before many weeks had passed. My employment number, 2299, indicated that 2,298 persons had been given work in advance of me, which was a very low figure when compared with the total number enrolled before the work covered by the original contract was completed. Besides the men, there were hundreds of teams employed as well as a large number of trucks. The idea of those in charge seemed always to be to build everything straight and strong, but to build it quickly, little time was wasted in smoothing the rough places, they being left to be polished by use. Taking into consideration the great number of men employed, the newness of the organization, the distance and manifold difficulties met with in the prosecution of the work, one cannot help but wonder at the excellent time made in the erection of the thousand and more buildings which now adorn the Camp Shelby hills. The water supply of the camp was very good and its cooking and distribution, especially during the months of August and September, taxed the executive ability of a number of water superintendents and the endurance of many men, trucks and teams. Water was obtained from spring creeks on the grounds and pumped by gasoline engines to a great number of distributing stations and centers of use.

The grading and graveling of roads through the camp, which work kept pace with the building, was of itself a stupendous undertaking. Many hundreds of carloads of gravel were used and now many miles of the finest drives in the state traverse the camp.

The road conditions between Hattiesburg and the camp was included in the work and hundreds of motor cars now pay tribute daily to the result achieved.

The camp was erected for the use of troopers from Indiana, Kentucky, and West Virginia, and with the arrival of the first contingents from those states the Mississippi boys who had been doing guard duty for many weeks folded their tents like the Arab, and silently stole away.

And it also can be said to their credit that they stole nothing else, at least not from me.

We felt like kin to the Mississippi boys and regretted to lose them, but we soon learned that real soldiers were not less than 100 percent human, and that if treated at all square they would respond in kind regardless of whether they hailed from the pine punctured hills of Mississippi or the banks of the Wabash.

Considerable good natured chaff has been thrown at us Southerners in regard to the lack of merry sunshine. We have been rationing out to our guests through the weather bureau.

Our weather man admits he did make sort of a mess of it, but his intentions were good all the while, when he threw the cold into high, he expected to hear all the soldier boys from the latitudes remark that it was just like the weather from home, but it seems that their woolies were a little slow in arriving and their enthusiasm for ice and snow was at a very low ebb and as a consequence some of the compliments they paid us for our atmospheric exhibitions would not bear repeating here.

In their hearts though they know there is a wide difference between the temperature here and in their home towns, but we're not going to be mean enough to even suggest their owning up to it.

We will plead guilty to having staged a change of temperature of over forty degrees on one occasion within twelve hours and admit that it appeared like an unhospitable proceeding and one likely to shatter the faith of many of the boys in the authenticity of the Sunny South, but when they take the trouble to compare notes and realize how little the weather at Camp Shelby has interfered with drilling and outdoor maneuvering and how greatly it has interfered with such work in camps situated farther North, we believe they will have a good word or two for "Dixie" when they swap tales with their comrades from other camps when they meet somewhere or nowhere in France.

Everything considered, Camp Shelby is one of the most desirable in point of location from an army standpoint. The climate conditions are much more agreeable than at most other camps. The natural drainage of the grounds is excellent, the water supply is very good. Transportation facilities to and from the camp are now adequate and the statewide ban on the liquor traffic make the maintenance of law, order and discipline a comparatively easy matter. The amusing and entertaining of the boys in camp by means of sports and games and by the conduction of reading, writing and recreation club houses at central locations under the direction of the YMCA while very satisfactory, will from now on be speeded up and added to from time to time until this feature of the camp life will be a credit alike to the department and to the community.

The city of Hattiesburg has raised a fund for that purpose and other organizations besides the YMCA are giving substantial assistance. One of the most attractive buildings on the grounds has been erected by the YMCA and is known as the hostess house. From it will radiate a gentle, but powerful influence that will tend to soften the harsher actions and speech of men only when thrown together in large numbers.

It is indispensable that our fighting forces must be kept in good spirits and to insure this they must be entertained and amused and

we must bear in mind that the same pleasures that they indulge in in civil life will most strongly appeal to them in their new environment. Consequently, it would seem best to give them anything they want in the way of recreation and amusement, so long as it is not vicious or immoral. It is estimated that there has been expended in the building of Camp Shelby approximately three million dollars, and the end is not yet. There is ample room on the present site for the doubling of the capacity of the camp and in my estimation no wiser move could be made unless the Kaiser "kwits." Meanwhile, let each of us do his humble task a little faster and a little better than we ever did it before and the eventual assertion of right by might is assured.
Sincerely,

R. E. Rosenberger

....

HENRY PAUL CAPDEPON, PARRIS ISLAND, SOUTH CAROLINA, TO CHARLES G. MOREAU, EDITOR, *BAY ST. LOUIS SEA COAST ECHO*, JANUARY 24, 1918 (*BAY ST. LOUIS SEA COAST ECHO*, FEBRUARY 2, 1918)

Henry Paul Capdepon (1898–1979) joined the US Marine Corps at age eighteen and served with the 4th Marine Brigade Headquarters in France. He later worked for the US Post Office in Bay St. Louis (*Bay St. Louis Sea Coast Echo*, June 14, 1979, 2).

Dear Mr. Moreau:
Noting the willingness in which you publish letters from lads in the army and navy, I would like to have a little space to say something about our well-picked clan, "the Marines," of the numerous advancements one can obtain in the Marine Corps and also to say a word to my many friends of Bay St. Louis.

I am a volunteer, enlisted in April 1917. This is a great life. Every man should grasp the opportunity to attain a military education. Glad to note that we have the best cantonment in the USA, everything modernized in every way. We being noted for our trench digging and self-service are worthy of such praise. If that is not satisfactory come to Parris Island, SC, and make a tour of our camp.

This island is situated off the coast of South Carolina, the Atlantic washes its shores, sixty miles from Savannah, Ga. The Marines put it on the map. When I first came down it looked desolated, but it happened to be under supervision of the best officers in the service. Within two weeks it was a city of barracks.

Our officers, most of them are from the ranks and they are fully qualified for such honorable positions.

The camp is divided into four separate barracks. A recruit first enters the quarantine, where he is physically and mentally examined, then sworn into service and receives his uniform and equipment. After learning the principal foot movements of our method of drilling he is advanced to the "manoeuvre grounds." The recruit takes his first hike under heavy marching order, a distance of two miles, he also takes his first lesson in modern trench digging and learns squad movements. After two weeks training at this barracks he advances to the "new camp." This is the place where he enjoys the life of a "Boot Marine." Drills from six to six and do police work in between. This continues for six weeks. Then for the rifle range. All qualify for sharp-shooter or better. Our coaches are the best obtainable. Spend about two weeks on the range learning the parts of the rifles, throwing hand grenades and again he learns some more trench digging. First line trenches and communication trenches are our specialty. Takes from fourteen or sixteen weeks to complete training. After that a man is fit for service abroad.

When the training is completed one has a chance to take the position he enlisted for. For instance, I had an opportunity to enter the post-office as clerk, I am now assistant postmaster.

Been down for ten months. Often wished to meet a man from my home town. Out of the many thousands of men who go through training here monthly, the only man I met was our well-known friend, Clement Bontemps, who is now transferred.[1]

Just received The Sea Coast Echo, for which I look for patiently and am disappointed if I don't receive it.

Am glad to say that I am from such a prosperous little town as Bay St. Louis, Miss. Can readily see that the Red Cross Chapters are doing their bit. Hoping the good work will continue, with regards to all, I am, Yours truly,

Henry Capdepon

1. Clement R. Bontemps (b. November 6, 1893) of Bay St. Louis served in France with the US Marines 6th Regiment and died on June 15, 1918, of wounds received in the Château-Thierry Sector.

VICTOR SYLVESTER ASHMORE, CAMP BEAUREGARD, LOUISIANA, TO A. F. HERMAN, EDITOR, *PONTOTOC SENTINEL*, JANUARY 1918 (*PONTOTOC SENTINEL*, JANUARY 31, 1918)

Pontotoc native Victor Sylvester Ashmore (1891–1970) was a farmer when he registered for the draft in June 1917. He was inducted on October 2, 1917, and served in the AEF infantry forces at the Second Battle of the Marne, where he lost two fingers. He went on to become a teacher at the agricultural high school in Kossuth, Mississippi, and later a supervisor for the Prentiss County Farm Service Agency.

Dear Editor:
Will you be kind enough as to print a description of the life of a prisoner in the army. Would it surprise you and my friends back there to know that I am in the guard house for thirty days for going home without a furlough and I want to ask those of you that I told a story about my pass to please forgive me for telling such an untruth. It is absolutely impossible for any one to get a furlough home, even if some of our people should die we could not go home as we are under a very strict quarantine, realizing that in a short time we would be leaving for France and that perhaps I would never get to see my people and friends again, I went home anyway and as a result I am in prison, some of you may consider me disgraced for life and will never associate with me again. I don't care who knows that I am in here when I did nothing more than go home to see my people and if you care to think any the less of me you have that privilege.

Some of you may not know what a guard house is, it is a row of tents just like the other boys stay in except they are guarded at all times to keep any one from escaping, as soon as we are put in here they take our hat cord away from us. We have been digging trenches for the past few days, but nearly every soldier has to dig trenches some time during their training. There are about sixty boys in here now and quite a number confined to their company street for ninety days and a sixty dollar fine, they have to help dig trenches too, several new ones are brought in every day so there isn't a chance to get lonesome. As far as the work is concerned I had rather do this than drill as it is much easier, but we have to work every day and Sunday too. Most of the boys that are in here are nice, well educated Christian boys that never paid out a fine in their life. They just got home-sick and went home without a furlough,

Victor S. Ashmore, ca. 1918
(findagrave.com)

and if anyone back there ever see their boys until the war is over they will have to do as we did. We are not permitted to talk to any one, of course we do but are not supposed to, also cannot salute any officer of "The Star Spangled Banner" when it is played, in other words we are supposed to be treated as convicts should be treated. Every morning we get up at 5:40, go to breakfast each one goes to their own company for their meals and they always send a guard along with a loaded gun to see that we be sure to come back. At seven o'clock we are lined up and marched out to dig trenches with a number of guards along, they are stationed all around the trenches to keep anyone from running away, however I don't think anyone would escape even if they had the chance, they do not work us hard at all, fact is, we work as we please almost. If it wasn't for the name of it, I had rather be here than in company street. We only work eight hours a day. Today is Sunday but we hauled wood this morning but it is so cold we are not doing any thing this afternoon.

Mr. Herman I would like for you to publish this for the simple reason that every one may know I am in here and why. I don't want any one going around whispering "have you heard the latest news? Victor Ashmore is in the guard house!" I can only say one thing. I certainly did enjoy my visit home and don't regret my trip in the least as I think it well worth thirty days in here and we are not treated as bad as you might think.

Most all the boys from home are getting along just fine but they are drilling them pretty hard. I wish for every one a happy, prosperous 1918 and a world wide peace.

Victor Ashmore

....

HENRY PERRY SUDDUTH, US NAVAL BASE, HAMPTON ROADS, VIRGINIA, TO EDITOR, *PONTOTOC SENTINEL*, FEBRUARY 25, 1918 (*PONTOTOC SENTINEL*, MARCH 7, 1918)

Born in Pontotoc, Mississippi, Henry Perry Sudduth (1895–1976) was working as a farm laborer in Greene County, Arkansas, prior to the war. He subsequently returned to Pontotoc and became a dairy farmer (*Pontotoc Progress*, November 11, 1976, 12).

Dear Editor:
If you will allow me space in your valuable paper I will give you a few glimpses of navy life. I enlisted December 15, at Memphis, Tenn., and was sent to Norfolk, Va., training station. On my way here I came through Nashville, Tenn., and Atlanta, Ga. There were 240 of us that came from Nashville. We stopped over in Atlanta for breakfast and the officer in charge had lunches fixed up for our supper and breakfast. We arrived at Norfolk December 17, at four o'clock and were given one blanket and mattress and a suit of underwear, ordered to take a bath and go to bed. The next day we were given a hammock and sixty dollars worth of clothes. I have eight suits, two blues, two dungers or overalls and four white ones. We were then put in a Company and assigned our bungalos. All our clothes were stenciled so we will know which garment is ours when we hang them on the clothes line. I enlisted as a fireman, therefore have not had very much drilling to do. We stayed at the

Norfolk Training Station a little over a month and then we were moved over to the Naval Operating Base at the old exposition grounds.

We have to scrub our hammock and clothes bags every week. While we were drilling we were inspected every day. We have to keep our clothes clean and neat and our hair cut short, go clean shaven and our shoes shined all the time. We have plenty to eat such as "spuds," beans, meats, fruits, cakes, bread and coffee. We do our own washing and sewing and take our turns in working in the mess hall. We are mustered every morning and march to the mess hall for our "chow." There is about two hundred of us quarantined as spinal meningitis germ carriers.

This is going to be a beautiful camp when it is finished. There is an aviation camp, there too, the hydroplanes are flying every day. If any of you boys back there want to enjoy life, have an easy time and see the world through a port hole, join the navy. We are paid twice a month, a fireman gets $36.20 a month, a seaman gets $32.
Yours for service,

H. P. Sudduth

RANDOLPH WILLIAM NICAISE, CAMP BEAUREGARD, LOUISIANA, TO CHARLES G. MOREAU, EDITOR, *BAY ST. LOUIS SEA COAST ECHO*, MARCH 11, 1918 (*BAY ST. LOUIS SEA COAST ECHO*, MARCH 16, 1918)

A native of Kiln, Mississippi, Randolph William Nicaise (1891–1972) was a graduate of Mississippi State University who served in the military from September 25, 1917, to March 6, 1919. He went on to work for the US Department of Agriculture (*Bay St. Louis Sea Coast Echo*, November 9, 1972, 4).

Dear Mr. Moreau:
Five months and a half have passed since I've been with the Colors. I am now in the 155th Infantry, US National Guard, which used to be the 1st Mississippi Infantry, so I may as well tell of my experiences that the boys at home, who will soon be called to service, may learn what they are missing or, rather escaping, for I mean what I said. A part of this original document to my older brother, Albert, who is now back at home making sweet faces at pretty girls, but he will soon be called to service to make some other faces, that is, "right face," "left face," and "about face!" which is about the first thing they teach a recruit.

Being with a Mississippi organization and lots of the boys I've known, time hasn't been so dull as perhaps it would have been otherwise. Anyway, I have tried to conceal my surprised appearance at the wonderful sights I've seen, because the boys would have made it public to my girl whom I've always made believe that I knew everything.

Some of the boys have kind of grumbled because of the poor accommodation we get, but as for myself I really feel like I had gone to a big picnic, gotten lost and never been found yet. It may be that it is because I never expected any "accommodations." One thing, I have not had to aggravate Pa this year for a pair of new overalls and coat and vest off the "cheap counter," when he made the annual trip to town. 'Spect though as spuds and beef are so high that I'd stood a poor chance to have gone with him to town this year.

I'm learning so much though that the folks will think when I go back home that I am perfectly polished.

The first thing that I learned was to do what I was told, so when they said "frog," I jumped. The next thing I learned was to always be on time. I think the school teacher said once that the adverb should not be placed between the word "to" and the infinitive, lest I get knocked out of something to eat, and then to be on time saves a guy "extra duty." Now I am learning to dodge all the work I can and "get by with it," but woe to the soldier who gets caught dodging, for he shall catch thunder the rest of his army life. I think I'll quit dodging and play "safety first."

Some of the boys have been talking about going to France, and fight the Germans, but I have not lost any sleep about it at night, and the dog-goned bugle calls me too early at morning for me to think about anything except "fall out," and answer roll call. When I get back home I'm going to have sister blow a bugle and whistle while I lie in one of Mama's soft beds and laugh at the "calling." I don't know just what all I have planned to do. I think I will teach my sister and little nephews to stand attention while I proceed to get "um" told.

Was kind of late about getting in line this morning. I saw "top" (first) sergeant write something in the little red book as I hurried out with my rifle; guess I get to spend the next two days in the kitchen. Took a bath today. First time I've been wet since I stood guard the other night in the rain. Uncle Sam has gone to a great deal of expense for us boys bathing facilities. I guess though he has a lot of money. I think I'll get another bath sometime as I felt pretty fresh and strong after that one. It sure is ahead of the "swimming pool" back home on the creek.

It's getting about time to blow out these white lamps, so I'll wait till some other time and write more.

Randolph Nicaise

EARL DOUGLAS COTTON, BOSTON, ABOARD THE USS *SIOUX*, TO "FOLKS AT HOME," MARCH 15, 1918 (EARL DOUGLAS COTTON PAPERS, FOLDER 2)

Cotton served as a radio operator on the *Sioux*, a cargo ship built in 1916 by the American Shipbuilding Company that was acquired by the US Navy on December 1, 1917, and commissioned as a unit of the Naval Overseas Transportation Service. The ship carried coal between stations along the East Coast for several months (*Dictionary of American Naval Fighting Ships*, 6:516).

Dear Folks at Home:
Whenever we are in port or during my spare time at sea I will try and write you as often as possible, but you must all accept the letter as meant for the whole —— family, for what I write in one is about all there is to say and that is very little for one sees very little at sea but a wide expanse of water and white capped waves. This scenery is of course very interesting to you but it is very hard to describe. We left Newport News, Va. Monday and arrived at the dock here in Boston Thursday at 11:30 A.M., so you see that we have made pretty good time. The distance from Norfolk to Boston is six hundred miles by sea, so you can imagine my thirty-five hundred mile trip across. Oh, yes I am a seagoing sailor, as the rookies in camp would say, I am well past the sea sick stage and now stand any kind of tossing, also eat like a young horse, dainty oatmeal for breakfast don't go anymore, it's something a little more substantial. I cannot kick about the eats as they are pretty good, better than some stations that I have been to, of course we still have our fish days—but thank the Lord no more heatless ones, I could stand the others but the "Heatless" ones got my nanny.[1] I used to curl up in a figure eight knot in hammock and wait for the bugle to blow, believe me that is not a very comfortable feeling. Now I don't have to sleep in a hammock and get cold for we have bunks, in the form of shelves, one above the other, and with my two blankets sleep pretty comfy. My watch at sea is from twelve to four A.M. and P.M. but all the same I manage to get my full amount of sleep, eight or nine hours, and while

we are in port we have no watches to stand, because our aerial is taken down so that the ship's cargo can be loaded, the only inconvenience is that one man has to be aboard ship all the time, this means that we can go ashore two nights out of three, even at that it is not bad, I guess otherwise we would be drawing a pension.

At present the ship is detailed to relieve the coal shortage along the coast, so that we will be held here for the spring and be relieved this summer so that we can go over with a cargo to the troops in France or England. Gosh, I can hardly wait for the trip to come, I want to go over so bad, but orders are orders and beggars cannot be choosers, we must bide our time. Our sister ship has already been sent over so that means that we will wend our way to the other side in the near future. We have a gun mounted aft and a detail for a forward gun which as yet has not been erected. There is a distinct difference between the arming of the British, or Limy, as the American sailor calls the Britisher, British ships have only one gun mounted aft while American Ships have two guns one forward and one aft, these guns are mounted on poop decks which are extreme forward and aft decks of any ship, a well deck coming between them and the poop deck amidships.

What else can I write about? My topics are about all used up, for my range of life is just about inclosed in the limits of a ship. To-morrow is my night ashore so that I will immediately take myself over to the US Naval Radio School and visit some of my friends, incidentally Mr. Petty.

How are things going along at home? How are the kids coming along in school? Is Louis studying, also is Mr. Wilbur doing his strenuous amount of studying, be careful and don't let the poor child overstudy himself, you know it's bad on the liver. Tell Miss Coralie that I am expecting some great things from her in the near future and that about the 8th of April I will see if I can spare her that long promised Christmas present. Money you know is pretty hard for us to get out here in this Navy. I am hoping that I get a second class rating by the end of this month, that means, as you may already know, an increase of ten simoleans, making my total pay fifty-one plunks per month, who said Earl couldn't make a living in this world. Guess it will be a shock, falling back into the old tracks of small pay for more work at home. I've got an idea that electrical work would be interesting, and maybe I'll take to it in preference to Miss Whitaker's College of Oratory. By the way, I dropped her a line quite a while ago and have not heard the outcome of it, do you know whether she received it or not?

Well I guess I'll close this awful amount of pounding as it must be monotonous by this time. Tell all the folks hello for me, tickle Bur under the chin and let him pull Coralie's hair, maybe Louis could do that pretty good though. Tell "Pop" to drop me a line as I think that he writes an interesting letter, and of course always like to hear from him. Tell him to give my regards to Mrs. Fitchett and that I am awfully sorry to hear that Jim has died. I don't suppose that it will be very hard for her as he had been away from home so much. Tell the Pettys, young, old and any new additions, also Grandmas Cotton and "Callie," and of course the pa, hello. Also make a general assertion that the Kaiser Bill will very soon bite the dust, and that Uncle Sam will walk through the streets of Berlin on the shoulders of the Navy, Army and Marines. (You notice that this letter is typed, well we have a brand new Underwood aboard for the exclusive use of the Wireless operators. There are three of us, the other two fellows are great boys and come from Santiago, Cal., we get along tiptop, and are leading a life of eating, working and sleeping.)

Good-night, 7:15 P.M. pretty late for me to stay up, am going to crawl off to my bunk, au revoir from
Yours in general,

Earl

1. In January–February 1918, the US government announced a series of "fuelless" days when Americans would do without heat or electric light to save coal for the war effort. In addition, President Woodrow Wilson decreed that Americans should do without meat on Tuesdays and without wheat on Mondays and Wednesdays so that additional foodstuffs could be sent to US servicemen abroad as well as to starving Europeans.

THEODORE J. AMES, 123RD INFANTRY BAND, CAMP WHEELER, GEORGIA, TO A. E. LEE, EDITOR, *OCEAN SPRINGS JACKSON COUNTY TIMES*, MARCH 15, 1918 (*OCEAN SPRINGS JACKSON COUNTY TIMES*, MARCH 23, 1918)

Ocean Springs, Mississippi, native Theodore J. Ames (1876–1927) operated a livery stable in his hometown before enlisting in the National Guard in Mobile, Alabama, in June 1917. He served in the military band section of Company A, 123rd Infantry, from February to December 1918. After the war, he returned to Ocean Springs and worked as a carpenter until his death in a shooting accident (*Ocean Springs Jackson County Times*, October 1, 1927, 3).

Dear friend Lee:
I guess you think I have forgotten you. I see a good many of the boys have written you from the different camps and ports, so I'll make a try, if the censor is willing. We have a real nice camp and naturally think it is the best—but say, if there was more water I'd be better satisfied. I can't fish. The camp is about horse shoe shape, every thing is arranged for convenience and very sanitary. We have a splendid lot of boys. Boys they really are. Why they act like kids, except when drilling, then they are men. I will pay any Fritz to get mixed up with our boys in their games, he had better be a mighty good friend of the Lord when he faces any of the DD (Dixie Division) in a scrap. Why, you insult the boys—they want to scrap—you if you tell one of them he is no better than at least three Germans. All the boys are satisfied here. No, they are not either. The eating is good, so is the treatment. Where the trouble lies is in having to stay here. They are like hounds on a leash at a hunt. They think they are fit, but of course, the men in command know best. When we do go the regulars will not have any thing on us. Our officers are good, as soldiers and friends of the boys.

The drafted men did not like it at first, but they soon got over that. Some of them got disability discharges after being with us two or three months, then you'd hear them howl at having to leave, as they were getting to understand it.

We are glad to get furloughs, naturally, and when we get back here blow about the big times we had. Gradually it leaks out that we wanted to get back.

Got a little lonesome, missed first this one then the other, till finally we missed the whole bunch—Reveille, mess call, drill or band rehearsal, the banter, games and all athletic sports.

Now we have baseball. We—the 123rd—propose to fly the pennant. O yes, we have a league and regular scheduled games. We have played two and won them. The boys believe in the band. We help all we can from the lines. I believe we can put any of them in the air. We played some of that music I brought from home at a dance in town recently. "Hula Hula Girl" made a hit. We had to play it four times. They don't mind keeping you busy, but we don't mind it either, as that's about all we have to do, except litter drill and first aid work, for that will be our work while the boys are fighting. Say, it would surprise you to see the difference in some of the men now and when we first got them. Not all, of course, but some were sallow, stoop-shouldered, sickly looking and negligent. They soon begin to pick up weight and get straight. I bet some of them measure a couple of inches taller. They got a good complexion and springy step. I suppose the first aid (hook worm) treatment has something to do with it.

We hiked Monday and Tuesday, not far, just a little to get the boys used to it. I guess about fifteen miles, not counting the maneuvers. Some of the boys got a little tired. I heard a couple saying they had not appreciated music before. When we played them in they were feeling tired, but as soon as they heard the music they livened up and forgot all about it. Why it would do you good to see the difference in the boys. While we were on the hike from Mobile to Montgomery we would play the regiment out of camp, then get ahead and play them in. It was July and hot. As soon as we would strike up they would straighten up, cheer and wave at us. Made us feel good too, like we were really helping. We have eight bands in camp and it is not much trouble to start a fuss if you criticize the other fellow's band.

It is surprising the number of men in camp and so few fights. You very rarely see any one mad enough to fight. When ever they do, they go at it fair and shake hands after. That's the last of it.

Well, this is about all. I think I'll turn in it's getting pretty late—nearly ten o'clock. You will have to excuse this pencil. While I don't know if there is anything in the regulations about it, it is easier for the censor, if he has to erase anything, and you know I'm not lazy.

By the way, I see the fish kept their word this winter. You know they promised me not to bite much, but to stay out in deep water and come next winter so they would be there when I get back. T'was nice of them, don't you think? You know we expect to have the Germans whipped in time to eat Thanksgiving dinner at home. So wish us luck and tell any of the boys at home that are anyway dubious about getting in the service that it is great. It will make men of them, physically and morally. You are taught nor allowed to do wrong. There are lots of boys in this country dodging about that would make good men if they would do their duty to the stars and stripes and their mothers and sisters.
Your friend,

T. J. Ames

LESS THAN FOUR MONTHS AFTER THE *PONTOTOC SENTINEL* PRINTED Victor Ashmore's letter (page 38), the paper printed a letter from the head of the camp where Ashmore had been stationed.

MAJOR GENERAL H. C. HODGES JR., COMMANDER, CAMP BEAUREGARD, LOUISIANA, TO GOVERNOR THEODORE BILBO, MAY 9, 1918 (*PONTOTOC SENTINEL*, MAY 16, 1918)

> My Dear Governor Bilbo:
> As the Chief Executive of your state and as a patriotic citizen of this nation, I know you are interested in the welfare of the soldiers of this Camp, thousands of whom are from Mississippi.
> It is impressed upon my mind every day that many mothers, wives and sweethearts of our soldiers are, unwittingly, bringing upon themselves and upon their soldier relatives the great misery and disgrace.
> "I want to see you,
> Please come home."
> The eight words of affection compose hundreds of messages that are received by men in this camp each day. Despite the fact that they appear as tender tokens from home, they are the cause of more misery and anguish on the part of the soldiers of Camp Beauregard than any other cause. They engender homesickness and discontent in the hearts of the boys who go, with or without leave, to their loved ones. In these strenuous times of war the crime of being absent without leave is a serious one its punishment is well known, especially to the men in the army.
> Because the folks at home are the innocent cause of so many of these crimes, I want to make a direct appeal to relatives and friends of the men to refrain from addressing to them messages that make them believe that things are not right at home—that they should return to their firesides even without leave or permission.
> It is natural, I know, for a sick wife or mother to want to see her soldier boy. In every one, except in the most extreme cases, the desire should be suppressed, for the soldier, not being a physician could accomplish no real good by a visit, but could, on the other hand, such a visit without getting himself into a predicament from which he cannot extricate himself in months and in some cases years. A soldier should not be written discouraging letters, but instead, he should be sent words

of cheer. He has important duties to perform for his country and he can do them better with a light heart.

The sight of a prisoner wearing a ball and chain is a pitiful one in private life. That of a soldier boy being driven to unpleasant duties of a prisoner under guard is just as shocking, but it is not an infrequent sight in this camp. The soldier receives such a letter and gets homesick of "blue" and decides to leave, with or without permission. After he arrives at home, he begins to realize what his actions mean and decides to stay. Desertion in time of War is punishable by the death penalty. Deserters from this Division are sentenced to confinement in the Federal Penitentiary for long terms ranging from ten to twenty-five years.

If mothers, wives and sweethearts could be made to understand what misery and disgrace they may bring upon their messages of good cheer instead of those which make the son, husband or sweetheart downcast and homesick.

I appeal to the Governors of Mississippi, Louisiana, and Arkansas to see that this matter is brought to the attention of their people.

You have my permission to use this entire letter for publication or in any other manner you may bring the desired result.

Thanking you in advance for your consideration of this and with sentiments of highest personal esteem, I am
Very sincerely,

H. C. Hodges, Jr. Maj. Gen. Commanding

HERBERT J. REMONDET, CAMP BEAUREGARD, LOUISIANA, TO FAMILY, MAY 17, 1918 (*NATCHEZ DEMOCRAT*, SEPTEMBER 27, 1918)

Herbert J. Remondet (1893–July 30, 1918) was the first soldier from Natchez, Mississippi, to fall in action in World War I. A printer and former employee at the *Natchez Democrat*, Remondet volunteered in 1916 and served in Europe with the 168th Infantry Regiment, 42nd Division. He is buried at the Oise-Aisne American Cemetery in Fère-en-Tardenois, France (*Natchez Democrat*, September 22, 1918, 1).

My Dear People:
I have received two letters from father and one from Mother and Alphonse and was glad to receive them all. I enjoyed reading them all especially the one father wrote in answer to the letter I wrote to mother.

It was grand I only wish it was longer but don't know whether I could have stood much more for it was playing on my heart strings. I received the medal and have it on and will wear it with me. I don't know how much longer this letter will be but will write as much as I can. Am awfully sorry to know that Josephine and Genevieve are sick and do hope and pray that they will soon be well again. I was in the hospital for thirty-two days and heard that my company was getting ready to move and I asked to be sent back to them. At first they didn't want to let me go back, they wanted me to remain at the hospital longer but I told them I was alright and could do duty so they sent me back last Thursday May 10, and we were transferred to the isolation camp on last Friday and have been here since. I would not advise you to answer this letter for we may move any minute.

If you do not hear anything about my insurance policy soon, write to our Congressman and get him to look after it. It is a ten thousand dollar policy and is worth writing for. I also have a one hundred dollar Liberty Bond that will be paid up in July. It will be delivered to me I suppose, for it is made out in my name.

I don't know just when we will leave here it is liable to be at any minute if you write again put your return address on the letter with the word notice *above the address and you will get it back. I wish we were leaving here tonight, I am tired of the detention camp, we cannot go anywhere, not even out of our company street.*

You said we may be going on a rifle range to practice up. I don't think so for we have one of the best rifle ranges in the country right here in this camp and I hardly think they would go to the expense of outfitting us in all new stuff just to go to a rifle range. We are well equipped and can move at a moments notice.

I am glad to know that your garden is doing so nicely and only wish I could come to Natchez and eat some good vegetables out of your garden and cooked by Mother, it would certainly be a pleasure. I was going to ask for a furlough when they let me out of the hospital but I wouldn't like for all my friends and comrades to go off to France and leave me behind, so I thought it would be useless to ask for a furlough anyway, for they would not give anybody one, that has passed the overseas examination. I could have gotten one by laying around the hospital until all the boys were gone but I did not want to be a slacker.

I don't think I will have time to write Eugene much of a letter, but will drop him a few lines.

We have a big, high barbed wire fence all around this isolation camp and have guards walking up and down on the outside. We cannot go out, but there are lots of pretty girls on the outside all the time that are talking to their relatives. I do not drop my letters in the box in the company, but I give them to one of the pretty girls to mail for me.

Well, father, mother, sisters and brothers, I must close for this time. Hoping I may be able to write again before I leave here. I will write you again before I leave the United States so don't be surprised if you receive a letter from another postmark than Camp Beauregard on it.

I will close with love to all.
Affectionately,
Good-bye—God bless all,

Herbert

AS THE UNITED STATES RAMPED UP EFFORTS TO AID ITS ALLIES, LARGE numbers of troops, supplies, and materiel needed to be transported to Europe. In wartime, the usual hazards of sea travel—among them inclement weather and icebergs, as demonstrated by the April 1912 sinking of the *Titanic*, which remained fresh in Americans' minds—were augmented by the threat posed by German U-boats. That risk dropped dramatically in mid-1916 when the British Admiralty introduced the convoy system of protecting ships. By the following year, the system had become widely used. Between eight and twelve vessels would be grouped together, with smaller naval ships—cruisers, destroyers, chasers, submarines—and aircraft escorting larger transport vessels and frequently drawing fire so that the cargo would reach its destination. Between June and December 1918, eighty-eight convoys made their way across the Atlantic, with the voyages averaging twelve days each (Welsh, *USA in World War I*, 16; "Transporting the Troops").

JAMES H. SEALE, NEW YORK, TO PARENTS, JUNE 1918 (*MEADVILLE FRANKLIN ADVOCATE*, JULY 4, 1918)

Dear Father and Mother:
I have just arrived here in NY, safe, sound, well and hearty; I weigh 175 pounds. I did not get seasick one bit on my trip. It is so nice on the sea.

We were eleven days going over and nine coming back. We sail in a convoy of sixteen ships; our ship carried about thirty-five hundred soldiers across there being about seventy-five thousand in the sixteen ships. We will be here two or three weeks, going over the ship. The boys are going over in a hurry. The people in England sure were nice to us, especially the girls.

I like the Navy better all the time. I did not like it at first for I was sick for two months but sea life agrees with me.

My work is firing a big steam boiler and I'm getting to be a second class fireman. I like my job.

Don't you all worry about me I will get along all right, we saw one Sub and took a few shots at her, our ship has five big guns on her and they are putting on three more. I can't tell you all I want to in this letter for we have just arrived and I am just writing a hasty letter for I want you to get it as quick as possible.

I will tell you more about my trip over there when I can have more time. I will send you all some of my pictures before I sail again. Write me all the news, tell me about the crops and everything. Give all the children my love and except a liberal share for yourselves, your loving boy.

James H. Seale

....

JEAN BREVARD, NEW YORK, TO MOTHER, JUNE 1918 (WORLD WAR I SCRAPBOOK [NATCHEZ], FOLDER 1)

My dear Mother:
At last I am back in the states and able to write you again; and by the way, mother, I certainly have some columns to write. I am going to start right from the first, when we left Norfolk, and tell you everything.

Well on the eighth day of April we left Norfolk on a collier, the USS Orion, thinking that we were only going down the east coast.

After sailing for ten days we encountered a storm off the coast of Puerto Rico. I got seasick for the old collier certainly rolled and pitched. Then after sailing four more days we arrived at Bahia, Brazil, South America. We stayed here four hours and then got under way again, and after a couple more days we arrived at Rio de Janeiro, the capital of Brazil, and one of the most beautiful cities in the world—two million population. It has second to the prettiest harbor in the world—Sydney, Australia comes first.

We stuck around here a week and then set sail again and after four days we arrived at Montevideo, the capital of Uruguay, also a very pretty city. Here we coaled four ships of the South Atlantic fleet, and sailed for the Falkland Islands. On arriving here we discharged the remainder of our cargo of coal (twelve hundred tons) and then headed for Buenos Aires, another pretty city, and it seemed more like the states than any of them. We stayed here a short while, and then sailed for Santos, Brazil, where we took on a two million dollar cargo of coffee.

From Santos, we went back to Rio de Janeiro, and from there we sailed back up to Bahia. By the way this city is just a little south of the equator and we went out and pulled bananas, oranges and pineapples and coconuts from trees they just grow around wild everywhere.

I got four letters from you here, which were brought down by the USS Nebraska. She was taking the Argentine consul home.

On the 31st day of May we set sail back to the States. When we were eight days out from Bahia we cracked up a wireless SOS call from the transport Hancock. She said she was being attacked by four raiders (as we call the submarines), and of course our skipper could not afford to take the chance of us being sunk too, as there were four raiders, and as the Hancock was only one degree of latitude west of us, we changed our course and beat it for the Bermuda Isles and arrived there safely two days later. We were some glad bunch to see land again.

While here we received a number of submarine warnings to the north of us and also to the west. The skipper wanted to stick around Bermuda until the sub scare was over, but we got orders from Washington to sail for Charleston, SC, at once, we did, and were just a half a day off the South Carolina coast, when we received our first submarine attack. I shall never forget it. It was 4:20 A.M. on the 17th, almost daylight, when we first sighted the raider. She was way out on the horizon and to keep us from seeing her she was making a smoke screen. I just happened to get up early, as I had some work to do. When we first saw her we thought she was a submarine chaser, as they look very much like a raider, and then, too, we were just ten miles off the coast, but soon we noticed the make of a torpedo boat, almost two miles off, coming straight towards us, and, mother, I'll tell you the truth, I was sure scared. Well, the skipper heaved our bow around, and it only missed us about sixty feet. They fired two shots at us, the first falling about two *thousand yards short and the next going just over us. In the meantime our gun crew was on the job and we fired fourteen shots at her just as fast as we could. The fourteenth shot knocked off her periscope and set her on fire. She sent up a flame of fire and smoke, and we did not see any more of her.*

A ship coming along later reported having seen debris and wreckage, and finally it was officially known that we sank her. We were very glad when we arrived at Charleston, about an hour later.

We only stayed there a short time and then came up here, and I have been transferred and am now stationed at this island.

Listen, mother, has Warren gone to station yet? I am sorry he had to go for it is such a hard life until you get used to it. However, I am glad he joined the reserves, as they have the preferences. I wish I was a USS NRF, instead of a USN,[1] but, oh well, the war is going to be over pretty soon, and we will all be out of it.

I don't know when I will be leaving here. Old New York is certainly some burg. I know how to get around pretty well. I am going up in the Statue of Liberty just as soon as I get a chance.

Mother, did you get your money from the allotment? By the 5th of July you should have seventy-five dollars, and if you don't get it please let me know and I will see that you do get it, because they take it out of my pay each month.

You know, I wrote you at first they might be a little late about sending it. Write me just as soon as you can and tell me everything.

With lots of love for all of you, your devoted son,

Jean

1. After World War I started, US leaders realized that navies would play a significant role in modern warfare. In response, they created the US Naval Reserve Force (USNRF) in 1915. It remains distinct from the US Navy (USN).

....

ROBERT H. DEKAY, 60TH COMPANY, MARINE BARRACKS, PARRIS ISLAND, SOUTH CAROLINA, TO A. F. HERMAN, EDITOR, *PONTOTOC SENTINEL*, JUNE 9, 1918 (*PONTOTOC SENTINEL*, JUNE 20, 1918)

Illinois-born Robert H. DeKay (1898?–1968) returned to Pontotoc, Mississippi, after the war and worked as a bank teller before becoming the town's postmaster in 1930. During World

War II, he was the chief air raid warden for the Mississippi Civil Defense Council. DeKay was also the state service commissioner and the executive secretary of the state Veterans Affairs Commission (*Pontotoc Progress*, September 19, 1968, 8).

> *Dear Mr. Herman:*
> *Hope you have not been under the impression that I had forgotten you and the bunch entirely. Down here they look on letter writing as a frivolous and unnecessary indulgence and we don't get very many opportunities for it. They are giving us in six weeks the training the draft armies get in six months. I have been here about five weeks and am almost ready to shove off. Have been on the Rifle Range for about ten days and will shoot for record in a day or so. It is a wonder to me how a Springfield rifle weighing nine pounds can have a kick of nearly fifty. I am a light weight myself and when I fire from a prone position I have to dig in my toes and hold her with both hands. Sounds scary but really is great fun. Since the submarine raids I have seen a good many Enfield rifles such as the British use. They are wicked weapons in close fighting.*
>
> *The South Carolina sun is beginning to bear down heavily these June days. I am tanned to about the same shade as Rufe Walker. Saw Herron Mitchell one day last week. Gone is that fair complexion of his. It's a great life.*
>
> *If there are any of the boys at home of draft age subject to call I would advise them to get into the Marines. They will have the advantage of training at a long established port under the finest drill instructors in the world. Every man here comes in as a volunteer and has the fighting spirit drummed into him from the start. Whenever trouble breaks out anywhere, any time the Marines generally show up soon and squelch it. They are everywhere from Haiti to Honolulu and always holding down the lid.*
>
> *Have you noticed what branch is bearing the brunt of our fighting "over there"—somewhere in France? Marines, of course. They were the first to hit France and will be the first to hit Berlin. That's their way of doing things, "First to Fight" has always been their motto. So boys, come on in and do your bit.*
>
> *Give my regards to Mrs. Herman, Will T., "Shorty" and everybody else. Would be glad to hear from any one at home.*
>
> *Private Robt. H. DeKay*

SARAH CATHERINE ANDERSON, RED CROSS NURSE, TO MRS. GREENLEY, JUNE 1918 (*GREENVILLE WEEKLY DEMOCRAT-TIMES*, JULY 25, 1918)

Sarah Catherine Anderson served in the Army Nurse Corps and was stationed at Camp Beauregard, Louisiana, beginning in the fall of 1917 ("Nursing News and Announcements," 418). She continued her career as a nurse after the war, eventually moving to Houston, Texas, and serving as the superintendent of nurses at the Methodist Hospital.

> *Dear Mrs. Greenley:*
> *Probably you will be a bit surprised to hear from me from this part of the country. My leaving Beauregard was rather sudden and quite unexpected. When the call came I just could not stay out any longer.*
>
> *We arrived the 23rd. Have been very busy. Being in the army now, everything, of course, is uniform. Then, too, the government equips us (though there are many things we have to get).*
>
> *The traveling suit is a Norfolk, very nice material, blue serge. The heavy coat is made of what they call "army serge." Hat "blue beaver." Shoes are from the "Coward," high laces, army regulations; three pairs, tan for parades, mahogany for dress, black for duty. They are very nice, too. Uniforms "gray ginghams," aprons "butchers." Also half dozen work hose, half dozen cotton suits underwear, woolen tights, flannel outing pajamas, gray sweater, two white shirt waists tailored, one blue flannel, one blue silk (we buy $5.50) raincoat, rubber boots, blanket roll.*
>
> *These are the most essential things. The trunk we are allowed to take is not to exceed thirty-six inches. In our blanket roll or carryall we are allowed our raincoat, rubber boots and sweater. Nothing can be slipped in. They are examined.*
>
> *Have had measurements for everything, shoes fitted. In all probability it will be more than a week before we get our entire equipment. Had one dozen photographs made. Have been to Hoboken, NJ. Had fingerprints for my passport. All this is complete. After this being done I got busy on my identification "tags." Got a "sterling silver" one for my wrist, name, no, unit, and so on. Aluminum for neck. There is no little work attached to getting ready. The most minute detail is given careful attention.*
>
> *We are warned for our safety and others not to tell anything or give a probable date when we will sail or on what steamer.*

Seven nurses came up from Beauregard, one from New York. She is a captain. Pretty nice. She knows New York as well as you do Greenville. We are not losing much time. Have seen everything from vaudeville to John McCormack. He sang at "The Hippodrome" last Sunday night benefit of Catholic Orphan Asylum. Seat sales [were] twenty-five thousand dollars. A number of his records were auctioned, six selling for one thousand dollars each, one for two thousand dollars, several for two hundred dollars and one hundred dollars.

Services at eleven A.M. today at Grace Church. We were anxious to go but were at 69th armory, busy. We who are going think we have work, but I'm sorry for the officials. Their work and responsibility is more than I can conceive. Though things are running smoothly.

We were sent to Bristol for one night only. One week has passed. Still here. Our trunks were sent to Judson. Were told today we would be leaving this hotel the last of the week. Hope so. Are too far away from headquarters. These hotels, where all the nurses are staying, are not the best. However, the government is doing its part by us. A time like this every one is accepting everything handed us cheerfully.

Miss Cartledge, from Greenville, is here, and at my hotel. She came up from Camp Shelby. Nurses from all over the USA. are here. Makes one realize we are really at war.

Tuesday morning at Hoboken we were lined waiting to go. Whom should I see go in? Mr. Lowry Jayne. I spoke, but in the excitement I fear he did not recognize me. I never saw him again. He had insignia on of a "field clerk." It is a new branch of service. I know very little about it. The way I understand, it is clerical work. He had leather puttees on, an officer's hat cord, though no bar. I learn it's a rank between "top sergeant" and second lieutenant.

Will you please send me interesting clippings from Daily Democrat? I do miss the paper.

Hotel Holly is the mobilization station. Judson just across the street. Address me to the former.
Kindest regards to all, I am,
Sincerely,

Sarah Catherine Anderson

Lucy Chamberlain, Red Cross Nurse, to "Aunt Sallie," July 1918 (*Greenville Daily Democrat-Times*, July 13, 1918)

Dear Democrat-Times:
I am sending to you some parts of an interesting letter from Miss Lucy Chamberlain, written on the eve of sailing from an Atlantic port.
   I shall give it in her own words, as her style is attractive in itself.
   Have the girls written you about the wonderful "send-off" the Red Cross of Jacksonville gave me? It just happened that my orders came on Saturday during the Red Cross week. On Monday the Red Cross was giving its final luncheon at the Mason Hotel. At the luncheon the final reports were to be read. There were probably between five hundred and seven hundred of the most prominent men and women of Jacksonville present. By special invitation I was present as an honored guest, and presented by the chairman of the woman's committee in the assembled audience in a very beautiful talk, at the conclusion of which there was such applause as I have never heard before, for myself, and then I arose to speak, and just as I did one man jumped up and waved his napkin and suggested that they give three cheers for me. Well, you can imagine what it sounded like—those several hundred men cheering me. After that they quieted down long enough for me to thank them, and, at the request of Mrs. Denham, give to the public the total sum raised by the woman's committee during the drive. That banquet certainly sent me away with a warm feeling in my heart.
   Aunt Sallie, it was the funniest thing to see the Boy Scouts begging me to let them carry me on a board in the parade from the Mason to headquarters. However, one of my boy friends was waiting outside in his car. How I escaped the boys while they were looking for the board. We are very beautifully situated at present [censored] Club of [censored]. It is owned by a very wealthy woman [censored] who turned it over to the Red Cross as a mobilization station for its girls, going into foreign service. Mrs. B[censored] pays all the overhead expenses. In the basement there is a most wonderful swimming pool in a room white tiled, with walls of plate glass mirrors. On the first floor are the chapel, roll call room, tea room, surgical dressing room and huge reception room, with piano and victrola, where we dance.
   Above are the five floors of dormitories. On the fifth floor there is a huge wash room where we wash our clothes. Also there is a gas stove with several irons and ironing boards.

The first night I slept in one of the dormitories with about thirty other girls but later the six civilians and the assistant to the chief nurse were moved up here to the fifth floor annex, where we have a suite of seven tiny rooms and bath. We are quite cozy and having a great time together. I had fun in the dormitories, though, it being my first experience. However, I was beginning to realize what Irvin Cobb meant by the expression, "no more privacy than a gold fish."[1]

The six civilians consist of secretaries (to the officer force), a dietitian, an anesthetist, and a pathologist. They are all dandy girls, and it goes without saying, experts in their line of work.

We are now very busy, being equipped. Our much desired uniforms have been fitted out and we will have them in a few days. Our uniforms are the same models as the nurses, except they are grey instead of blue.

These Coward shoes are big enough to fit our grandmothers, but are solid comfort. You realize how wonderful they are when you are drilling. Don't laugh when I say drilling. We really do. Every afternoon we go to the armory and drill madly for an hour and a half under the command of a terribly efficient officer, who really scalps any one so unfortunate as to err from the straight and narrow path. At first is was very difficult to grasp the military tactics, and the slowly moving Southern girl, especially, finds it difficult to learn to obey a command on the instant. However, death itself is almost preferable to being yanked out of line and openly humiliated before the whole company. We give most respectful attention to our stern officer than we would to a dozen kings and queens.

Rapidly we are assuming quite a soldierly appearance and military formations are becoming quite easy. The early part of this week we posed [passed?] in review before the sweetest, most wonderful nurse—a Red Cross nurse—just back from the front—wounded severely several times, the last time losing one foot. It gave you a thrill of pleasure to drill before her, for indeed, she looked like a saint in her beautiful uniform, with the Cross du Guerre over her heart.

After the drill she gave us a most inspiring talk, and in conclusion said she would be the happiest girl in the world if she could go back with us to the other side.

Singing is as compulsory as drilling. After the drill we form a platoon around our instructor and sing all the war songs, popular songs, songs of the different sections of the country, etc. At drill a few afternoons ago we listened to several of the units singing their different songs, and when they had finished our band of Southern girls answered them with "Dixie," and you should have heard the applause. Our instructor, a northerner, said he had heard "Dixie" before, but he had never really heard it sung till we sang it for him.

Drilling is compulsory for many reasons. We could vacate a hospital in a few minutes and have a complete report of the whole company from the reports of the corporal in charge of each squad. There may be times that we will have to do this—when the hospital is under shell fire, or in danger of capture, or something of that kind. Also, we do everything in military order. We go on or off a boat as soldiers do, etc.

Singing is compulsory because of the cheer it brings, because recreational effect, and most wonderful of all, because of the marvelous cures it works on shell shock patients. A bunch of nurses have gotten together and sung for an hour or two straight, and in some hospitals as much as 80 per cent of the cases. Think of that!

My time here has been with interesting meetings, but I must not keep you longer. Besides, I have to get many additional things that compose my equipment this morning. One's friends must be careful in times like this. Information that appears to be absolutely innocent may be the connecting link that some spy is looking for. You realize the seriousness of it here more than you do at home. We are guarded night and day by secret men.

Good-bye, dear—This may be the last letter I'll have time to write you, but you will have to admit it's a book. Love to all of you, and don't worry. Remember I am not afraid.
Yours as ever,

Lucy

1. In his 1915 best seller, *Speaking of Operations*, American humorist and author Irvin S. Cobb (1876–1944) wrote, "I was not having any more privacy in that hospital than a goldfish."

SARA M. F. BABB, NEW YORK, TO MRS. TAYLOR, JULY 14, 1918 (*GREENVILLE WEEKLY DEMOCRAT-TIMES*, JULY 25, 1918)

New Albany, Mississippi, native Sara M. F. Babb (b. March 16, 1873) worked as a visiting or community nurse in Greenville, South Carolina, as well as Greenville, Mississippi, before resigning to join an Italian unit attached to the AEF. After the war, she moved to New Orleans and worked at the city's Charity Hospital before becoming a nurse with the US Indian Bureau and working with Native Americans in Oklahoma (Babb, "Washerwomen"; "Sarah M. F. Babb, R.N." [biographical sketch], in Daughters of the American Revolution, Belvidere Chapter, Washington County World War I Scrapbook; *American Journal of Nursing* 31, no. 9 [September 1931]: 1112).

> My Dear Mrs. Taylor:
> I am tremendously interested in everything that is happening to me. Every nurse is ordered to report on arrival to Holley hotel, then the various units are sent out to hotels leased by the government. Our unit is fortunate in being sent here as we are in the midst of things and so near as to be able to walk to almost every one of the various departments. Every hour of the day we are kept busy reporting for various equipments, for passports, for vaccinations and drills, singing lessons and Italian. So there isn't very much time for sightseeing. We have a drill master, Capt. Russell, who says he gives us exactly the same drill the soldiers take. Our unit is a company divided into platoons and squads. We have a Captain, Miss Fitzgibbons; three lieutenants, Miss Surgent, of New Orleans; Miss Tarpey, of El Paso, and myself, besides sergeants and corporals. I enjoy the drills very much and am always thinking how splendid it will be for my school children when I get back. Our singing master is a lieutenant and teaches the songs of the soldiers and sailors. Each unit has a song. We have chosen. "Dixie." The Colorado unit sings "The Battle Hymn of the Republic." The chorus is always an improvisation, as "Glory, Glory, Colorado, as we go marching on." The Maryland unit sings "Maryland, my Maryland." Units come and go and are never noticed, the New Yorkers tell me, but our unit has made New York sit up and take notice; perhaps it is because we are so country and odd. We have had write-ups in all the leading papers. I think, too, it is because of the Sisters being in charge that has been unusual; ours are the first American Sisters to be sent over. They receive so much deference and consideration from all the officials. Sister Chrysostom, our chief nurse,

is a very remarkable woman. She has a genius for organization and the happiest and kindest ways of exacting strict obedience. Almost all of our Allies are represented in our unit. We have five or six British subjects; our dietitian, one girl from Yorkshire, one from Scotland, three from Ireland, many Italians, French from New Orleans, and, most interesting of all, an Indian girl from New Mexico. She is very true to type in looks, in dress and manner. Delights in gorgeous beads and bright colors, and is very solitary and apart. Sometimes we go out sightseeing in groups but she always manages to lose herself and wanders through New York alone, very fearless and taciturn.

We drill in the Armory of the famous New York 71st. Four units usually drill at once. We have several captains who drill us; and day by day we find a unit absent that never comes back again. They have been shipped away in the night or the dawn. The utmost secrecy is observed. We know nothing ourselves but are continually reminded if we should give out any information as to the names of our ships, the date of our sailing, we will be dishonorably discharged. There is so much of human interest all about me—various types of nurses, many shades of religious beliefs, viewpoints fashioned by many varied environments. Yesterday I sat at lunch with a nurse from San Francisco whose father was an Italian and mother an Englishwoman, who had lived in Italy, South Africa, New Zealand and finally drifted to San Francisco. She is an astrologist, and very seriously told me that as soon as the planets get into a benign aspect we will have peace. We are living in the House of Argol, the Evil Star that rules in the constellation Perseus. Next year, she says, peace will surely come. I hope God will permit her prophecy to be fulfilled.

Monday, 8:20 A.M.
We have so many distractions we can never finish letters. Please give my love to all Greenville, and beg them to take this letter to you for them all. It is so impossible to write letters. I am so anxious to know all about your work, and if your new nurse has come. I am so interested in everything that is happening to you. You will please address me like this:

Miss Sara Babb, ARC
ABH No. 102
Hotel Holley,
Washington Sq. West
New York, NY

and if we shall have disappeared it will find me somewhere, sometime. Give, too, your return address on letter. And now I must report for the day. How quickly events move; and how insignificant we all are, blown about like leaves on the winds of fate!

Please write me. I want to hear from you before I am too remote. Yours affectionately,

Sara Babb

ROBERT JEFF MCWHIRTER, COMPANY K, 149TH INFANTRY, CAMP SHELBY, MISSISSIPPI, TO A. F. HERMAN, EDITOR, *PONTOTOC SENTINEL*, SEPTEMBER 2, 1918 (*PONTOTOC SENTINEL*, SEPTEMBER 12, 1918)

Robert Jeff McWhirter (1890–1954) was living in Springville, Mississippi, and working as a farmer when he registered for the draft. After the war, he returned to farming, moving to Winston County.

Dear Sir and Friend:
I will write a few lines to The Sentinel *as it is my old paper. Will proceed at once to tell a little of army life, tho' I fear I may not give an interesting recital. We left Pontotoc on July 17, and reached our destination at midnight that night. We marched three miles to the Detention camp where each of us were given a mess kit, a blanket, a bed sack and cot, towels and scrub brush. Then we were shown our tents, eight in each tent. I was placed with seven other fellows from Pontotoc County. On Sunday we were called out to attend church, most of us going.*

Camp Shelby is a nice place. It is on a big hill in a dense pine woods, you can see nothing but pine trees and tents as far as your vision reaches. Of course there are some buildings, such as the Infirmary, base hospitals, theaters, YMCA and mess halls, but all the boys sleep in tents.

At five o'clock every morning we were called out and lined up for roll call and physical exercise lasting about forty minutes. Then we would "fall out" and at six we would go for breakfast, after which we cleaned our tents and drilled until eleven. An hour later we ate our dinner and until three that afternoon permitted to rest at the YMCA, or the "Canton" [Canteen?]. We then practiced in the drill field until five, at that hour everybody took a bath and got himself ready for supper. From six until seven we were entertained with music, boxing matches, (by

Robert Jeff McWhirter writes of Camp Shelby, "nothing but pine trees and tents as far as your vision reaches." (Bernays Photograph Collection, Box 22, Folder 48, No. 4)

both white and black), singing of war songs, dancing, picture shows and all kinds of funny plays, enjoying the entire list of amusements. At ten o'clock every fellow was required to be in his tent and the lights out.

No doubt some of you are wondering what we had to eat. Well, most everything, you could think of, such as beef stew, spuds, beans, fishes, fruit. Had it been served like we have it at home it would have been fine but was all stirred up in a pan together and not being accustomed to eating that way it was rather tough. We bravely made the best of it, however.

I like South Mississippi very much, except it is extremely dusty, being a sandy soil and soon dries. After a hard rain of two hours you could kick up dust. There comes a cloud not much larger than your old hat, the wind blows and the dust so thick you could not see which way you were going. Then what a rain follows! We got soaking wet several times on the drill field. On August 5, they called us to regular company. They marched us all together—more than a thousand of us, all marching to the band stand where we were called out a company at a time. It sure was some hot and some stood there all afternoon before they got through with us. Only one other Pontotoc Countyite and myself were in the same company. Don't know where the others went except Morse Woods. If any one reads this knows the address of Judson Ellis please send it to me as I want to find him. I like the boys in my company, most of whom are from Kentucky except forty and they are from Mississippi. Earl Dillard is in my company, he is from Pontotoc County. He is now in the base hospital sick with measles.

I have been twice to the Rifle Range, a distance of twelve miles. We carry our pack and our rifles. Twelve hundred of us went together. We drill only five days in a week. On Saturday we have inspection, which is finished at ten o'clock and are then off until Monday. Today is a holiday and everybody is having a good time, some enjoying the match game of ball.

I've been quarantined twelve days but will be released next Thursday. Will be glad when we get back to our company. I am on guard tonight for the first time. As it is growing toward evening I will draw my letter to a close. Please send The Sentinel to the address given below. I've missed a copy or two and I regretted it greatly as the paper is like getting a letter from home. With best wishes for everybody in that part of the State and especially to Mr. and Mrs. A. F. Herman, I remain,
Yours truly,

Robert Jeff McWhirter
Company K, 149 Infantry
Camp Shelby, Miss.

WILLIAM S. STRAUSS, CAMP HILL, VIRGINIA, TO "FOLKS ALL," SEPTEMBER 2, 1918 (DAUGHTERS OF THE AMERICAN REVOLUTION, SHUK-HO-TA-TOM-A-HA CHAPTER, LOWNDES COUNTY WORLD WAR I SCRAPBOOK)

William S. Strauss (b. November 8, 1887) was a merchant in Columbus, Mississippi, before joining the 1st Provisional Mississippi A & M Training Detachment in May 1918. By August he was attached to the 326th Quartermaster Company, which was assigned to the 101st Division. Strauss went overseas later in September and died on October 10, 1918, from acute pneumonia.

Dear Folks All:
Your three letters, Uncle Simon's, Leopold's and Albert's, all received. Each one was read over and over and surely enjoyed and appreciated.

Letters mean much to soldiers for you know our spare time is usually a matter of moments and we can always grab out a letter and read it, in between calls. This brings thoughts of home and why we are "in" instead of allowing us to brood and figure on work ahead.

Sunday, one half of our company was granted a pass, the balance a holiday.

I was like a kid with a circus ticket and five dollars to spend. I went to Old Point Comfort, watched the passenger vessels come in, all crowded with sailors and passengers. Then I inspected the Chamberlain Hotel, a luxurious place and just newly refinished. We then (suppose you know we each have a regular buddy) went to Fort Monroe, and no part of this is restricted to "over sea" men. We got to examine coast guns, carriages, shells and ammunition store rooms. We climbed upon parapets and saw the patrols and battle ships. Then the coast guards showed us ends of sub nets and how the mines were set. They claim a sub cannot come within one hundred miles of the fort. These coast guards are trained to handle all kinds of water and land weapons of destruction. They handle from a two inch to a sixteen inch cannon. They claim an accurate range of eighteen miles for some of the guns. I also saw a hydro-plane hit the river then rise and fly away. The inside of Fort Monroe is now used for officers' training school.

It is quite an impressive place, the homes and barracks being typical of our ideas of "Ole Virginia." They also have a wonderful YMCA. We then hiked about three miles along the coast trying to detect which were real and which artificial defenses. The anti-aircraft guns are not as impressive as coast guns. I guess they must be lighter to be handled quicker. You should see these searchlights sweep the sky and ocean for air machines. When you actually see these sights you wonder how any nation can carry on offensive war fare and yet we are told we are out to capture Berlin and must be prepared to walk the whole way.

Some transports brought in 167 wounded soldiers yesterday. The sailors tell most interesting tales but do not claim the Germans are whipped. They state that our first troops have done so well that we must bend every muscle to uphold the American soldier's enviable record. The Germans have learned to expect a charge whenever they meet Americans and up to date we have been the better wielders of the cold steel.

We have a company fund for musical instruments and athletic goods, to carry over seas, so will be made amused.

Our company boasts of a piano and quite a few musicians of ordinary amateur talent. They meet in the office where I am located and the music in turn makes me home-sick and lonesome or lightens my spirits and puts in pep—just according to what they play.

Will

ANDREW M. PICKETT, FISK UNIVERSITY, COMPANY A, TRAINING DETACHMENT, NASHVILLE, TO DR. L. COSTLEY, SEPTEMBER 15, 1918 (*MEADVILLE FRANKLIN ADVOCATE*, SEPTEMBER 26, 1918)

Andrew M. Pickett (1897–1971), an African American from Meadville, Mississippi, was a farmer until his induction into the army on August 1, 1918. He was assigned to the Students Army Training Corps (SATC) at Fisk University in Nashville until December 17, 1918. The SATC allowed men to attend school while receiving military training, and in June 1918, Fisk president Fayette Avery McKenzie persuaded the school's trustees to allow the school to host the program beginning in August as a means of raising funds (Nicholson, "To Advance a Race," 227–28). After the war, Pickett moved to Chicago, where he worked as a janitor and laborer.

Dear Friend:
It is a pleasure for me to write you and inform you how all the boys and myself are getting along.

I am as happy as a bee and you know a bee is happy so long as his provisions last.

Doctor, we've had more than six hundred young men qualified to do the work that I signed to do which caused me to be here.

We came here for the purpose of learning a mechanical trade that we might serve our country, but lots of our comrades have gone to various parts of our native land to pursue other studies in order to fit themselves for future events.

I am proud to say that our Mississippi boys are second to none in the number gone. Even some of our Mississippians are on their way to France, one of whom was my room mate, and several others of the company to which I belong. I belong to Company A, which has the distinction of being conspicuously known as the best. I am proud of my job.

Dr., I could have gone to France with the boys that left last night providing my line of trade would have been as theirs, but as there are some differences between my trade and theirs, it forces me to resume my studies, because I am going to France anyway, and be engaged in helping tear asunder Kaiserism—because we don't mean anything less than to do him as much harm as possible. We've got the power and we've had him agoing from our boys on the front, and we are going to maintain our position as we've got him going, until we hear him squall out "calf rope"! Then we are going to "Hang the Darn Kaiser to the Sour Apple

Tree"[1] *as we soldier boys usually sing, and love that song because it's one of our thrilling favorites.*

I for the Stars and Stripes of course!

Andrew M. Pickett

PS Give my regards to Mr. Forman
Editor's note: Andrew was sent off some time ago under the call for colored registrants of grammar school education to take a mechanical course.

1. A popular World War I song that adapted a verse from the Civil War tune "John Brown's Body":

   They will hang Jeff Davis to a sour apple tree,
   They will hang Jeff Davis to a sour apple tree,
   They will hang Jeff Davis to a sour apple tree,
   As they march along!

- 2 -

CROSSING THE POND AND GETTING READY

JAMES GERVYS LUSK TO UNKNOWN, OCTOBER 1917 (*GREENVILLE DAILY DEMO-CRAT-TIMES*, NOVEMBER 1, 1917)

James Gervys Lusk (1893–1954) of Greenville, Mississippi, fought in France with the 2nd Machine Gun Battalion, 16th Infantry, 1st Division. He returned to Greenville after the war and worked as a cotton broker (*Greenville Delta Democrat-Times*, July 14, 1954).

> We have moved again from where I wrote you last, and rode in a motor truck fifty miles to this school, where all nationalities are stationed. We have little huts to live in and the weather is very cold.
> We are being taught the British drill, and it seems so funny after learning our own. I went out yesterday and saw some excavated trenches and a lot of captured trench mortars of the French type; they blow holes in the ground large enough to put a small sized house in, and kill everything within three hundred yards of it. (I am speaking of the British guns.)
> I also saw a number of German prisoners and among them were kids, not near as large as Segare. There is a terrific battle going on near us, perhaps you will know of it by the time you get this letter, the great drive started three days ago. The British have the Germans on the run, and they are so glad to see us and are expecting the United States to finish the job.
> The Colonel of the school asked us not to tell the other officers here that America was going to win the war, as it might serve to dishearten them after so many years of fierce fighting. He said they all knew that the United States was the most wonderful nation in the world and that it would take her money and men, with their brains to do the job

proper. General Haig[1] *predicts the war will end by January, and he is considered a wonderful man.*

You might think it a joke, but I can sit here and hear the roar of the big guns as plain as anything; they jar the whole ground under you. It is a fearful noise, and at night you can see the flare of them just one after another, all day and all night.

The raid we were in, the one I wrote about before, we are permitted to tell of. The Huns came over and gave us a delightful welcome that night. We were at a British camp eating supper, but we were told what to do when it started, so, you see, they know exactly when they are coming; they have a trench all ready for just such emergency.

We Americans did not want to get in them, as we wanted to watch the raid go on, but we were ordered in. Instead of lying down, as ordered, we stood up to look for them. They caught one machine by a search light and it looked so pretty, and we were pulling for him to be brought down, so he unloaded all of his bombs and went as high as he could—but no use. A shell hit near us and you should have seen us duck.

1. Field Marshal Douglas Haig (1861–1928) served as commander of the British Expeditionary Force from 1915 until the end of World War I.

....

JAMES PERCY WALL, THIRD CANADIAN CASUALTY CLEARING STATION, BRITISH EXPEDITIONARY FORCE, FRANCE, TO "NONNIE," OCTOBER 23, 1917 (J. PERCY WALL PAPERS, BOX 1)

A graduate of Millsaps College and Columbia University Medical School, James Percy Wall (1878–1952) was a Jackson, Mississippi, physician who served in an American hospital unit that was attached to the British Medical Service.

Dear "Nonnie,"
Recently I visited a near-by city, famous for its wonderful tapestries, and a city where four great treaties were made.[1] *Where normally it has a population of over seventy-five thousand, it now has not more than one thousand of civilians, and for the most part they were unable to get away at the beginning, and now since there is very little danger in this city, these same civilians are running little shops, which, if the war lasts much longer, will make them immensely wealthy, for every thing*

The Ruins of the Basilica of Notre-Dame de Brebières, Albert, France, ca. 1914–18

they sell has a profit of 200 or more per cent, and it is notorious how the "Tommies" spend their shillings for trifles, regardless of whether the article is needed, they buy it, because they are really miserable when not spending their money.

In walking thru and about this old city, there is an abundance of evidence as to the accuracy of the gun-fire of the enemy—entire roofs blown away, entire streets leveled with the ground, while there is not a house in the city that does not show broken windows, etc. The great cathedral here is a wreck,—its roof gone, while broken in walls, columns knocked down, yet in its accustomed place, untouched by shell, while there is all manner of destruction about it, stands the statue of "The Virgin," and the devoted people worshipping this image, feel like God's hand saved it from the ravages of the Hun.

A few miles distant is another cathedral that has been pounded by the Boche shells. On the steeple of this cathedral there is a huge wooden statue of "The Madonna and Child." The base of this statue was struck by a shell, but instead of being broken or knocked down, it was only tilted over, and now hangs suspended down the steeple at an angle a little over ninety degrees from its original position. It looks as if a strong gust of wind would blow it down, but according to the beliefs of the *faithful, this statue is not going to fall till the Germans are defeated, for God has put this precious image in the perilous position as a constant reminder that His Hand has not been withheld, and that the effectual and fervent prayer of the righteous still avail much. Be this as it may the fact remains that these two images were unhurt, and these people get a great deal of comfort and an ever present hope from this fact.*[2]

Since coming to France, I have seen every kind of service it is possible for a medical man to see, namely:
1) Attached to Staff of a Base Hospital, seventy miles from the front.
2) On Staff of a Field Ambulance, eight miles from the front.
3) Medical Officer to a Brigade of Artillery, one mile from the front.
4) In charge of Advanced Dressing Station, half a mile from the front.
5) Have made routine inspection of the Trenches, at times less than fifty feet from the enemies' trenches.
6) And am now on the Staff of a Casualty Clearing Station, twelve miles from the front line.

The Base Hospital is where all of the post-operative cases from a Casualty Clearing Station, or the less severely wounded and sick are sent as soon as evacuation is made possible. As a place for the after care of the patients it is ideal, but for a man wanting to do surgery it is not a desirable place, because all of the work has been done before the patient reaches this station.

In a Field Ambulance service the work is principally seeing to the early evacuation of the sick and wounded to the Casualty Clearing Stations,—there is plenty of opportunity to get all the excitement one might want, and many times a great deal more than he bargained for in his over-optimistic moments.

As medical officer of a brigade of Artillery, my duties at first were mostly of an executive and sanitary nature for the greater part, and it was no trouble to keep "cool." In this position I took the place of a British Officer who had been killed only a few hours before, and put my cot down in the dug-out where he and his two helpers had been killed by a shell striking a tree and ricocheting into the dug-out. It did give me a "creepy" feeling to be lying over this poor fellow's blood, and wondering every time a shell went over or burst near me, whether the next one would get me.

One drizzly afternoon I saw a German observation plane come over, because of the clouds he had to fly very low, at times not over one hundred feet above the ground; his job was to locate our batteries, he flew over me, and waved a defiant hand, and if I had been a good shot I could have plugged him with a revolver; he went back of his lines and in less than half an hour the German guns began to shell our batteries. It was indeed exciting to stand behind a row of sand bags, and watch the enemy's shells gradually get closer and closer to our guns, and then get so close that the men had to abandon the gun, because it would soon be struck, and was so it could not be moved fast enough—I saw twelve inch gun blown up this way, and it was not more than a hundred yards from me.

Our immediate command in this Brigade of Artillery consists of forty-eight four and half inch guns, four nine and two tenth inch guns, and two twelve inch guns, and I want to tell you that when they get into action, there is "some action."

As Officer in Charge of a First Aid Dressing Station, my work for the greater part was "first aid" dressing; direct my forty-six men how to bring in the wounded, and then after dressing how to evacuate them to the rear. While in this station one afternoon the enemy put thirty-one big shells over near us inside of thirty minutes, the fragments of shell falling about us, and the vestibule of our dressing station had many fragments scattered about it and in it, and they were still hot after the barrage had ceased. When the shooting started I ordered all of my men to take cover. Somewhere in Physics there is a law concerning falling bodies, that with a given velocity a falling body accelerates at the rate of thirty-two feet per second. If that band of stretcher bearers of mine had had a few minutes to go before getting to cover after my command, they would have been going so fast that they would have made a falling body appear as if it was going upward, and I can tell you that I was not long in coming after them.

While in command of this station I saw the bravest boy I ever saw. He was brought in with his right arm practically blown off at the shoulder; he had walked over a mile, had lost quite a lot of blood, and was practically exhausted. Tho suffering great pain he did not complain, but he looked anxious; I went over to him, and upon my asking him if he wanted something, he took his other hand, put it inside his tunic, brought out two telegrams and said "Sir, will you please see that these are delivered?" This boy was only nineteen years old, yet his sense of duty was so great, that tho only a dispatch rider, he could forget his own suffering to the extent of delivering his messages so that they could be carried onward to their destination. I dressed this boy, and shall always *remember him as the grittiest fellow I ever knew. He got well and tho he has now an empty sleeve, I would rather be this Scotch laddie than the War Lord of Europe.*

Just to the rear of my station there is one of those nine and two tenth inch British Naval Guns (they are called "nine point two" for short); and when it blazes away, it does cause some disturbance both at the origin and where the shell lands. Somehow the artillery officers choose dressing stations for their gun-emplacements—they must have some place to conceal the flare from the guns, but it does seem to me they could choose another place than immediately behind a dressing station, because such a position draws enemy fire, and if the shell should happen to hit a dressing station we all go up in the air about the barbarity of the Germans, when at fact we are to blame for putting a dressing station in front of a gun or permitting a gun to be placed immediately to the rear of our dressing station.

With[in] fifty feet of this big gun there is a newly made grave, with a crude cross, made out of two sticks of wood, undressed, and unpainted, but on this is the most appropriate epitaph I have ever seen; this man was serving the gun when a shell struck the crew, and he was so badly wounded, among several others that his identity was never known (his identification tag and all identification being removed by the shell), and he was buried close to the gun position where he lost his life. One of his comrades, not knowing this man's name, rank or any means of identification, wrote on an old envelope his epitaph, pinned it to the crude cross—and this is what it said, only three words, but expressive of the thought that carried much to us—"SOME MOTHER'S SON."

As inspector of my trenches, it was my duty for either me or my first sergeant to go up to them every day. There is considerable misconception of what a trench is—they are not nearly so dangerous or uncomfortable as ordinarily regarded—the great danger is getting into them and getting out again, for if a man shows his head he is sure to attract the enemies' fire.

My first morning of inspection (we choose the time of day when we thought the Germans were not shooting, and this is easily calculated, because these fellows shoot according to the clock) in company with my sergeant I went up to the system to be inspected—it was about half or three quarters of a mile from my dug-out. As we got in the open we got down on our all fours and crawled along till we got into the trench, after getting into a trench, I asked the sergeant where we were headed to, he pointed out another trench not over fifty yards away, not caring to walk around thru the connecting trench, I crawled out to walk across, not even dreaming what would happen, and as I raised up out of the trench a machine gun of the enemy's began to sputter at me,—well, you can believe me or not I got back into that trench at the rate of considerably better than a half hour in one minute. For this foolish action of mine I was criticized very severely by the sergeant (of course he was polite in his criticism) and informed me that I was subject to a courts-martial for unnecessarily exposing myself to enemy fire. I was not hit, tho scared awfully badly, and there is absolutely no danger of my ever being court-martialed for a repetition of that kind of an offense, because after that first morning's experience the only way one could get me to repeat such a fool act would be to make it hotter in the trenches than it is "over the top," and I do not believe that is possible.

The soldiers have dug-outs along the sides of the trenches, thus they are protected from rain, and exploding shells, while along the bottoms of the trenches there are board walks (called, euphuistically, "duck boards") to keep the men's feet out of the mud and slush, the land (they call it "terrain," from the French) is so soft and the water seeps up from the ground, as all of this section is below the sea-level or so near it that it amounts to the same thing.

Having had my "school experience," I was transferred about one month ago to a Casualty Clearing Station, and in this class of work I am to remain till transferred back to the Americans, among whom I am supposed to be qualified by that time to do war surgery.

I do not know of any reason for putting American doctors in the various kinds of work I have been doing, unless it is a matter of policy of putting untrained men in the dangerous posts is a matter of economy in men—for if a doctor gets killed early in the game, he is just one doctor less, but if he gets killed later on in the campaign he has lost all of the training he has acquired in the different stations in which he has served, for there is no doubt the longer a doctor keeps alive over here, the more valuable he becomes in every way to his command.

My present position at this Casualty Clearing Station offers great opportunity to see, learn and to do. Such a station is a mobile hospital near the front. Here we operate on all serious cases, keep them till they are able to be evacuated farther back to a Base Hospital where they are kept till well, or die, or able to be evacuated to England, if they are not to be of service any more for several months. The work here is heavy, we have five operating teams working five by day and five by night, the major operations will run from 40 to 180 in twenty-four hours according to the activity on our immediate front. We are one of four similar stations on this immediate sector. Here we do everything from shining the shoes to cutting the hair. Our work is primarily life-saving, leaving the functional restoration and cosmetic beautifying for the backward areas to do after the men are sent to them.

Tho we are some distance from the front we are by no means out of danger, because the long range guns can reach us, and nearly every night enemy planes come over bombing everything in sight. A few weeks ago one of these planes dropped a bomb within 150 yards of my tent, killing sixty-two people (nineteen of whom were German prisoners) and wounding twenty-nine others. Consequently the doctors in our hospital (there are thirty-two of them) are rather "gun shy."

Always thought I had a generous streak of yellow in my make-up but to see how some of these officers act when a Bosche plane comes over that they did not have a streak of yellow, but that they had been smeared with yellow ochre—these men (and they are showing their sense too) will lie down flat on the floor, get behind banks of dirt, in holes, any where they think they have protection from flying fragments of shell—our only hope is that flying fragments will not hit us, because nothing will save us if a direct hit of the original shell strikes us.

A few days ago our men made a successful attack, and drove the enemy back for one to two miles over a six mile front. Late that afternoon the soldiers coming back from the front were feeling rather good, because they had given "Mr. Heine, his'n," and tho it was cold and raining, the band sitting on a flat car was playing "When we come to the end of a perfect day."[3]

Our hospital trains are marvels of construction and service for the wounded and sick soldiers. Instead of using the little coaches so common on the European railroads, these trains have large steel coaches so arranged that they are able to care for thirty-six stretcher cases each or seventy-two sitting cases per coach and there are sixteen coaches to the train. These trains are in many instances individual gifts from rich people back in England, and represents a great war service to these poor men who are so badly in need of just this kind of help.

Each train has an isolation ward for transmissible diseases, thus protecting the other men from additional contagion; a dressing ward for slightly injured cases; an emergency operating room; a drug store; a kitchen, serving hot drinks to those able to take them—all of this run by competent doctors, efficient nurses, and capable orderlies.

The religious side of the soldier has ample opportunity for expansion in this unit. We have with us all of the time a Roman Catholic priest, a Church of England rector and a Presbyterian minister.

These men do good work, encounter all kinds of creeds, but the word "Padre" is applicable to every chaplain, be he Conformist or Non-Conformist, and he is ever welcomed by the soldier, and tho some few men assume the air of agnosticism they soon come to the belief that "God is our refuge and strength, a very present help in trouble."[4]

In one section of our Casualty Clearing Station we care for a regiment of East Indian soldiers, and the "care-for" is advisedly used. Because of their religious rites, their food must be kept separate from that of Christians, be prepared by their priests and cooked in a certain way. To illustrate, whenever mutton is sent to these troops, the sheep must be brought to them alive; it is strung up by the hind feet, and after the Mohammedan priest goes thru some incantations and a prayer, the priest severs the sheep's head with a sword, lets him hang there till all of the blood has run out, then after some more incantations and prayers the sheep is ready for the cook. Without all of this, the Mohammedans will not touch the mutton, and because the cow is sacred to these people, their meat is all mutton, and because the memory of the Sepoy Rebellion is well kept alive the government carefully guards their religious prejudices.[5]

Another illustration that people are the same the world over where the same conditions exist, is the British way of handling the wounded negroes in this war. From the West Indies there are a number of negroes, and tho there is no direct opposition to them, most of the soldiers want to be regarded as separate and detached from them especially on a social equality idea, therefore the government has a modified "Jim Crow Law," and when they are evacuated they are put into separate sections, thus avoiding any probability of trouble between the races.

The other day I "wangled" (that is some nationality's way of saying, "bummed a ride") an automobile ride up to the sea coast town; the journey being thru territory held in common by the French and British. Tho the trip was only thirty-three miles, I passed 473 automobile trucks in going up. On this trip I could not help from contrasting the English and French wagon trains—the one looked clean and bright, and the horses as if they had just been groomed for a horse show, while the other looked dirty and the horses poor and ill-cared for. Such a condition of affairs is to be expected, because the French have borne the brunt of this awful war for three years, and I caught myself thinking about how our soldiers are going to look after we have been at this war game for three years.

The French officers were all neatly and loudly dressed, every one had on one or more medals, and some of them had so many that they really looked like a color bearer in the Emancipation Day parade staged by the Jackson negroes.[6]

Along the beach for over a mile (this is on the English Channel) there are magnificent villas and casinos, built of stone and tiled brick, but are all now deserted, and barbed wire entanglements run down to the water's edge, for the Germans occasionally make sorties out from the bases with their torpedo boats and shell this coast city; only the tonight before my visit they succeeded in breaking thru the patrol, and put over two hundred shells into the city; the next day a German spy in a French uniform was caught on the street, he faced a firing squad as soon as preliminary courts-martial could get him to that desired place.

The spirit animating our allies is sure to win. Tho worn and tired after three years of an awful carnage and suffering, everybody today is determined more than ever not to let up till Germany is completely beaten, and like Babylon has "fallen to rise no more,"[7] to push the world into such a cruel war, all because of the ambitions of a mad, war nation, dominated by selfishness, puffed up with vainglory, urged on by arrogance and nurtured by hate.

1. Amiens, France, known for its tapestries and its cathedral, was the site where several notable treaties were signed.
2. Early in the war, German shells hit the Basilica of Notre-Dame de Brebières in Albert, France, dislodging a statue of the Virgin Mary holding an infant Jesus. The statue did not fall but remained hanging precariously. After German troops took the town in 1918, British guns finally brought down the statue.
3. Carrie Jacobs-Bond, *Perfect Day* (Chicago: Jacobs-Bond and Son, 1910).
4. Psalm 46:1.
5. Sepoys were Indian soldiers in British military regiments in imperial India. To load their guns, the sepoys had to bite into greased paper rifle cartridges. In 1856, rumors spread that the grease contained a mixture of beef tallow, which Hindus are forbidden to eat, and pork lard, which Muslims do not eat. The rumors sparked a massive May 1857 revolt against the British Empire in which hundreds of thousands of people were killed.
6. Emancipation Day commemorates the day in 1865 when African Americans learned of their freedom. It was celebrated on various dates in different parts of the South but most commonly on May 8 or June 19.
7. Revelation 14:8.

CREW OF THE USS *PENNSYLVANIA* TO C. B. TORJUSEN, OCTOBER 31, 1917 (*PASCAGOULA DEMOCRAT-STAR*, NOVEMBER 9, 1917)

C. B. Torjusen's son, Cornelius O. Torjusen (b. December 1889) was a US Navy seaman who had enlisted in April 1917. He and seven other men died when the SS *Motano* was torpedoed off the English coast on July 31, 1917.

> *Dear Sir:*
> *On October 28th memorial services were held onboard this ship in honor of those men who had died since the commencement of hostilities. There were about 350 Blue Jackets and Marines present. After the reading of the honor roll, it was unanimously decided to send a memorial of their respects to the nearest relatives of those who have already gone down fighting for the nation.*
> *We, in the navy, feel a very strong comradeship for our brothers in the service. Our duties, our hardships and our ideals bring us closer together, and at this present time when we are eagerly awaiting the chance to fight for our great American ideals of world wide liberty, justice and peace, we want to show our gratitude to those who have sacrificed all they had—their lives—for those ideals. We know that you are now deeply troubled in your recent loss and so we extend our most sincere and great sympathy to you; but more than that we would have you feel that the sacrifice has not been in vain, for it is through the example of such men as these that we, their comrades, may fight until our cause shall triumph.*
> *With the sympathy and best wishes of the men of the USS Pennsylvania.*

THE CREW

AS THE AEF GREW TO MORE THAN ONE HUNDRED THOUSAND MEN, British and French leaders pressed General Pershing to commit his troops, ready or not, to relieve the struggling and exhausted Allied lines. By October 1917, the Americans had had extensive training in the use of grenades, trench raiding, and gas warfare, and Pershing believed that his troops could be eased into the lines, rotating them after a ten-day trial period. Both the

French and the British were desperate for replacements, but Pershing stood by his decision to have his men fight in American units. The first American shell to fall on German lines was fired in the early morning of October 23, 1917, a few hours after the first US contingent had taken up its position opposite Bavarian troops (Welsh, *USA in World War I*, 20).

SEGUINE ALLEN "BEPPO" ARNOLD, FRANCE, TO MOTHER, NOVEMBER 28, 1917 (*GREENVILLE DAILY DEMOCRAT-TIMES*, DECEMBER 27, 1917)

Greenville, Mississippi, native Seguine Allen "Beppo" Arnold (b. December 6, 1889) attended the US Naval Academy and worked in a packinghouse before volunteering to serve in the war. He went to France with the Sewanee Ambulance Unit in July 1917 and died of a cerebral hemorrhage on May 2, 1918, making him the first Greenville man to give his life overseas (Everman and Fort, *History of St. James' Church*).

> Dear Mother:
> Am now in the worst post we have, have been here four days and will leave after two more and go back to headquarters. There is not much to do here, just an occasional call, generally "malades" (sick patients). But the place is a regular mud hole down between some high hills. Our quarters consist of a shack about fifteen feet square, where there are four bunks raised up off the ground, a fireplace and a very small table which six of us eat off at the same time, so you can see how much room is left for moving around in.
>
> We have had a very interesting visitor with us every night since I've been here. He is a Frenchman who operates an air compressor near here, speaks four languages, including English and was a mining engineer in British East Africa before the war. Yesterday there was an inch of snow on the ground and he took us up to his place, loaned us his saw and showed us where we could get some good wood on a hill that has been heavily shelled by the Germans. It was just covered with shell holes and the wood we got was from a tree that had been cut down by a big one.
>
> Yesterday your letter dated the 18th of October came, last week I got one dated the 26th. Guess they came by different routes. I will never forget mine and how near I came to not getting here, just one little old US destroyer was all that made it possible, but it certainly was a beautiful piece of work, was all over in about two minutes, during which we all thought we were done for. I went so far as to take off leggings, shoes and coat.

Tomorrow is Thanksgiving and we are going to have some extra things to eat, though there won't be any of Uncle Sam's turkeys, which we read about in the papers. We will give the French cook about fifteen francs and will get some extra rations from our section fund. May have some champagne, which we can buy for only five francs, just a little more than a dollar a quart.

I have decided not to try to send you anything [for] Christmas, since there is so much chance of its not arriving, but would like to know what you would like to have. There are so many things I could bring back. The soldiers are making all sorts of souvenirs from shells, etc. One of the boys bought a pair of vases made from a French 75.3. They are very pretty, have a rough finish from a blunt punch and have a flower beaten out, engraved around the edges and polished. These would be very pretty on the mantelpiece, but I'm sure they are going to be so numerous and cheap after the war. Maybe you would like some lace; saw some handkerchiefs yesterday with very pretty lace but they were too loud.

Dinner is being served from our large can under the table. C'est la guerre.
Devotedly,

BEP

BY THE BEGINNING OF 1918, BOTH THE ALLIED AND GERMAN FORCES were running out or steam. The French and the British had suffered heavy losses on several offensives, and the Central Powers were suffering economic strains, with populations hungry, workers disgruntled, and strikes increasing.

EDWARD HINES JR., FRANCE, TO EDWARD HINES SR. AND LORETTA HINES, JANUARY 18, 1918 (*BAY ST. LOUIS SEA COAST ECHO*, MARCH 2, 1918)

Edward Hines Jr. (b. July 24, 1896) was the son and namesake of the president of the Edward Hines Lumber Company, which owned extensive tracts of land in Mississippi. He enlisted while a senior at Yale University, and his unit, the 4th Machine Gun Battalion, sailed for France on December 24, 1917. He died of pneumonia in June 1918 ("Edward Hines, Jr."; Fickle, *Mississippi Forests and Forestry*, 88).

Dearest Mother and Father

Well, here I am, somewhere in France. How I wish I could tell you where and all about it; all the interesting things that have happened and the wonderful opportunities over here.

I suppose you have been wondering why you have not heard from me. The truth of the matter is that I ate something which did not agree with me, a couple of days after I left and was quite sick for a couple of weeks. I never got out of bed while on the boat. Am fine now, but you can probably understand how busy we are. Capt. White has been just like a father to me, especially while I was sick. There was nothing he would not do for me and I know that you people are not worrying while I am with him.

We had one slight submarine scare going across, but there is really very little danger now as the English and Americans have the Germans pretty well scared. After landing in England, we went to Winchester which is called an English rest camp but which is more like Dumont in its purpose. We were quartered the first night in a barn with three boards, straw and blankets to sleep on, so you can imagine we did not sleep much not being used to it. It was a pretty place but we were there only a day.

Mother dear, if you know any boys coming over here please get in touch with them and tell them to bring American Express checks to France in place of money as they are worth even more than American money. They are now worth 57 francs on $10 and before the war they were worth only 51.25. $10 in US money is now worth 55 francs.

I am in the best of health now and exceptionally busy as I have been assigned Adjutant Pierson's position who will leave us shortly, I am sorry to say.

Major Mills has been wonderful to me and is putting a load of responsibility on me which I know you will be delighted to hear and which really suits me well.

I am quartered in a nice French house in this small village and all in all am most comfortable. We eat at a butcher shop where we can get a nice steak and French fried potatoes when we have the money to pay for them, which, thanks to you, dear Mother and Father, I have a sufficient amount of and only wish it were the good fortune of all boys under me to be able to share some of these comforts.

Outwardly at least England seems to have felt the war more than France, as here the people are cheerful, happy and hopeful. They have enough to eat and it is hard to realize that there is a war here. Personally I admire the French beyond words.

Speaking about sending things over. It is not possible to obtain candy, cigarettes and other luxuries here so if you know anyone who wish to send the boys comforts, they all long for these things.

You will laugh when I tell you I am in politics. I have the title of being Town Mayor. Wouldn't the fellows at Colony House (Yale) laugh at this? If you see the boys be sure to tell them for I know they would enjoy the joke as much as I do. But now, Mother, this is truly a responsible position, as I am supposed to run the town and have a private office—and, as you know, I am Assistant Adjutant of our battalion, so you can see I am kept pretty busy. The details of the work, however, are wonderful training and I more than appreciate the opportunity I am having for development in this line. We are anxiously awaiting for peace convention; the people here are all expecting great things from it. War may be alright, and we are now at it, but one cannot help but look at the pitiful side of those who have been nearly four years suffering all the agonies of this horrible world conflict.

Tell the boys you know who come over to bring warm clothing, rubber boots and any luxuries they desire as they cannot be had here. Have the officers bring their sand belts from US.

I want to tell you that it takes four or five weeks for my letters to reach you and longer for yours to reach me. This is a pity and seems so unnecessary. If we were permitted to use the French post I could get a letter to you in about ten days. I wish the newspapers at home would take up this matter and see if something can be done so that we can get mail in less time. If they realized how we boys watch the post I am sure they would gratify one great desire of our lives. We are not criticizing a single move of our Government as we know what they have had to do and when we compare the work at home it is with the greatest pride we say "We are Americans," but a matter simple as this could be corrected if our Government would realize how much it means to the soldier boys to know that you get our letters promptly and that yours come right through to us.

We miss sweets and pastries, etc., dreadfully. We can get some of it, but it is frightfully high. A package of dates costing five cents over there cost forty cents here; a small bar of very poor milk chocolate costs a franc to 1½ francs.

Our week days are filled with routine from morning to supper time, after which we study French for two hours, and military lectures by French officers. We are so tired when we turn in that we have no trouble [hunt-around?] for sleep. We are thoroughly accustomed now to the booming of cannon and the buzz of aeroplanes and pay very little attention to it.

I went to mass Sunday morning at 8:30 and never was so mystified in my life. I thought I had some comprehension of the right thing to do at the right time. The church was filled with American soldiers and French women, and we stood up when the women sat and kneeled when they got up; it was so different from our service. They take up a collection but once a month which I presume is on account of the war. Then the strangest thing of all was during mass they pass bread around for every one in the church and, needless to say, we boys did not know what to do. We wondered if we were receiving Holy Communion without going to confession, but we concluded we would take the bread and later we learned it was customary for everyone to break their fast together. It is pitiful to look about the church Sunday morning and see all the dear good women in black, a few wearing colors, and it is plainly seen that the strain of the war has told on them. They all believe France will win and make Germany pay heavily for her sins. Believe me, I sincerely hope we all have a whack at her to make her feel more the horrible crime she has committed. You are here but a few moments when you are inoculated with a fierce hatred for Germany.

Your cigarettes were a God send to all the boys whom I divided with, will not be hurt if you send more. Our captain is entirely out of the allotment he brought over.

Also, Mother dear, we say God bless the Red Cross for all of our boys. I suppose we officers would have had full and plenty were it not for the work that you succeeded in getting from the Red Cross and the great kindness of Mrs. Charles Dawes[1] and your good friends. I may have had to see my men suffer instead of being fairly comfortable.

I must now close, my dears, with all the love in the world to the best father and mother a boy ever had.
Your loving son,

Edward

---

1. Caro Blymyer Dawes (1866–1957) was the wife of Charles Gates Dawes (1865–1951), a prominent Chicago banker and politician who went on to serve as US vice president

from 1925 to 1929 and was a corecipient of the 1925 Nobel Peace Prize. Charles Dawes served in World War I with the 17th Army Corps of Engineers, and his wife organized an enormous volunteer effort to provide clothing for his unit.

....

CARL WALZ SCHWEIZER, FRANCE, TO MRS. METCALFE, JANUARY 24, 1918 (*GREENVILLE DAILY DEMOCRAT-TIMES*, MARCH 16, 1918)

Carl Walz Schweizer (1894–1976) was born in Cincinnati but was a resident of Greenville, Mississippi, prior to the war. When he registered for the draft in May 1917, he was a student at the Citizens Training Camp at Fort Logan H. Roots, Arkansas, a voluntary program that offered instruction in military skills for potential officers in the coming war.

Dear Mrs. Metcalfe:
Am writing to let you know I have received the Christmas package sent to me by the ladies of the Belvidere Chapter, Daughters of the American Revolution. Please give the ladies of the Belvidere Chapter my warmest thanks for their very welcome gift. The package was a complete surprise as I had no idea it was coming. All the articles will be most useful and those I did not need I gave to some of the fellows who haven't received their Christmas packages yet. The lump sugar is a luxury, as sugar cannot be bought here for love or money. The diary is handy and the two speeches are most welcome, as I am forever getting into arguments about Greenville and Mississippi. There is only one other Mississippi boy here with me, and I have to do all the talking. Am nicknamed the "man from Mississippi" by the other fellows, because of my defending the state in our debates.

Cannot give you any war news, but will give a short account of our life in camp. We live in "Made in USA" barracks and have good bunks. Our meals are excellent and we had big turkey dinners on the holidays, with apple pies, nuts, cakes, etc. The men I am with are nearly all college men and we get along fine and have good times together. There are quite a number of mandolins, ukuleles and violins and lots of good musicians, so we do not lack for music or singing. Have electric lights.

Am at a training camp for aviators, but I hope to get to the front some day.

There is a large YMCA here and they give entertainments and movie every week. Have musicales and singing and have services on Sundays. They run the Post Exchange where we can buy chocolate bars, jam, cakes, tobacco, etc. We had several football teams and our cadet team won the championship. Are having a basketball tourney now in YMCA. So you see we do not lack for entertainments. Also have boxing and wrestling.

The American Red Cross have a hut here where they run a cafeteria for officers and sell sandwiches and coffee to the men. Have real American women, too, so we feel more at home when we walk in. Have a piano and good players for most any instrument. Have a camp paper, besides we can buy the foreign edition of famous American newspapers.

Looks like the folks at home are beginning to feel the effects of the war. I think it will do the people a lot of good, teach them to be more economical in many ways.

I have had some good times shopping in the French stores. See very few men not in uniform, and all the women are dressed in black. See some good looking French girls, but I like the Greenville kind best.

All the houses over here are built of brick or stone with tile roofs, are most picturesque. Wouldn't care to live in them as they are too dark and dreary.

We have had several heavy snowfalls and cold days, but are having spring weather now. Guess I had better close, as I have written several pages. With best wishes and a Happy New Year to all, I am, Very truly yours,

Carl Schweizer

JAMES PERCY WALL, 13TH GENERAL HOSPITAL, BRITISH EXPEDITIONARY FORCE, FRANCE, TO "NONNIE," FEBRUARY 8, 1918 (J. PERCY WALL PAPERS, BOX 1).

Dear "Nonnie,"
You ask why, if our unit is an American one, my mail should be addressed in care of the above hospital.

This is one of the first six American hospital units to come to France and was attached to the British Medical Service and because of its efficiency has been kept by this government, and in as much as our troops did not need us we were permitted to remain under the British control so that we could learn War Surgery and War Medicine. Nominally we are part of the British Expeditionary Force, but we are all Americans, from our Commanding Officer down, and rarely ever do we miss an opportunity of letting this fact be known.

These six American Hospital units now serving with the British will be taken as "models" for the units in our Army, and this is no more than it should be, for we have been over here over eight months, have learned how the war game is played, and naturally know more than the new comers will know for a while after beginning to work under war conditions. When we are to be returned to our forces we do not know and suppose we will know only a few days before we are transferred, and this is as it should be because of military reasons.

Here at a great base every thing is done, that is humanly possible, to make the soldier's time pleasant—boxing matches, wrestling matches, hockey, and amateur entertainments—in fact there is a distinct department that looks after the entertaining feature for the sick and convalescent soldier and those on leave.

Tho I am practically out of the danger zone at the present time, I have taken out another ten thousand dollar insurance policy in your favor. It is so arranged you need not worry about premiums, and I do not believe that you will get a chance to collect it, tho the disability clause may become effective before this great struggle is over.

Most of our men are unwilling to go home till the Germans are licked "good and proper," but every body will be glad when that time does come, and from the way things are now humming that time is not very far distant.

A few nights ago our Commanding Officer "requested" ("requested" is euphemistic for "ordered") me and two other officers to make arrangements for a dance in honor of twelve new doctors who had just taken examinations to enter the regular army medical service. I have no idea why he "requested" me to serve in such a capacity for when it comes to dancing I know absolutely nothing; could not tell the difference between a waltz and a "break down," and never could differentiate a "two step" from a "goose step." Somehow I am lucky because every thing worked out to make my efforts produce the desired results, as the program moved along smoothly, and everybody seemed to enjoy the evening, but Gee! I was glad when I got this out of my system.

We have a new identification card in the army. Orders were issued to have our pictures taken—no mention being made as to whether they should be with or without hats. After a lot of discussion we decided, as our passport pictures were made with our hats on, that that would be the proper procedure, and accordingly we had them "took" with our hats on, and very proudly did we turn over the pictures to the Adjutant, *congratulating ourselves that the other disagreeable task had been performed without any casualties; however the next day an order was issued stating that these pictures should be made without hats, accordingly we had to go thru the "look pleasant" performance again. We must have shown very plainly our displeasure at the enforced return engagement, as the photographer in the most bland way asked, "Est-il tres terrible?"*

On the 13th I go to Paris for a two week leave—American Officers are not permitted to spend over twenty-four hours in Paris, but being attached to the British we do not come under this restriction. If I can get my passport vised, I want to spend a part of my leave in Rome, and if I can get permission from the British and American Ambassadors and the permission of the Prefecture of Police in Paris, and the approval of the Italian Ambassador, I most surely am going to the land of spaghetti for a few days anyway.
Lovingly,

Percy

ABOUT TWO HUNDRED THOUSAND AFRICAN AMERICANS SERVED OVERseas with the AEF, most of them in all-black labor or stevedore battalions.

....

JESSE J. LEE, COMPANY I, 303RD STEVEDORE REGIMENT, FRANCE, TO ADERTON B. NANCE AND MARGARET B. NANCE, FEBRUARY 27, 1918 (*GREENVILLE DAILY DEMOCRAT-TIMES*, APRIL 20, 1918)

Jesse J. Lee (1887?–) served overseas with the 302nd Stevedore Regiment from December 1917 to July 1919. This letter was written to Aderton B. Nance, a Greenville bank executive, and Margaret B. Nance. Their son, Rutherford Lanier Nance (1896–1963), was an electrical engineer on the US steamer *President Grant*.

Dear Sir and Madam:
I feel it my duty to write you all and explain to you all my feelings toward your son who accompanied us on the voyage to France, being so very much impressed with his manly conduct and behavior towards me on the trip, and too, I think that you will be glad to hear from him and that I met him.

He accorded me the kindest treatment on board ship which no more could be expected of him, being of the royal blood he is. I cannot and never will forget his kindness towards me. Now before you begin to wonder who I am I will try to tell you. I am Jesse J. Lee, the ex-mail carrier of Greenville, also the recent laundry solicitor for Messrs. Leon Fletcher and Harris.

My home is 409 O'Hea Street, my family also resides there. Mr. David Armstrong, the present mail carrier, will better explain to you who I am. I am with the forces in France to assist in winning the war, if such can be, and I am putting my whole heart in the work, as you know, too, well that I will do. I am not exactly on the firing line, but I am back of those who are there. I have received the highest honor that my company can award one for service. I hope this will find you and your family well and prosperous in your affairs. It leaves me well. I hope to be back home again some day and meet you all face to face and talk over the times now happening. I also hope your broad-hearted son will be home to make you and his mother glad in your old days.

This is not all I could say, but for fear that I will say too much or more than you will have time to read, I will come to a close. I hope to hear from you all some time if I can.

So hoping again that all is well, I am your very truly,

Sergt. JESSE J. LEE (Colored)

ON MARCH 1, 1918, NEARLY A YEAR AFTER THE UNITED STATES HAD ENtered the war, only six American divisions were stationed in France: two of them had no combat experience, while the other four had been assigned to relatively quiet sectors. With the Allied forces near exhaustion after three years of fighting, the inexperienced Americans would soon be tested (Stamps and Esposito, *Short Military History*, 272).

Back home, people were still being encouraged to participate in the war effort in whatever way they could—by knitting scarves and socks, collecting reading materials, and writing encouraging letters (*This Fabulous Century*, 228–33).

BENJAMIN M. BAILEY, FRANCE, TO MRS. FRANK, MARCH 7, 1918 (WORLD WAR I SCRAPBOOK [NATCHEZ], FOLDER 1)

Benjamin M. Bailey, Regular Army, was the battalion commander of the 2nd Division, 15th Field Artillery (Hallas, *Doughboy War*, 20).

> *My Dear Mrs. Frank:*
> *I shall identify myself as the fortunate soldier who now wears your sweater. I lost all of my field equipment and was handed a sweater bearing your address by another regiment that had been supplied to the last man.*
>
> *It may be of interest to you to know that if your garment had eyes and could talk, it might tell you of the grandeur of the snow clad Alps of Switzerland—you might be initiated in to a few of the mysteries of the deep recesses of the German terrain beyond the battle lines, as seen from an aeroplane five thousand feet above old mother earth. You might be given a picture from a balloon of how American shells look when they fall.*
>
> *Last but not least you might be given the gratification that every true American woman finds in knowing that her efforts have helped to warm a heart whose beats quicken at the thoughts of home and the loved ones who may some day be called upon to bear the heaviest burdens of victory.*
>
> *I thank you and the other good ladies of Natchez for myself and for the many of my men who do not always discover the name of the earnest worker at home.*
> *Very sincerely,*
>
> *Benj. M. Bailey*

PHILIP G. DAVIDSON, FRANCE, TO L. PINK SMITH, EDITOR, *GREENVILLE DAILY DEMOCRAT-TIMES*, MARCH 13, 1918 (*GREENVILLE DAILY DEMOCRAT-TIMES*, APRIL 11, 1918)

The Reverend Philip G. Davidson (1865–1946) was born in Carthage, Illinois, and served as rector of parishes in Colorado, Missouri, and Nebraska before coming to Greenville in 1904 to serve as rector of St. James Episcopal Church. When the United States entered the war,

Davidson took a leave of absence to go overseas with the YMCA, which was the first social welfare organization to offer its wartime services to the government. General Pershing tasked the YMCA with providing amusement to the soldiers and overseeing their moral welfare. The organization operated "huts" or "canteens" designed to serve as substitutes for home, school, theater, and church and hired more than twenty-five thousand workers, at least one-fifth of them women, to operate the facilities (*Greenville Delta Democrat-Times*, June 3, 1946, 1; "YMCA with the A.E.F.").

Friend Smith:
I am now at the work assigned me which consists in ministering to four camps, two of which are occupied by negro troops, scattered over an area of about ten miles. Our association is just starting in at the larger of the camps which I have made my headquarters and we have a tent 25 × 50 with a piano, Victrola and some athletic supplies. We are still awaiting part of our equipment as the other camps have not yet received anything. This is on account of the fact that the rapid expansion of the YMCA work has outstripped all expectation. Of course the necessary equipment will be received within a few weeks.

We are located somewhere behind the fighting lines and this fact, in reality, offers the best field for our work. Secretaries and chaplains can share the life of the men under somewhat normal conditions and exercise a leadership and influence along moral and spiritual lines as well as in camp playground activities. It is in such camps that the men are first brought in contact with the temptations of this new life, while at the front there is no time for temptation or for thoughtlessness. It is there a grim fight in which the ministry of the Y is that of creature comforts and encouragement. The biggest moral work of the YMCA as well as its most strengthening service is being rendered in just such places as this.

Officers and men have welcomed me heartily and with the best spirit of co-operation, and I want to assure you that I have never met a finer body of men. They are manly, clean and temperate to a degree that places them in high comparison with any similar group of men in our country. I have never been as proud of America as the past few weeks have made me. If I could get such a crowd of virile young men out to an evening service in St. James as I had last Sunday evening at the Y, and have them singing, responding and showing earnest reverence as these men did, I should certainly not care a great deal if they did move back the benches and have a lively boxing match. We have a lot to learn about Christianity from our army.

I have not seen Mr. Percy since I left him in Paris, but I know that he is going at his work with thoroughness. You will probably see him before I do as he plans to return to America a few weeks before my contract with the YMCA expires. I hope to put in most of my time here in the four camps, or until the work has become well established, then to make at least a short visit to the front and to one of our great YMCA rest camps for the soldiers before getting back to America. I plan to study the work of the YMCA and to learn what I can of the need of the men. In this way I believe that I can render the best service to our boys and to the government. I have already learned a vast lot over here.

Please extend my regards to friends and my appreciation to those who contributed to this work.

Very sincerely, P. G. Davidson

....

ROBERT WALTER RUPP JR., LONDON, ENGLAND, TO PARENTS, APRIL 1918 (*OCEAN SPRINGS JACKSON COUNTY TIMES*, MAY 4, 1918)

Robert Walter Rupp Jr. (1893–1958) was a farm laborer in Ocean Springs, Mississippi, prior to enlisting in the US Navy on May 7, 1912. He remained in the service after the war and was stationed in both London, England, and the Panama Canal Zone. He also served in World War II and was discharged from the navy on October 27, 1944.

Dear Father and Mother:
I arrived safely in Liverpool, two days ago and am all settled down to work once more.

We had quite a trip across. The first few days out it snowed and then hail would come flying along. The weather cleared after we got out in the Gulf Stream.

When we arrived in the war zone every one was on the lookout for German U-Boats and on the last day out we encountered two.

The submarine was seen first, on our right side, by an American destroyer, who was part of our convoy, and it wasn't over two hundred yards from our ship. The destroyer swung around and when she was directly over the German U-Boat, she dropped a depth-bomb. You ought to have seen the remains of that submarine going up in the air.

The second one we saw fired a torpedo at us and it would have sunk our ship had it not been for the man at the wheel. He saw the torpedo coming and swung our ship around. The big torpedo missed us [by] only a few feet.

This submarine came to the surface to see us blow up after she fired the torpedo at us. Well as soon as she showed herself, a six-inch explosive shell from our ship took off the whole conning tower and she went down like a rock.

So you see we got over here with a "whole skin" and sunk two of the Kaiser's "tin fish" to boot.

I like my new work fine. It is somewhat different than what I have been doing on the Connecticut, but there isn't anything about the work I am afraid of.

I am well and have a good appetite and can sleep like a log. Haven't seen much of London yet, as there has been so much to do. Will write to you all at home over there, every week.

Love from your son,

Robert Rupp

HENRY J. GOOLSBY, COMPANY C, 5TH BATTALION, 20TH US ENGINEERS, FRANCE, TO MOTHER, MAY 12, 1918 (*PONTOTOC SENTINEL*, JUNE 13, 1918)

Henry J. Goolsby (1892–1973) was a railroad brakeman living in Louisville, Mississippi, when he registered for the draft on June 2, 1917. After the war, he returned to the railroad, living in Madison County, Tennessee, and working as a conductor.

My dear Mother:
I am sure that you know today is Mother's Day and Gen. Pershing sent us a message it was the duty of every soldier boy to write his mother today, and that he would see that the post office department would make every effort possible to get the letters to their destination, if it was properly addressed with "Mothers' Day" written in the right hand corner of the envelope; said it would be given the same attention as a special delivery letter in the States.

Of course I intended to write to you today anyway, for it is Sunday and that is about the only time I have to write except at night when my bed appeals to me so much that I can't stay out of it. And when I do plan to write the lady stops us downstairs and keeps us up until 10:30 or 11 o'clock talking to us, and of course we have a drink or two of wine during that time. It is customary for everybody to drink wine and beer in France, for they all drink it, young and old, and think it is perfectly all right.

The lady that owns the hotel is about forty-five years old and she has a daughter nineteen years old. There is another lady here about thirty-three, I would judge, and the maids. The daughter plays the piano so you see we have lots of good music along with the many other good things we have. There are four of us who room here, two in a room, and the people are certainly good to us. They are always asking us if our rooms are suiting us and they say that they want us to feel as comfortable as possible. Well, I think they ought to when I think about us coming away over here to help them out. One of the boys that rooms with us is a corporal and they say they are not afraid to stay in the hotel with us officers.

Let me tell you about our beds. They are fine and it is certainly hard to get out of them when morning comes and anyway you know how I always like to sleep in the morning. The beds are a little higher than our beds at home and they have a straw mattress and a big feather bed on top of that, so you see we almost have to have a step-ladder to get in them and we have two quilts and a sheet to cover with, and then on top of that there is a feather tick about one and a half feet thick and about four and a half square. It is made like a big sofa pillow. We use that to cover with too. I don't know where they got that idea, but it is hard to tell about these French people because they have so many funny ideas about everything to we Americans.

This is certainly a beautiful country, especially through this section. I am crazy about it, but it is pretty cool yet. We have had only one or two warm days since I came here and it has rained almost every day. The French say before the war they always had pretty weather by this time, but since the war it rains nearly all the time. Well, they are right. But when you think about it, it is very natural that it would.

Well, I will tell you something about our work. Every man in the outfit is a lumberman. As the western fellows express it, a "Lumber Jack." A woman who watched our parade in Washington called us "wooden headed," possibly she was right but at any rate we are doing some excellent work here in France.

Company C. of the 5th Bn. of the 20th Eng. has the best record of any Company in the Regiment so far and we are going to keep it for *everybody in the company pulls together. We are doing logging with Auto trucks and horses. We have two big white trucks and each of them pulls a trailer loaded behind it, and when they come in that means four loads, then we have other trucks, they are English trucks. We have about fifty head of horses, but we use most of them in the woods skidding the logs out, only two teams hauling with wagons.*

There have been two crews on the job ever since I came here, one day and the other night. Rivalry exists between the two crews, one trying to saw more than the other. My crew has been leading from a few feet to a couple of thousand every day, until one day last week they out cut me a few hundred feet, and you know I couldn't stand that, so you ought to have seen me getting busy the next day. I ran that little old mill for all she was worth and I out cut them by about four hundred feet. I want to tell you I was some tired when six o'clock came. For running one of these French mills is not like running one of our good old American type mills. We haven't got our American mill yet but we are expecting it soon. There are several French mills in this section of the country. It astonishes them when they see us cut thousands of feet in a day when they only cut a few hundred feet. They don't seem to understand the hustling, strange Americans. The lady here where I am rooming says one American can do as much as two Frenchmen can do.

I must stop and go to supper. I am feeling fine and in the best of spirits. Guess the service agrees with me as I am taking on lots of flesh and if I continue to gain will be a two hundred pounder soon. France may look good to some people but the old US will be good enough for me when I get back. Love and best wishes to the people of Pontotoc County.
Affectionately your son,

Segt. Henry J. Goolsby

....

JAMES EARL WATERS, FRANCE, TO FAMILY, MAY 27, 1918 (DAUGHTERS OF THE AMERICAN REVOLUTION, SHUK-HO-TA-TOM-A-HA CHAPTER, LOWNDES COUNTY WORLD WAR I SCRAPBOOK)

James Earl Waters (1893–1961) was living in Columbus, Mississippi, and selling cars for a Memphis dealership when he registered for the draft on June 5, 1917. He returned to Columbus after the war and went into business with his brother, Ray Waters Sr. The company they founded, Waters Truck & Tractor, remains in business today.

Dear Mother and Brothers:
Have lots of news for you this time.

First am enclosing money order for eighty-five dollars which you may add to our account.

You cannot guess who I saw the other day. Was sitting down thinking about home, when who should come up but Sam Kaye. He saw me about same time I saw him, and useless to say we were both overjoyed at meeting. He is a first Lieutenant aeroplane pilot. He immediately asked how you and Ray were, and seemed glad to hear that Ray had been appointed superintendent of the plant. After we had a long talk he invited me to take a ride with him, which I gladly accepted. Tell Ray that Sam is making just the kind of pilot that everyone back home predicted—an exceedingly good one. Met a number of his friends, who all spoke highly of him, not only as a friend and good fellow, but as an extra good pilot. I have watched him fly for two or three days, and I can say that he handles a machine wonderfully. Was also pleased to note that he is the same old "Democratic" Sam.

I have just gotten out of the hospital after being there for a week. Had some kind of fever; don't remember just what the doctor called it. I think it was just plain old "Mississippi malaria." Feel fine now after getting it all out of my system. Was at an American Red Cross Hospital, American girls as nurses, and the treatment I received there couldn't have been better, unless it had been administered by dear old mother's hands. With out a doubt the Red Cross is the greatest institution of its kind in the world today. Don't fail to contribute to the cause, when ever the opportunity arises. Wish you would donate some for me out of the money I send home.

For fear some of my letters have gone stray will tell you again that I have been stationed in and around Paris for quite a long time—it's a wonderful city, and wish that all of you could be with me to visit same.

Had a nice letter from Todd the other day. Said he expected to soon enlist. If he does do not worry about him, mother, for it will be great training for him and at the same time he will be doing his "bit," which he will always be proud of in the years to come. I know you are just like other mothers [as] all hate to see their sons go to war, but am sure you and others would send their sons away with a smile, if you only know more about this war and of the horrible crimes the Germans have and are committing every day. And it is directly up to the young Americans to step in and put a stop to it.

Tell Ray to make it a point to see Mr. Kaye and tell him about meeting Sam. He can't praise him too highly, and don't be surprised if you soon hear of him making a record for himself.

Must close, and with lots of love to all,
Lovingly,

Earl
Censored:

WILLIAM ALEXANDER PERCY, FRANCE, TO CAMILLE PERCY, JUNE 16, 1918 (*GREENVILLE DAILY DEMOCRAT-TIMES*, JULY 30, 1918)

William Alexander Percy (1885–1942) was a Greenville, Mississippi, lawyer and poet whose father, LeRoy, was a US senator from the state from 1910 to 1913. William served as a member of the Commission for Relief in Belgium in 1916 but returned home and joined the army when the United States declared war. He subsequently returned to Mississippi and became a noted writer.

Mother dear:
I'm a soldier man now. I hike, make up my own bunk, clean my rifle, dash at dummies with a bayonet, go through gas clouds with a mask on, take notes on map making, machine guns and counter attack—in fact am getting generally primed to be a terror to the Bosche. It's rather strenuous, but entirely satisfying. All this talk about getting a place in the army that fits one's particular qualifications is rot—there ain't no such place. One's previous training goes pretty much for naught, and the only satisfactory part of this game is the scrapping part, not because scrapping itself is pleasant, but because that's what all the rest of the game is created for, it's the end of everything, the whole point and object. And the best job in the army is a platoon leader's, he guides the fighting of the men, shares their hardships, lives with them, gets all the cussing, none of the credit, and is perfectly satisfied with himself. A captain's job isn't so intimately human, has more general responsibility and is the only one approaching a lieutenant's in interest. If I can get through this school, be assigned to troops and finally get into the lines, I'll be happy, and being headed in that direction at the present I am happy now. The line is a long way off, but it's in sight. You should see the gorgeous contempt of these lieutenants for the rest of the army in

general and for those who will never get to the front in particular. They have unlimited pep and are completely satisfied with life. Don't think I'm alone in wanting to get to the line, everybody of any real nature has this same desire. And don't think I could be of more value to the cause in the SOS, I could not—I know because I've been there. My own special qualifications are those of a poet and they are equally worthless in this business, front or rear—they'll keep, I hope for "après la guerre."

I'm so delighted at getting away from Paris and desk work that I think I've gained in weight and I certainly have attained a wonderful tan. We all wear overseas caps these days and present a most jaunty appearance. The men in the school are very likable. The army is the most unselfish institution the race ever invented. Everyone is doing something they don't want to do for a cause they believe higher than their own wants, and as it works out in detail, no man alone can do his part, every one helps every one else; self-sacrifice is quite casual and impersonal, an every day matter. In all the horror and pity of the thing it's certainly well to remember this—it's the shining and the splendor of it all.

Tell father those rosaries of his were wildly packed with most of my clothes, books and valuables when I received my hurry call from Paris and put them in my trunk. I hope Adah's and Aunt Nana's spiritual welfare will not suffer for their lack and I promise to ship them the first opportunity.

If our voters could hear these soldiers talk of La Follette and Vardaman[1] they'd never let the election be a matter of doubt.

As to shipment of socks, I believe it impossible to send them over now, which is a pity, as these home-made socks are much better than the bought ones.

Please send me kodaks of you and father. Also have the Literary Digest and New Republic sent me. My love to everybody. I can't cable from here, but don't worry. With heart full of love for you and father. Your devoted son,

W. A. Percy

---

1. Robert M. La Follette Sr. (1855–1925) was a US senator from Wisconsin and a vocal opponent of World War I. James K. Vardaman (1861–1930) was elected to the US Senate from Mississippi in 1912 but was defeated in his 1918 reelection bid largely as a result of his opposition to the war.

VICTOR SYLVESTER ASHMORE, INFANTRY COMPANY 7, AT SEA, TO "HOMEFOLKS," JUNE 19, 1918 (*PONTOTOC SENTINEL*, AUGUST 1, 1918)

Dear Homefolks:
Well, we have been sailing over a week and no land in sight yet. I am told that we will be on the water several days longer before we reach land and when we do I will be one glad fellow. Not that I am afraid of our ship being sunk, but there are so many on here and we are not enjoying every luxury imaginable, though everything is as well as could be expected. Anyway, land would look mighty good to me now.

I had often heard and read about the great Atlantic Ocean, but I never realized what a big body of water it is until I have been riding day and night and am only half way across. We are not the only troop ship along by any means, and one of "Uncle Sam's" battle cruisers is convoying us across and we are expecting the English fleet to meet us when we get into the sure enough war zone.

The first day we were out at sea was very rough and at times the waves would dash over the deck and wet us, also the ship did a great deal of rocking. As a result we all got sea sick, and if you have ever been too sick to die, then that was the way we felt. I didn't eat a bite for three days and some were even sicker than I was, but I am feeling fine and able to eat all I can get.

Yesterday I saw a whale come up about fifty yards from our ship. Later in the day we ran into a school of fish, although I did not know their names. They followed our ship several miles and would all jump up out of the water at the same time, which interested us greatly. I have also seen a few flying fish and birds of different kinds living a thousand miles from land.

This is an English ship we are on and it is over two hundred yards long though there are other ships along that hold three times as many passengers as this one.

Sunday. June 23, 1918—As I awoke this morning and went up on deck I got my first glimpse of land which looked mighty good to me after seeing nothing but water for the past two weeks. There is land on either side of us and I am told that it is some island that belongs to England.

I think we have been up near the North Pole for the past few days [as] it has been mighty cold. We will reach our destination tonight or in the morning some time and it will be somewhere in the United Kingdom.

June 25—We arrived yesterday after two weeks of sailing and I was glad to get here. Had a fine voyage and did not see any submarines, though I am told one was sighted about twelve miles from us. Before we reached here about twenty-five torpedo destroyers and chasers met us and convoyed us into port. Forgot to tell you we are in the United Kingdom and are out at a rest up camp for a few days before we travel further. I am of the opinion we will get the rest of our training here in this country, though can't tell. We are in a beautiful city although everything looks strange and quaint to me, even the people. They marched us from the ship out here through streets which was five miles. All the people lined up along the streets to see us pass, and seemed pleased to see American soldiers and did everything in their power to make us feel that we were welcome. Every time we stopped to rest the good ladies would bring us out cake and hot coffee, and other things to drink.

Everything is quite different to our American towns. Each street and house is built almost alike; every one red brick and two stories high. On every corner there would be a store or two of some kind operated mostly by women, and I noticed that all the street car conductors were women. In fact they have taken men's places in almost every vocation of life.

These people speak the English language, but some we cannot understand, and also some say they cannot understand us, but believe after we get better acquainted and learn their ways we will get along just fine together.

The only thing I don't like, our money is only worth half as much as theirs when we exchange it for English money, and everything costs more, too.

The nights are very short here or it seems to me they are. Last night at eleven o'clock we went to bed and the sun had only been down a short time. We got up at six o'clock and the sun had been up quite a while. It is pretty cold here at nights. If they call this summer time, I would sure hate to be here in the winter time.

I wish it was possible for me to tell you everything I have seen since I left Camp Beauregard, but that would take a week, then, as you know, we are not permitted to write everything that we would like to write, so I will just wait until I get back to America to tell you the rest, which I hope will be in the near future.

Now if you should not hear from me when you think you should, don't worry because it takes a long time to get there and sometimes they fail to get there entirely.
Love to all,

Victor Ashmore

....

RICHARD THORP CARR, US BASE HOSPITAL NO. 67, LIVERPOOL, ENGLAND, TO MOTHER, AUGUST 15, 1918 (*PONTOTOC SENTINEL*, SEPTEMBER 19, 1918)

Richard Thorp Carr (1890–1935) was a Pontotoc, Mississippi, planter who registered for the draft in June 1917. After the war, he worked in the commodity division of the local Federal Emergency Relief organization (*Pontotoc Progress*, July 25, 1935, 1).

My dear Mama:
We are in the harbor at Liverpool, but have not left the ship. Think we will land some time this afternoon, and I am not sorry one bit. This is the fifteenth day we have been on board this ship but I have enjoyed every minute of the time. The trip has been a delightful one, without the least bit of trouble in any way. We may have passed a good many submarines but failed to see any, but we were well guarded all the way. There were about twenty ships in our convoy and a good many submarine chasers and battle ships. The ocean is a beautiful place but there is entirely too much of it. It is much larger than the ponds I have been used to fishing in. Saw the most beautiful sunset at Halifax on our third day out and wished that you could have seen it. Our ship spent the night there, where our full convoy was made up, and the next morning started on our long trip over here. I was not sea sick one bit but a good many of the fellows had an awful time. Of course, they were not very sick but felt as if they would die. Our ship is the Mauldings *and she brought over about two thousand soldiers.*
    A few of us have had charge of the hospital all the way, which made it nice for us for we had a good place to sleep and plenty of good things to eat. The rest of our bunch slept down in what they call the hole, which is two decks below the water mark and crowded as could be. I slept down there for the first few nights before I came to the hospital which was no pleasant experience at all. How would you like to go to sleep when you could hear the waves leaping against the ship away

above your head? But that didn't last long and the rest of the trip I enjoyed very much.

The only sad feature of the trip was one of our boys died of pneumonia Tuesday night and was buried at sea Wednesday morning. A nurse and I sat up with him for four nights and did every thing we could for him but to no avail. We were relieved at seven in the morning and could sleep the rest of the day if we wanted to. The sun rise was beautiful and every morning I would open the port hole and watch it come up.

There are about seventy-five nurses on board ship and the hospital was near their quarters, so we had plenty of girls to talk to. They are not the nurses who belong to our unit for our nurses have not come yet.

I can't say how long we will be in England but I don't care how long, for I had just as soon be at one place as another, as long as I have got to be away from home and you. I have thought of you all the way and hoped you were not worrying about me. If you know how good I feel and how nice every thing has been you would not worry one bit. I would like very much to let you know right now that I have arrived safely and hope that this letter will soon reach you and find you all in good health. Take care of yourself and always know and feel that I am where I should be and that it will not be long before I can come back to you. A heart full of love to you all.

Richard T. Carr

REUBEN T. CLARK, PARIS, FRANCE, TO C. J. MILLER, SEPTEMBER 7, 1918 (*NATCHEZ DEMOCRAT*, OCTOBER 19, 1918)

Reuben T. Clark (1877–1960) was born in Virginia and educated in Chicago before coming to Jackson, Mississippi, in 1892. After stints as a bank clerk and a newspaperman, he turned to the study of medicine, and he began practicing as an osteopath in Natchez in 1904. He served with the 1st Mississippi Volunteers in the Spanish-American War and with the YMCA during World War I (Rowland, *Mississippi*, 143).

Dear Mr. Miller:
I am at the office waiting for the safe to be opened so that I can go to work. I have gone back to my "first love"—handling the other fellow's money. Of course, everything in this department is money—dollars, pounds, francs, liras or fractions thereof. We do about ten million

dollars per month, or as about as much as all of Jackson, Miss., combined. Just to give you an idea: The YMCA has swamped the banks of Paris—many times we give them deposits faster than they can take care of them; so recently we have prevailed upon the American Express Company to take some (a few million) from us. We have twenty-five people in connection with the treasurer's office, sixteen of whom are busy making out deposits in the receiver's office for the local banks. This money comes in the head office in Paris, located at 12 Rue d'Aguesseau, by registered mail, special messenger trucks, etc. It is carried in grips, gunny sacks and even packed in boxes as large as small steamer trunks. We keep one man (the vice-president of a Richmond, Va. Bank) busy in an automobile carrying money for deposit to the banks.

A great deal of the money received, especially the French currency, is in bad order. We keep five French girls busy patching it up with mending tissue. The [fifty] franc note is a work of art as is also the [old] one hundred franc note.

Before coming to Paris I heard that there was a scarcity of water. That is a mistake; there is more water used in Paris for its size than any city on earth. There is no dust here; every street is paved, and washed—washed and then washed. Paris is very clean. Early in the morning the garbage and trash [cans] are put out in front; a big buck Moroccan negro precedes a big auto truck and dumps every other can in the one next to it; then another red cap negro picks it up and throws it up to a negro in the wagon. The driver is usually a woman. In each cart is a boy who picks out the rags and paper and puts it in large baskets. Following the wagon come the women sweepers; the water flows down the gutters (they always sweep down-grade), and with long brooms made out of some kind of brush and small tree branches bound together, and they clean up in a hurry; the work is usually finished by nine or ten A.M.

I have been here one month today. The weather is about like it is in Natchez at this same season.

We YMCA men are all in uniform—that of an officer, but we have no rank. I don't know what effect the new draft law will have upon us who volunteered, and are still under forty-five years of age. The Red Cross men are in the same class as we are—officers without rank. I don't know what the Red Cross men are allowed. We get no salary in a salary sense; we are allowed $120.00 (584 francs) per month and our clothes. In addition to this we are allowed a home allowance to take care of home obligations. (In my case it is $100 or 570 francs per month.)

Ordinary board here costs a little over $75.00 per month; whereas a nice place would cost from $100 to $125 per month.

A meal about like one would get at the Bon Ton of Jackson for seventy-five cents would cost two or three dollars here. A good Bordeaux, a French wine (practically all French wines are sour), will cost from fifty to seventy-five [cents] per quart plus fifteen cents for the bottle, which is refunded upon its return.

The parks here have those of the world beaten. The statuary is fine, and in every nook and corner. France need never go broke on the war; just throw her art and statuary upon the market and the millionaires of the world would refill the depleted war chest of France.

I am nicely located. Get a half holiday and all of Sunday each week. I have all of everything I need. We get good American cigars here at four to six cents each; but no chewing gum, no cake, no white bread. (I would give a dollar for a loaf of Mrs. Miller's nut bread.)

By the way, I want you to look out for one bushel of extra nice pecans (medium size but a good flavor). Perhaps they can be shipped on Christmas; if not, then I will get you to ship to Mrs. Clark.

With love and best wishes. I hope Francis is all right again.

We get the same war news you do.

Dr. Reuben T. Clark

SARA M. F. BABB, US BASE HOSPITAL NO. 102, ITALY, TO MRS. TAYLOR, SEPTEMBER 23, 1918, (DAUGHTERS OF THE AMERICAN REVOLUTION, BELVIDERE CHAPTER, WASHINGTON COUNTY WORLD WAR I SCRAPBOOK)

My Dear Mrs. Taylor:
After a voyage of three weeks, I found myself so busy and absorbed in the most distracting and interesting events I delayed writing you. There is, because of the strict censorship so little that I can tell you of the things you are most anxious to hear. I am busy and very content and glad I am here; I wouldn't have missed the experience for anything. We are more comfortably settled than I had hoped to be. We have electric lights and cold water, and the greatest fun furnishing and making livable our quarters. The dietitian and I have taken up our residence in

a little shed that hangs high up on the side of the centuries old house in which we are quartered. I have dubbed it the "Crow's Nest." We climb five flights of stairs and pass from a narrow hall on a small stone terrace, then down a flight of five steps into the "Crow's Nest." We have one door and one small casement window. Our furniture consists of two cots, two camp chairs and a camp table twelve inches square. I use my trunk for a dressing table and every time I go into it, I put all my toilet articles on the floor. I am very happy because my floor is not made of stone but of broad, rough boards. I shiver when I think of others so unlucky as to have to get out of bed on cold winter mornings on stone floors. We never dream of the luxury of a fire. That would be impossible. From the narrow ledge of the little stone terrace I have beautiful glimpses of blue mountains and through the little casement window the moon beams softly and the Great Dipper and Polaris smile on me with all of their old friendliness. I am glad I love the stars and learned to find my way about the skies. To see the same familiar constellations that shine unfailingly through their appointed seasons upon the cotton fields of Mississippi, makes me feel less far from home. But to return to the Crow's Nest. The great wooden beams over head are very artistic and our walls are cement that were once tinted rose color. And, too, the Crow's Nest is a splendid point for observation. At first the deep roar of big guns was awesome, but now I am so accustomed to it that I seldom think of it—and the airplanes make me very sick for Greenville and the Mississippi—the noise to so like those throbbing little gasoline engines on the river.

The army is a school in which Socrates would have delighted. We learn from the relative value of things, that we are often happiest not when we have most but when we possess least, and what tremendous joy little things give us! One of the Sisters gave me as a great treasure, a piece of plank for a wash board, and I came home so overflowing with happiness for an hour I did nothing but exult over my treasure. Finally my roommate, the English dietitian, who came out of one of Thackeray's novels, said resentfully, "Miss Babb, why should I be bored to extinction about a miserable piece of plank?" I retorted, "But Miss Oades, that is the very first wash board I ever owned, and why can't you have a little of the milk of human kindness and enter with sympathy into another's joy?" Whereupon, she muttered something about vain repetitions and I silently clasped the wash board in my arms. We do our own washing so that when I come back I will know all about sanitary inspections

of washerwomen, practically as well as theoretically. I am sure I'll be more sympathetic and can appreciate all their difficulties. All the skin is rubbed off my knuckles and my fingers are raw and bleeding, so you see why the wash board is such a great treasure. We adopt the Italian style, a smooth plank on which the clothes are laid and then a heavy stiff brush against the clothes. We make wonderful inventions in the way of clothes lines, putting twine strings on pulleys and stretching them across from one window to another, some lines four stories high. Our court yard looks like a tenement house. And another discovery for breakfast, when you haven't bread, cold boiled potatoes and syrup are not bad. Yesterday afternoon we had a baseball game followed by a football game played by the British and Italians. An Italian band gave beautiful music and the spectators were very enthusiastic. Sometimes amid the wild clapping and shout of the players one would hear a low ominous roar. I am sending you a requisition for some things, as we are allowed only to write one requisition to each person once a month. I have sent one already to my sister. This letter is for all my friends in Greenville. Please tell everybody to write me. Do tell me everything that is happening at home and my best love to all my school children and indeed all Greenville.
As ever, Yours,

Sara Babb, ANC

....

EMANUEL BRANDON MOUNT, AT SEA, TO MOTHER, SEPTEMBER 1918 (GREENVILLE DAILY DEMOCRAT-TIMES, NOVEMBER 8, 1918)

A native of Pond, Mississippi, Emanuel Brandon Mount (1892–1982) was a veterinarian. He practiced in Douglas, Georgia, before the war and later worked in Cleveland, Mississippi, and Memphis, Tennessee.

Dear Mamma:
Well, I guess this is the first letter you have received written at sea, and I know you are glad to hear from me.
We are on a very nice ship but cannot tell the name of it. All the officers have nice rooms for quarters, and we are served at tables just as if it were peace time. Same dishes and accommodations. The men are served just the same as if they were in camp, but sleep in hammocks.

The second night we were on board ship I was on guard in one section and the men were very sea sick. Although I felt sorry for them, it was a good show, as you could hear all kinds of remarks. One of them said if his people ever expected to see him they would have to come over there. Another said he would give a year's salary to be able to get a hand full of dirt. Another fellow said he could see why Columbus kissed the earth when he landed.

I told one fellow to go upstairs and get a little fresh air, and he said, Lieutenant I do not want anything. I have come here to die.

Others would stretch out on the floor and groan.

I was lucky. I did not get sea sick at all, and I left the day after I wrote my last letter to you.

We have a fine bunch of officers on board. Also the ship crew are a fine bunch of fellows. We have a piano and several of the fellows aboard know how to play so we have plenty of music.

The only unpleasant thing about the trip was that three of our soldiers died and the law of the sea is that they be buried at once. They put the body in a canvas bag and tie an American flag around it and have the same ceremony as if on land, and then they are lowered over the side of the ship and weights tied to their head and feet and slide them off board into the sea.

It was a very sad affair but after all it is just as good as being buried in the ground. I don't think any more will die, as we are not far from land, and not so many more are sick.

Well, we will not be on ship so much longer, so will say good-bye for this time.
Love to all, your loving son.

Doc

THOMAS FOOTE, LONDON, ENGLAND, TO ANNA FOOTE, HATTIESBURG, SEPTEMBER 1918 (*HATTIESBURG AMERICAN*, OCTOBER 3, 1918)

Dear Mother:
I have purposely delayed writing you for a few days until I could write you something definite of my plans, but now that I know more of them, I find that for military reasons they cannot be discussed in the mails. I can say, however, that the prospects are that I will not get near the front

for several months, and I am afraid that my prospects are poor for any work near the front for some time at least.

The service to which I shall be assigned is not required at the front, so unless I can get a change of assignment I won't go to the front at all unless the front should by any misfortune very suddenly change for the worse, which I feel and sincerely hope will never happen again.

While in Liverpool I stopped at what is said to be the best hotel in all England, (the Midland Adephi). I have stopped at a great number of hotels in America where I thought the service better. This I suppose is due to war conditions over here.

I went to St. Paul's for services today and enjoyed both the service and the sermon very much. The choir was simply grand; some of the finest voices I ever heard were there. The building alone was an inspiration.

I have visited Hyde Park, the Tower of London, London Bridge, Buckingham Palace (from the outside), Westminster Abbey.

All these things are truly wonderful and full of most intense interest, but the most wonderful thing in all England are the English people. They are 100 per cent grit and perseverance. This is apparent everywhere. I noticed it first on the boat coming over. I was on one of the large liners that in peace times ranked well up among the good ones, and on this trip carried quite a few passengers and some troops. On board, serving in various capacities to which they were suited, were quite a few school boys who are giving up their holiday to this service, braving the dangers of the submarine, in order that the passage for their Allies may be made a little more pleasant, and they stuck to their jobs like real men, for the whole of the trip, and I am sure that every soldier and civilian on board enjoyed their trip more and found it a great deal more pleasant because of their presence on board the boat.

As we sailed into the harbor, we passed a ship in the docks, just completing its debarkation. On board were a great number of women and girls who had come aboard to do the clean-up work, so that the crew might go home for a short shore leave before returning to America for more troops, food, or munitions, and they did their work well and they did it cheerfully. As we passed, noting our soldiers, they all came to the rail and cheered our boys lustily.

When I got ashore I found this on a vastly larger scale. Girls are acting as conductors and drivers for street cars, cabs, and omnibuses. Boys, girls and women [are] putting into cultivation with their own hands out of the way places, and so well and on such a large scale are they doing this, that in spite of the absence at the front of their [?] time laborers, the production of England for this year will very largely exceed that of any normal year. To this end England's boys and girls have contributed their vacations and its womanhood their leisure. It is said that in normal years England only raised enough food to feed themselves twenty weeks; but, I am told this year her food supply will take care of them for a little more than forty weeks.

There is no pronounced scarcity of food over here. There is a very wise food administration that insures a fair distribution of food and prevents hoarding and speculation at the expense of the needy.

Every boy who is of mechanical turn of mind is employed during his vacation in some way in some shop, munitions plant or something of the land, and you may be pretty sure when you see a boy at play over here, he has done his turn for the day, or else he is not an English boy.

It is not a mercenary motive that prompts all this industry, but rather a [?] sense of patriotism that is permeating in the people. England has suffered some 2.5 million casualties during this war, but not one single boy or girl have I seen on the streets begging, who founded their claim to charity on the fact that they had lost relatives at the front (and I have been through the sections where the poorer classes live, too). So I say that there is no mercenary motive back of this but rather a contribution to the boys at the front by those who cannot go, of their very best efforts, their best energies, and their best brains.

This is not confined to the poorer class of people, but all classes are doing the same thing from titled nobility to lowly serf. All this they do without a single whimper, not a complaint. Yes, they are 100 per cent grit and as long as there is one alive they will be fighting this war until Germany is whipped and Prussianism banished forever from the earth.

Truly the most wonderful thing about England is its people.

Tell any of my children, you may see, that I couldn't get my class rolls which contained addresses through the customs at New York, so I shall only be able to write those whose addresses I can remember.

My address for the present will be: 12 Rue d'Aguesseau, Paris, France, Care American YMCA.

With love to all, I must close.
Your devoted son,

Tom

JOHN MORRIS BOES, AT SEA, ABOARD THE USS *ANTIGONE*, TO A. E. LEE, EDITOR, *OCEAN SPRINGS JACKSON COUNTY TIMES*, OCTOBER 1918 (*OCEAN SPRINGS JACKSON COUNTY TIMES*, NOVEMBER 2, 1918)

Born in Louisiana, John Morris Boes (1891–1940) was employed as a grocery clerk in Ocean Springs, Mississippi, when he registered for the draft in June 1917. He remained in the US Navy after the war before becoming a police officer in New Orleans. The *Antigone* started out in 1900 as the *Neckar*, and it was one of the German ships seized by the United States when it entered the war. Renamed the *Antigone*, the vessel ferried troops across the Atlantic between December 14, 1917, and September 15, 1919 (*Dictionary of American Naval Fighting Ships*, 1:50).

> *Dear Friend Mr. Lee:*
> *I have just returned from my seventh trip to France, and thought that I would write and tell you of some of my experiences.*
>   *I made my first trip over there in December, 1917. I ate my Xmas dinner in the war zone and my New Year's dinner in France. This being our first trip over we were more or less enthusiastic and when we gave battle with our first submarine on the 26th of December it caused a little excitement, but we [are] all over with that feeling now, and feel disappointed when we don't have any "subs" to feed our fourteen inch shells to, or to drop a ton or so of depth charges on. Well, submarines are few and far. Sam's Navy is on the high seas—they are hard to find. We have met very few of them and always gave them a warm reception whenever we did. I have only seen one ship torpedoed. That was the* USS President Lincoln, *on May 31, and the submarine that did it did not come up till the ship had been sunk for a couple of hours.*[1] *Neither ship in the convoy saw it, so it did its cowardly act and got away with it.*
>   *The convoy that our ship is in has not lost a ship going over, and only one coming home to the USA.*
>   *I am sending you a few copies of "The Theban," our ship's paper. This little newspaper will give you a very good review of life aboard a transport. We of the* Antigone *are very proud of our ship and her splendid record along all lines. For very obvious reasons our branch of the service is clothed in camouflage and shrouded with secrecy, but thanks to the efficiency of the officers and men the troops are going over safely and swiftly.*

We have gun crews on here that have been awarded the pennant for marksmanship, and they defy any U-boat out that we may meet.

Of course other ships are as equally prepared as we are, and are always on the job. Our convoy has taken over thousands of troops and only lost one ship, on our journey home.
Respectfully,

J. M. Boes
GSK Storekeeper, USN

1. The USS *President Lincoln* was the largest US Navy vessel sunk in World War I, though 689 of the 715 men aboard survived and were rescued.

AUGUST STERZENBACK TO JAMES LAMBERT, EDITOR, *NATCHEZ DEMOCRAT*, OCTOBER 1918 (*NATCHEZ DEMOCRAT*, NOVEMBER 3, 1918)

August Sterzenback (1887–1924) was a New York native who lived in Natchez, Mississippi, before the war. He served with the field artillery and then operated a mail boat between Natchez and Fort Adams until his death (*Natchez Democrat*, February 12, 1924, 1).

Dear Friend:
I will try and tell you a few things about my trip through England and France. We landed in a large port in England and marched through the streets of a large city to entrain and as we pulled out of the depot a British band played "America" and it was a great sight to see them all salute as we pulled out. We arrived in the wee hours of the morning at a rest camp and at nine A.M. we marched down to the dining hall and received out first British ration which consisted of bully beef, lovely cheese and jam, after which we lined up and picked out a detail whose duties were in hoeing potatoes and the rest of the outfit took a cold water bath and then a series of instructions started which lasted almost till dark. Its never late until two and then its too late and the next day drew rations at 7:30 A.M., and somewhere about 12:30 P.M. we really got the rations and then after talking to the British soldiers about the war for two hours we hit the hay expecting on the morrow to see France. At 4:30 A.M. his Royal Highness, the top cutter or first sergeant, with his never to be forgotten whistle, shook us out again and then another feed, jam, bully beef and cheese and made up our packs and marched

to the depot and entrained. The trains in England are not like those in the States. They are divided into compartments of eight and equipments and nothing more. After a few hours on the road, we landed at a seaport where we took ship for France. Yes, and it was an American ship that took us across the channel, and as the evening shadows fell we bid old England and our Tommies and friends adieu. The next morning we were at a port in France. We marched through the streets of a large city and were greeted by the inhabitants very warmly. The little children gave us flowers while the old folks cried with joy and after walking four long French miles and climbing about steep hills we landed at another rest camp and the only people who enjoyed a rest were the German prisoners of war, who are guarded by the British. After a few days at this place we marched to the depot where the trains were awaiting us and to my surprise, this train consisted of two coffee pot French type engines whose exhaust would remind you of an old horse with a bad case of the heaves. Then box cars or stock cars marked eight chevaux (meaning horses) or thirty-eight hommes (meaning men)[1] and in the center of the train we had three very poor third class passenger coaches for the officers. These coaches were in compartments just like in England. Then loading the supply of war bread, wolley beef and other canned goods, we rolled out into No Man's Land. The word comfort being unknown either fore or aft and after steen [seven?] days on the road we arrived at a French village in the foot hills of a well known mountain range and as we were the first American troops to enter this village the people at first didn't seem to realize that we were friends instead of foes. A French officer told them who we were and arranged for our billets and we landed in quarters which consisted of a large barn with lots of hay and our room mates were the cows, chickens, horses, oxen and etc.
The people of this village own a community wash tub which is located in the village square and it is a great sight to see the soldiers assisting the people of the village in doing their work. We call it the village bath tub. This is fed from the mountain springs, gravity system. No rain, no system. Speaking about Billies, well here they are with wooden shoes, some class. We also have a village crier who with his cap, boots and cape and armed with a drum, he brings the news and the Yanks have no idea of what he is talking about. But when he gets through, they all give him three cheers. The chief occupation of the people of this section of the country is farming. Methods are very crude; grain and hay are cut by hand and loaded on a large wagon drawn by the family milk

cow. We are now located in a section which has very little left. We get up in the morning and you can shake the frost off of the blankets and then is when I think of my little life in the bluff. I am just trying to give you a little idea of what we have gone through these past few weeks, as you know all this mail is censored, so will conclude for this time sending my best to all.

I remain as ever, the same,

Gus Sterzenback

1. Built between 1872 and 1885, these four-wheeled train cars weighed twelve tons each and measured twenty-nine feet long and nine feet wide. They were first used as general-purpose freight haulers before being converted to troop and animal transports for wartime service. In 1949, the French people sent the freshly painted and repaired cars to each of the American states as a sign of gratitude for their humanitarian aid following World War II (Société des Quarante Hommes, *Merci Box Car Memorial Book*, n.p.). Mississippi's "Gratitude Train" resides behind the Old Capitol Museum in downtown Jackson.

WILLIAM HENRY WOOD, COMPANY 15, CAMP FARRAGUT, NORFOLK, VIRGINIA, TO EDITOR, *NEW ALBANY GAZETTE*, DECEMBER 13, 1918 (UNION COUNTY WORLD WAR I SCRAPBOOK, BOX 1)

William Henry Wood (1886–1930) was born in New Albany, Mississippi, and was working as a farmer in Wallerville when he registered for the draft in June 1917. He returned to Union County and became clerk in a school dormitory and later a teacher.

> Dear Editor:
> If you will give me a little space in your valuable paper, I will relate to the readers of The Gazette a few of my experiences since I enlisted in the US Navy.
> One year ago last September I entered school at Mississippi Normal College at which institution I would have finished the Teacher's Certificate course the following July. After I had been there eight weeks, I decided to enlist in the navy and carried the decision into execution the 21st of November 1917.
> In company with two other recruits, I landed at the Norfolk, Va., Training Station the 24th of November. I spent my first night in the "bughouse" and had to sleep on the deck with at least fifty other recruits.

Next day we (all new recruits) got our clothing, a sea-bag, a hammock and a mattress. It took most of the day for us to get our clothing fixed in regulation style and stowed away in the sea-bag. After we had finished this task, we were assigned to company 79. The next day enough men were entered in my company to make the required amount, 140 men. The next day we were put under the command of chief petty officer, C. N. E. Fountaine, a man who has been sixteen years in the navy. He was a good fellow and every man in the company liked him. Next morning he had us to "fall in" in two ranks and march out to the drill ground. After a few preliminaries we started on my first military drill. We had to drill eight hours a day when the weather was favorable. When I had drilled two days my feet went on the "bum." The chief excused me from drill for two or three days until my feet got better. After I had been on the station a week, I was detailed for the Mess Hall as a mess cook. A mess cook's duty is to put the food on the table and wash the dishes. Most every man in the navy has to do a "hitch" as a mess cook. A "hitch" on the station is a week and aboard ship it is three months. I have served both of them.

While our company was at Norfolk we had some of the coldest weather I have ever seen. One of those cold days we had to go out on the field and stand attention for forty-five minutes and my feet froze. A week later they gave me quite a bit of trouble.

The cold made quite a number of the fellows sick, and I knew one fellow who froze to death in his hammock.

On the 23rd of December five of the best drilled companies were transferred to old Jamestown for further training. We were the first company to reach the new station. This was a much more desirable place than the Norfolk station. We had much better quarters and many conveniences that we did not have at Norfolk. Each company had its own "wash place," clothes line and mess hall. There were eight companies in a regiment and each regiment had a high fence around it. In each regiment was a sick bay, a canteen and a YMCA building. There were concrete walks all around each barrack and one leading from one barrack to the other.

After we had been here a few days, we were given Springfield rifles, shell-buts and bayonets. We were taught to port arms, shoulder arms, slope arms, present arms and order arms. It is a pretty scene to see several companies going through physical drill with arms.

We remained here until the 25th of January. By this time we had gone through all the necessary training before going to sea. On the above date three companies were sent to sea. Most of my company went aboard the USS battleship Kentucky. Here is where I learned what it was to be a fireman. We were on duty four hours and off eight. For four weeks I passed coal for the fireman and relieved him on the fires when he got too warm. The next two weeks I had the fires. When a fellow faces the fires four hours he is most "all in." At the end of two weeks I was rated second class fireman and transferred back to Norfolk station on the 7th of March with more than a hundred other firemen. Here we were put on general detail work. Some days we did not work; others we built roads, concrete walks and worked in the navy yard.

We were on the Norfolk station until the 26th of March. At this time more than a hundred of us firemen were sent to Charleston, SC. We didn't do much work here except guard duty. We had a good time while we were at Charleston and we were sorry when we were mustered out from there. 130 men left Charleston on the 16th of April and were stationed at Jamestown, Va. I was at this station three weeks. Most we did while I was there was guard duty.

On the eighth of May I and eight of my company were drafted for the USS Susquehanna. She is one of the German ships taken over by the government. She is over six hundred feet long, eighty-five feet wide, has eight decks, a crew of six hundred and could make fourteen and one-half knots. When she was loaded to her capacity she carried three thousand troops, eight thousand tons of cargo and thirty-five hundred tons of coal. We used most of this coal going over and back.

Sixteen troop ships sailed from Newport News, Va., for France on the 10th of May. When we were four days out, we struck a rough sea and here is where I got sea-sick. This lasted two days. The rest of the trip was smooth.

We landed at Brest, France, the 23rd of May.

On the 29th of May we sailed for the states in company with three other ships. The sub-destroyer came out with us two nights and one day. They turned back for France before daylight of the second day out. At nine o'clock that morning we were attacked by a sub. She sank the USS President Lincoln. This was the biggest ship in the convoy. She was hit three times with torpedoes and went down in thirty-two minutes. She lost several men but I never learned how many. The rest of us made our "get-away" and landed at Newport News on the 10th of June.

In all, I made five trips to France. Each time we landed at Brest. On our second return we were attacked by a sub. The destroyer's men were with us this time and they sent the sub to the bottom. On our return trips, we brought wounded soldiers who were not able for further duty in the trenches.

On the 7th of November I was transferred to the Norfolk station. I was here until the 11th. Then I was sent aboard the USS Wm. A. McKinney. *I was aboard her only a few days, leaving the 16th of November for the hospital with a dislocated shoulder. I was in the hospital until the 9th of December. Then I was sent back to the Norfolk station and I am still here.*

With this, I send a merry Christmas and happy New Year to The Gazette and all its readers. I am,
Your friend,

Will H. Wood

- 3 -

OVER THE TOP AND INTO BATTLE

ON MARCH 23, 1918, THE GERMANS BEGAN SHELLING PARIS WITH LONG-range guns nicknamed Big Berthas (Thoumin, *First World War*, 462). Parisians initially thought that the projectiles had been dropped by airplanes but soon realized that Germany had cannons that could shoot as far as seventy-two miles (Mitchell, *Memoirs*, 189). US general John J. Pershing believed that the attacks marked the beginning of new German offensive and on March 28 "placed at the disposal of Marshal [Ferdinand] Foch, who had been agreed upon as commander in chief of the allied armies, all of our forces" ("Story of War Is Told by Pershing," 2).

PHILIP G. DAVIDSON, FRANCE, TO "FRIENDS," APRIL 6, 1918 (*GREENVILLE DAILY DEMOCRAT-TIMES*, APRIL 29, 1918)

> Dear Friends:
> In my last letter I told you that I was located a certain distance back of the lines and acting as secretary to four camps of troops engaged in the service of supplies. This naturally did not convey any impression of glory or danger and those of my friends who expected me to come back in shape of a stained glass memorial window will be, I trust, happily disappointed.
> Your feeling in regard to the service of supplies is a mistaken one, however, if you think that there is no special romance about it. One of the boys had the wrong idea when he dropped into my quarters the other day with the remark: "This SOS business gets a man nowhere. Nowhere at all. The fellows up in the front get the service medals, the Sunday supplement stories, the Liberty Loan and Red Cross talk, and

hold the general attention. No one knows that we are over here. How about a transfer to the suicide club?"

This young man was in charge of one of the most important details of the operation upon which this especial camp of troops is engaged. His removal to the machine gun or aviation service would mean the slowing up of production here at a time when we are on forced draft now to keep even with the demand. This young man's work is equal—I consulted an authority about this—equal to the putting in of a mile of trench a day, or the laying of a thousand feet of railroad line or the moving of a loaded freight car a mile and a half. These are not the things that he is doing, but he is doing something quite equally as essential.

It is just possible that no one is going to write any stories about the service divisions, the engineers, the quartermasters' department, the hospital and medical and all the manifold operations that are going on. No one is going to tell about the magnitude of this work or of the miracles that our government is accomplishing, because the Huns might find it out and then people in the United States are not especially interested. They want to know about the boys that Empey and Hankey wrote about; the "Over the Top" lads.[1]

My men in the four camps do not have the incentive of peril to make them thoughtful. They are working with tremendous energy. Titanic labor is their daily contribution to the great victory coming some day. They are young. They are in perfect health. They are away from home, from church, from decent women, from all restraints and with no prohibitions except those of military law. All around are the country wine shops, infested with loose women. Yet I tell you that among these there are many moral heroes who have influence over the others.

It is right here in these service camps throughout France that the big work of the YMCA and of army chaplains is to be done. It may take some talent to hand out canteen supplies to men at the front or in the big receiving camps. It may take to amuse the men and cheer them with vaudeville companies from Paris or entertainers over from the states, in the Big Huts along the front or at the rest camps. But to go out into the woods where there are no huts at all, and brace the moral standards as well as cheer the life of lonely, tempted boys is the big job.

The four camps to which I have been assigned are just like this. We have one hut at one of these camps and it is only partly equipped. At the other four camps we have nothing, owing to the difficulty of securing *supplies, not to the neglect of the YMCA, for the authorities are only too willing to do everything. Our supplies will be coming in and we will be in better shape to take care of the men. I do not doubt that. But just now it is a matter of considerable difficulty to get any sort of meeting with the men except out under the trees when it is dry as it very seldom is.*

I do not flatter myself at all about any special ability to handle this biggest job I ever had. It is a job bigger than any man I ever knew. It is a job that fills a man with humbleness of mind. I have been tempted again and again to write the head office to send some one who really could do the job and let me go to waiting on the lunch counter somewhere. But I hate to go off and leave these fellows. I am just mean enough to want to stay on the job a while longer, even if it does deprive them of a better man.

Just to think of having a big crowd of men like this as friends. To go about from tent to tent and be greeted everywhere with a welcome. To have them come and discuss all sorts of questions, personal and otherwise. To be in the midst of this vital life as a part of it and to hope that perhaps some young fellow may be influenced right and that somewhere back in the States a mother's prayers have been answered by my coming to the camps. A man cannot give up this kind of job lightly although he may be perfectly aware that he is a hopeless failure on the work.

I am glad that I am here. How long I will be here I cannot tell. But as yet I see no good place to let go and really think that I will find it increasingly difficult. With best regards,

Philip G. Davidson

1. Arthur Guy Empey (1883–1963) was an American who served with the British and US armies in World War I. After he was wounded and discharged, he published a 1917 book about his experiences, *Over the Top*, that sold more than a quarter of a million copies and was made into a movie the following year. British soldier Donald Hankey (1884–1916) was the author of two popular volumes of essays on the war. The first, *A Student in Arms* (1916), was a gung-ho portrayal of the British Army's performance; its successor, *A Student in Arms, Second Series* (1917), was published posthumously and offered a less enthusiastic take on the war.

AS SPRING ARRIVED, THE AMERICAN TROOPS GOT THEIR FIRST TASTE OF battle. On April 17, American forces were ordered to relieve the French troops at Cantigny, an agricultural village with a population of about one hundred that had been occupied by the Germans. Over the next month, the doughboys endured heavy German artillery fire while awaiting further orders (*American Expeditionary Force: Doughboys in World War I*; Welsh, *USA in World War I*, 21–22).

....

HARRISON BRISTER, FRANCE, TO PARENTS, MAY 12, 1918 (*MEADVILLE FRANKLIN ADVOCATE*, JULY 11, 1918)

Tylertown, Mississippi, native Harrison Brister (1896–1919) was working as a factory laborer in Slidell, Louisiana, when he registered for the draft in June 1917. Unlike most African Americans who served in the war, Brister apparently saw combat, probably with either the 92nd or 93rd Division. The War Department created these two segregated units in 1917, and members of the 92nd served with the French, while the 93rd saw some combat in the closing months of the war (Hallas, *Doughboy War*, 218).

> *helo My Dear Mother and farther*
> *How er you to night I am will and I hope when thease few lines has reached your hands I hope that it fine you all well and Darning well tell John hello tell all the Boys hello ant rose hello tell all the girls I sad hello tell the Boys they auter to Be a Man lik me stand up an Be a Man Come over and tak Part with us I am in France I has cross the sea. It is thirty hundred miles across we wear sixteen Days an Night Crossing the Deep Blue sea the armey fine tell John that war is hell But I am a Brave man I has A solger in the Army I will be home some time I Don't when But it is Not gouing to Be so veary long I Don't think say I am sending you all fifteen Dolars Ever Mount her you getting it Ben sending it far 4 mounth rite an let Me no I want to see you all Bad we left new yorrk on the 5 of DEC and we landed at france on the 25 we took Christmas in france so Mother Don't worry abot Me far I am all rite Pray far me that I Mite hole out until the end I am a sharp shuter so I am getting along all rite so you all Be good so my time is short so I will close my letter so By By all from your sun,*
>
> *Harrison Brister*

HARRIS DICKSON TO COLONEL L. R. HOLBROOK, MAY 15, 1918 (HARRIS DICKSON PAPERS, BOX 2)

Harris Dickson (1868–1946) was a noted Vicksburg, Mississippi, lawyer, judge, and writer. Early in the war, he was a correspondent in Europe for *Collier's* magazine, but he had returned home before he wrote this letter to a colonel with the 7th Field Artillery in France (*Jackson Clarion-Ledger*, March 18, 1946, Harris Dickson Subject File).

> *My dear Colonel,*
> *I wonder if you know how anxiously I, in common with all Americans, am now watching the newspapers to see what happens along our front. From a knowledge of how men think and feel, I am quite sure that we at home are even more anxious than you at the front.*
> *When I first got back to the States I felt quite discouraged and disheartened at the apparent lack of appreciation and interest in what this war means. However within the last few weeks I have traveled a great deal, made a number of speeches in many different states, and have now come to feel quite exuberant and optimistic over the whole situation. Our people are certainly waking up, putting their shoulders to the wheel, and determining to do whatever may be necessary to win this war.*
> *As to our men at the front I have never had the slightest doubt I know darn well that they will do their duty to the very last atom of energy that may be in them. It was the folks at home, who found it so difficult to comprehend, who are so very far away from the war itself and from all knowledge of European politics—it was for the folks at home that I felt the disquieting doubt. That however, has now passed away. I know men by the thousands, the very men we have in this country—or in any other country—who have put down their private affairs and are devoting their talent entirely to war work. Whatever else may happen this great calamity is going to make a nation out of us.*
> *But this letter is not sent as an essay upon war and war conditions. It is simply to convey to you my earnest interest in your welfare, and my warm personal affection for yourself.*
> *I should be immensely grateful if you, or some of the younger officers around you, would send me just a little note telling any news of the regiment, or any personal gossip concerning things which may have*

happened to my friends. You do not realize how deeply I am attached to that regiment, to yourself and to your officers and men.

With the keenest personal interest and the abiding confidence that our Nation has in its boys at the front, I am,
Most sincerely your friend,

[Harris Dickson]

THADDEUS KINMAN WYNN, D COMPANY, 14TH PLATOON, 10TH CANADIAN INFANTRY BATTALION, FRANCE, TO MOTHER, MAY 16, 1918 (GREENVILLE DAILY DEMOCRAT-TIMES, JUNE 20, 1918)

Greenville, Mississippi, resident Thaddeus Kinman Wynn (1895–1964) officially joined the Canadian Expeditionary Force in May 1917 and served overseas during the war. He subsequently moved to Jackson, where he worked at the Exchange Oil Company.

Dearest Mother:
I have at last found time and writing material at the same time to write you a decent letter.

'Tis a most wonderful day and I am out in an old deserted apple orchard trying to monopolize the sunshine. My battalion is out a few days' divisional rest. 'Tis a God-send to get back here where 'tis partial peace and quiet. What a relief to not have those damn siege guns going off in your ears. Nearly every rest we have had since I joined this outfit has been right under some naval siege battery and they were in the habit of firing every five minutes of the twenty-four hours. We have started on a three weeks rest three different times and four days has been our longest time out of the line as yet. However we are doing pretty good this time, as we have been out for over a week now.

I am awfully sorry to say that I have been an awfully sick boy for the last six days. The MO [medical officers] call it French fever, but am glad to say that I am all OK again except getting my strength back.

How are you all getting along? Owing to my mail being addressed to the 1st Battalion and then my being transferred to the 10th Battalion, I have been out of luck for mail from home as it possibly will be sent to the 1st, then has to go back to England. Did you get my address correct? No. 2448325, D. Coy, 14th Platoon, 10th Canadian Inf. Batt., BEF, France.

As soon as my mail is addressed like that it will come through OK. The first letter I had from home was from sister, written in Nashville on March 26. How is Billie?[1] Is he still in the States? I do hope he is for I certainly do wish him the good fortune of not having to see any of the life over here. Can you imagine this?

I had sister's letter delivered to me while in the front line; in fact, it was handed to me by my corporal out in a shell hole in "No Man's Land." I was on patrol duty. This is a beautiful country over here and 'tis a shame for it to be overridden with soldiers. The French people do surely deserve a lot of credit for they have a wonderful spirit. You will see them cultivating their land right up in the forward area and then the military authorities will run them out and dig up their crops with trenches.

Everything over here is billeted out, and if you are lucky you get a roof over your head. At present I have a good billet. 'Tis an old barn, a big manure pile with sweet, healthy odor and three horses and two cows, nineteen chickens and sixteen soldiers. Oh, I forgot the most important lodgers, two dogs and one jackass. It's a dead certainty we don't get lonesome.

I guess I can call myself a real true soldier now as I can boil tea in my steel helmet over a "Tommy cooker," which is a tin can with rags and candle grease in it as fuel, when the wind is blowing hard and 'tis raining at a two forty clip, using what is left to shave in, as water is scarce.

I will try and give you my impressions of the first trip in the line. No one can tell you what it is like, no matter how many lectures I had on what I was going into I did not picture anything as awful, nor can any one, although everybody say 'tis the hardest trip the battalion ever made. When I joined the Battalion they were at a quaint little French village. 'Twas on a Friday. They were there for a three weeks' rest they thought as they had just come out from a long trip in. On Saturday about three P.M. I was over trying to parley vous for some eggs and potatoes, and word came for us to stand to in battle order. You could see the oldtimers shake their heads, for they knew something mean was in store for us. I was all anxious and elated at getting my first try at Fritz. At four o'clock we moved off, lumber carts, cook wagons, and all. About six o'clock we halted and waited until it got good and dark, and then moved forward again. Everybody in good spirits. Makes no difference what happens over here, you see everybody with a smile on their face, regardless. About nine o'clock we were marching along. No order had come to hush talking, but there was not a word being said above a whisper. We were in the real *danger zone, and a few big shells had burst not twenty feet from my platoon. No one even turned to notice except myself and a young lieutenant who was making his first trip, too. About ten o'clock orders came back for machine gunners to take over their guns and ammunition. Here is where I began to work. We leave timbers and cook wagon and transport carts behind and proceed on by platoons. Fritz begins to shell our road pretty heavy; two killed, four wounded, and I did not know about it until later. You could see the sky all illuminated with star shells and the noise of the guns going off right under your face was enough to run a person crazy. About thirty minutes walking and we leave the road, taking a trench. As machine gunners always take the lead and I am No. 1 on our gun I was the first man of our platoon excepting guide officer and sergeant. It was the darkest night I have ever seen. After going along for a while all the time shells were flying over our heads and bursting all around us, somebody whispered for me to duck. I did duck, believe me. Just as I got down a whiz bang*[2] *busted on the parapet above me, covering me with dirt. We continue on and on, in and out of trenches, turning to the right and then to the left all the time ducking shells. It seemed like ages and miles to me. Twice just before I would get there the trench was blown entirely in, so I begin to think I was pretty lucky. We pass stretcher case one after another, being carried back to the dressing station. Everybody talking in whispers. Everybody busy and doing their job, without questions or noise. After going these many miles and three more of fourteen platoons knocked off coming through the communication trench, we finally arrive at the portion that my platoon was to take over.*

The battalion we relieved was anxious to get out, as it was late, about three o'clock. The officer and sergeant take over. No. 1 and 2 are called to man the gun, so I go to work setting up my gun, getting my ammunition arranged. Sentries are posted. The fellows we relieved begin to file out and we are left the sole keepers of this trench. From the number of guns going off I thought 'twas a pretty lively night, but No. 2, who was an old head, says that this was nothing but just the same it was warm enough for me. But I was so tired and worn out that this standing on the firing step peering over into Fritz's line, which was about 125 yards off, was good stuff, for me and my hours' shift went by in no time and I was relieved. I hunt around for a cubby hole to crawl into to take a smoke. Just as I was about to get settled my officer came around and said that the battalion on our right was going to pull off a raid on Fritz and he wanted a Lewis gun out in No Man's Land to cover their return. Would

I take the job as he was going along, too. Yes. So off No. 2 and I start, loaded down with gun and ammunition, trailing along behind him. We finally come to a low place where we can crawl out over the top. We proceed to crawl and crawl through barbed wire and everything. A Fritz machine gun heard us and opens up, but he was just about a foot too high, so we continue until we come to a big shell hole and the three of us camp here. Star and flare shell had begun to go up in numbers on both sides. Our artillery opens up just as I get my gun set right and the three of us all ready for action. Our guns were just giving Fritz hell and the sky was the prettiest display of fireworks you could imagine. About that time Fritz woke up to what was coming off and started to shell. Well, thank God. I was out in No Man's Land and all those shells were passing over my head. A hot cannonading continued for some time. 'Twas about four o'clock and not long before daybreak. My gun was doing its share as we located a Fritz machine open and pot away at it all the time. 'Tis about time for the raiders to be coming in now and there were flare signals going up all down our line to show them the way and where to come in. We three carried on in our position until it got so light the officer begins to get worried if we are going to make it back all OK.

We started back, crawling about ten feet and then laying still for a bit until Fritz would lose track of us. Machine gun bullets were playing all around us. No. 2 had one to pass through his coat sleeve. We finally reached our lines OK but it 'twas good and light by this time. The report from the raid was good, as they brought in a big bunch of prisoners, a couple of Fritz machine guns and only had a few casualties of their own.

I have been two days writing this, so am going to close for the present and send this along. Will continue where I leave off in my next letter. Lots of love to you all.
Your devoted boy,

Thad

1. Thad Wynn's brother, William T. Wynn (1890–1951), was a student at the Citizens Training Camp at Fort Logan H. Roots, Arkansas, when he registered for the draft in May 1917 and was stationed at Camp Pike, Arkansas, at the time this letter was written. He returned to Greenville after the war and became an attorney, and he represented Washington County in the state legislature from 1924 to 1928.
2. *Whiz-bang* was a common term for German field artillery shells, which traveled faster than the speed of sound, meaning that soldiers heard the sound of the projectile traveling before they heard the report of the gun firing it.

GEORGE E. QUISENBERRY, SAUMUR, FRANCE, TO PARENTS, MAY 21, 1918 (WORLD WAR I SCRAPBOOK [NATCHEZ], FOLDER 1)

George E. Quisenberry (1892–1956) was a journalist with the *Kansas City Star* and Associated Press before resigning to enter the Signal Corps (Aviation Section). His parents, Everett B. and Fannie C. Quisenberry, lived in Natchez, Mississippi. After the war, he resumed his career in publishing and moved to New York (*The Fourth Estate*, April 20, 1918, 4B; *New York Times*, November 23, 1956).

Dear Folks:
This writing will surprise you, no doubt, but we have just gotten a new censorship ruling that permits me to tell you where I am now. The name of it is Saumur, about half way between Tours and Angers on the Loire River, southwest of Paris. If you have read this closely, you will see that I have been in the advance zone and, of course have seen something of the front. I know a bit of actual war conditions now, just what the French have been undergoing for four years and what we are to do.

Generally a mess of mud, dirt and desolation, ruined buildings and villages for some miles behind the front lines. You have no idea of the desolate look of a long destroyed village, stark, staring walls, crumbled dust and powder, sometimes with bits of old furniture, timbers, anything, everything.

The front itself was a zig zag affair of trenches, the Allies are one side of a hill, the Germans on another: endless map of cuts in the brown earth, going seemingly crazily everywhere, with barbed wire entanglements, debris, shell holes and such in between.

Sometimes, it was so quiet, in the peaceful sunlight, that all thoughts of war went glimmering. Then one side or another began a bombardment. The guns have a tremendous roar, and the deep dugouts seemed a wise precaution. Some of them are eight to ten meters deep.

At one time I heard a barrage that was continuous for three days both allied and Bosche guns were in the chorus. I was several miles away but our place was constantly being shaken and when it ended we missed the noise. Couldn't sleep for a few nights.

There is so much to tell about the front that I would have to write for a week to tell you all about it. The airplanes were a constant source of wonder; to see the shell bursting around a Bosche, like powder puffs, thousands of meters in the air, was most exciting.

I like to see Jury [Jerry] get his, and so would anyone who has ever heard his motor in the air at night bent on a raid. I have seen several knocked down and once there was a wonderful fight near us in which the Bosche got the worst of it. That also is very thrilling.

The Bosche's motor has a peculiar sound that we could detect quite distant. Practically always at night and when he came the whole front sprang alive to greet him. Great long searchlights playing for him high in the air; anti aircraft guns banging for him; star shells bursting, and signal rockets going. One night we saw a Jury fall in flames, it lasted only a few seconds, but it was a nice sight. Jury has many things to pay for.

Night, of course, is the most fascinating time up there, with the fireworks going, and sometimes, the plane sings the air with the machine guns whirling exactly like a typewriter. That is an odd sound, not easily forgotten. They try to sweep the roads, after darkness, in the hope of getting troops or supply wagons. Another stirring sight is the movement of long lines of troops, to and from the trenches.

This used to be a most aristocratic place, I am told. In former years, it was a famous French cavalry school and the elite of the country came here from miles around. The surrounding territory is very pretty and very fruitful. All the buildings are of stone or brick, with high walls surrounding them; gardens, close cultivation and all that stuff. The YMCA here has taken over an old nobleman's home, very beautiful and we are living as I told before, in a rather pretentious house.

Naturally, I am well, happy and contented here. But the most fascinating part of France is the north, near the line.

Send this to Maxine, please as it is too long to rewrite. With love,

George

ON MAY 28, AMERICAN TROOPS LAUNCHED THEIR FIRST SUSTAINED OFfensive action of the war. In his report on the battle, General Pershing wrote that the 1st Division "attacked the commanding German position in its front, taking with splendid dash the town of Cantigny and all other objectives, which were organized and held steadfastly against vicious counterattacks and galling artillery fire. Although local, this brilliant action had an electrical effect, as it demonstrated our fighting qualities under extreme battle conditions and also that the enemy's troops were not altogether invincible" ("Story of War Is Told by Pershing," 2).

WALTER ELZRA DOVE, FRANCE, TO PARENTS, MAY 29, 1918 (*MEADVILLE FRANKLIN ADVOCATE*, JULY 4, 1918)

Walter Elzra Dove (1894–1961), a native of Hamburg, Mississippi, earned a bachelor's degree from Mississippi A & M (now Mississippi State University) and a doctorate from Johns Hopkins University. He was employed as an agriculture researcher for the US government in Dallas, Texas, when he registered for the draft in June 1917. After the war, he worked as an entomologist/parasitologist.

> *Dear Mother and Father,*
> *Your letter of recent date was received yesterday and as usual found me in the best of health.*
> *Owing to the rules of the censor there are lots of things of which I cannot write and if you have noticed, my letters have always been written in such a manner that if they were intercepted nothing of military importance could be learned. We are obliged to refrain from writing anything which could give a spy a clue as to the location of movement of troops and supplies.*
> *In a general way I have told you what I am doing and you know that I am located in the Advanced Zone near the Southern portion of the line. Our camp is near enough the front to hear the big guns, but as yet we have not been shelled or bombed. The only attacks that we could expect would be from the German planes and for defense against these we are pretty well fixed. Our planes are in excellent condition, we are doing some co-operative instruction with the American artillery, and we have little fear of the (Boche) German planes. As you know, I trained in the Infantry in the States and was transferred to the Aviation section as a ground officer which was due to the fact that there was a shortage of ground officers for this branch of the service. By doing this I was sent "over here" much sooner, and I am very glad that I made the change. Not because I dislike Infantry, for such is not the case. I am still very much interested in Infantry operations, and at times I feel that I could be doing more in that service.*
> *Yesterday in company with some of our pilots and Aerial Observers we visited the front lines and had an occasion to see some real activity. We witnessed at least six attacks on air-craft by anti-aircraft guns, some of which were our planes being attacked by the Germans. A late type of a German bombing plane was brought down behind our lines by our*

Walter Elzra Dove, 1918
(ancestry.com)

men, but our planes returned safely. The clouds are used to good advantage by planes when they are attacked, as they easily conceal themselves when they are fired upon.

In going to the trenches we were unable to get gas masks and "tin hats" until we were pretty close up, and while we were without this essential paraphernalia we had an occasion to cross an open section in the automobile. A German observer balloon had just gone up and German artillery fire was directed upon our road, but the nearest shell missed us by two hundred yards. We did not lose any time.

Upon reaching battalion headquarters we were accompanied by an infantry lieutenant, who visited some of our strong points with us. We went to a "listening post" in "No Man's Land" which we found very interesting. It had been taken from the Germans on the previous night.

Our men were in excellent spirits and had become accustomed to heavy fire. They were well protected in "dug outs" and appeared to be at ease.

It seems strange but the residents of this section were cultivating their farms, children were going to school, and apparently they were not concerned with the shells which were constantly being fired over their heads. They felt as though they were sufficiently protected by our men on the line and I believe our men will prevent the Boche from doing anything. There is no doubt as to the outcome of the war, as "our boys are showing the stuff that men are made of." All we want is a little time, plenty of artillery, equipment, ammunition, and air planes and you can leave the rest to us.

Last night we took the planes out of one hangar, borrowed a piano from the Red Cross, found a few violin players in the "flight" and had a real entertainment. Had a few Mississippi negroes to dance for us, but as I expected our hypnotist could not hypnotize them. A couple of the YMCA ladies came down and seemed to enjoy the little show.

Our men are rapidly building our repair shop and soon we will have it equipped for repairs on aero motors, plane repairs, trucks, small clock like instruments, vulcanizing, and any other thing that needs repair.

With love to all and assurance that everything is going well, I am always,

Walter

FROM CANTIGNY, THE FIGHTING MOVED SOUTH TO CHÂTEAU-THIERRY, A town spanning the Marne River, and to Belleau Wood. On May 31, the Germans had reached the outskirts of Château-Thierry, within thirty-seven miles of Paris. In fierce fighting on June 3–4, American troops prevented the German forces from crossing the river. Then, from June 6 to 26, the Allies retook Belleau Wood from the enemy, suffering tremendous casualties. ("Château-Thierry: Overview and the Defense of the Marne River Line," *Doughboy Center*; *Battles: The Battle of Belleau Wood*).

....

THADDEUS KINMAN WYNN, FRANCE, TO FAMILY, JUNE 10, 1918 (*GREENVILLE DAILY DEMOCRAT-TIMES*, JULY 19, 1918)

Dearest Mother and Family:
I must say that I certainly was glad to receive you letter dated April 14, which reached me today.

The razor and glasses have not as yet arrived, but no doubt it won't be long before they turn up, and they will come just at the right time, as on my last trip in the line I had my glasses broke and the pair that I am wearing are not at all satisfactory.

The weather is simply wonderful over here now. Everything is all a bloom; honestly, it makes me sick to think that civilized people are at war and destroying each other in the grand old country. This wonderful weather makes me homesick and I long for Mississippi, my mother dear, family and friends. Oh! How I would love to be in Greenville for a while.

We have just come from a four day trip in the line and I picked a poppy from "No Man's Land" to enclose in my letter as a souvenir for you. We had a very hard trip, as things were pretty lively and I thank God once more that I am here to write you. Our casualties were pretty heavy and our platoon caught a big share of them. My number two on my gun got the nicest "Blightey," a rifle bullet through the right shoulder. I sure do envy him, as he is laying peacefully in a hospital back in England by now.

We are billeted in a wonderful old chateau which is all in ruins, the grounds, which cover about ten acres are very beautiful and the most wonderful of all, there is a creek running through it. This morning I stripped and washed all my clothes and did my best to catch all of my "trench-pets," and after a bath I will feel fairly decent, as this is the first time in three weeks I've been any ways clean. We will enjoy our few days of rest here if Fritz does not shell us too heavy, but 'tis not very far back and he has been banging way at the chateau about every fifteen minutes since we landed here. However, we are used to that by now. But 'tis lots nicer to go to bed and know you are sure to wake up again, tis'n't possible around here. But so much nicer than that damn line duty. I certainly will be glad when we go "over the top" on our own big show, as it is better than having to fight him off of ours. It is a living hell when he comes over, for if you are hit and only wounded, it's ten to one you won't live, for if he gets you he can't bother with you, as he has enough wounded of his own to look after, so it is finis with you, especially the Canadians, as he hates us like the devil. We are on his black list. We lost one platoon officer this trip, a young lieutenant who arrived about two weeks ago. 'Tis a shame, as we were just beginning to know him. A whiss bang made a direct hit on him, there was absolutely nothing left of him to carry out.

Don't think from the horrible things you read about that all is black for us over here in the uniform, for when we are out of the line things are done to try and entertain us as best as they can. Tomorrow night we have a game of baseball with a Yank outfit which is around close. You would be surprised to see how close up to the line these concert parties come and some of them are really very good. You take things as they come, if you lose your hold on yourself you are gone. A soldier's motto out here is "Live today, for tomorrow you may die," so everyone is always in good spirits as it is possible under conditions. 'Tis remarkable how some chaps stand it who have been out here two or three years. I take my hat off to them. We have several fellows who came over with the first contingent and have only been back to "Blighty" on leave, as every time they were wounded the hospitals here in France were not filled up, so they were held here in France. 'Tis certainly a shame. You can bet these chaps are glad to see the Yankees over here, for after they arrive in full force no doubt these chaps will be sent home on a long furlough.

Do give my regards to friends back home and tell them I am still kicking and Fritz hasn't got me and I still believe that he isn't going to get me either. I received a note the other day telling me of Beppo Arnold's death. 'Tis certainly sad and I certainly feel sorry for Mrs. Arnold.

Started this letter on yesterday with the intention of telling you the second chapter of my first experience on the line, but have used up all the paper that was in the platoon and the gang is growling because I didn't use both sides of the sheet.

You really run across more real humanity and good fellows out here in this war than you see in civil life in five years. "Believe me" this life will certainly change a person and in majority of cases all for the good. It will certainly make a Christian out of you.

Will drop Capt. Rielly a note. But tell him if I am the only one of his school out here that I am certainly catching enough hell for the whole lot. I sincerely hope none of the others ever have to see any of it. However, as bad as it is, am awfully glad I am in it and I still believe I am coming through all OK. Anyway 'tis the "best old war we've got" so let us make it do for the present. But just the same I would give a thousand dollars for a good hot bath, clean pair of pajamas, a soft bed with real sheets and a regular meal for three weeks. I am sure tired of sleeping out doors with an overcoat for cover, eating bully beef and hard tack and washing just now and then. 'Tis a good life if you don't weaken.

Give Robert my love. It looks as if you can't get time to write everyone. I did so appreciate the letter from Miss Maud. I gave you my address in my last letter. Censor won't allow us to give it more than once or twice and we have to sign our full name to everything. So Harper is a bloated bondholder. God bless him, how I wish I could see him. Bloing

Rest the place where we were billeted had a little boy and girl just about his age. I think I made a hit with their mother by playing with them when I was laid up. Quite often she called me in and gave me a couple of fried eggs and bowl of milk. I used to try my French on her.

A big hug and kiss for sister and lots of love for Billie and Margaret, and heaps for your dear sweet self. I think of you all the time. How I would like to see you.
Your devoted boy,

Thad K. Wynn

PS Lieut. Lovegrove is back in his bank at Sandwich, Ont. He was turned down on his eyes for active service.
PSS We just lost our Colonel, he was promoted to Brig. Gen. Major Ferguson, now our acting Colonel is a young Yank from New York and I am crazy about him. He was my company OC [officer candidate] when I joined this battalion.
T.K.W.

MITCHELL J. SEALE, COMPANY K, 167TH INFANTRY, FRANCE, TO FAMILY, JUNE 15, 1918 (*PONTOTOC SENTINEL*, JULY 25, 1918)

Alabama native Mitchell J. Seale (1892–1971) received the Distinguished Service Cross for extraordinary heroism for his actions on July 26–27, 1918, during fighting near Château-Thierry (US Adjutant General's Office, *Congressional Medal of Honor*, 45). He returned to Alabama after the war and became an electrical engineer.

My dear Homefolks:
Two or three letters from you came while I was in the trenches last. I would have answered before now had I had time. Any time you fail to hear from me for several days don't be uneasy about it, because there are times when it is very inconvenient to write.

Everything is fine over here and we are winning the war as fast as we can.

The weather is nice and warm now and we have plenty to eat and plenty of good clothing to wear.

I have never seen a more beautiful country than this. I like England, too, but of course there are none like the good old USA.

I have been in the trenches several times but nothing has happened to me yet more than being scared almost to death a few times. The worst of all I was going down a trench one day when I heard something that sounded like a Ford automobile. I tried to go in a rat hole and couldn't and about that time a high explosive shell struck right near me. It bounced me around like a rubber ball at the same time knocking my helmet off. I picked it up not knowing whether or not I was dead or alive and started on down the trench but at a much more speedy gait than I had been going.

Before I went to the trenches I expected to find them half full of mud and water but found them different. There are a lot of crooked trenches running every direction. They are walled up and floored with lumber and dry when it isn't raining. The dugouts are dug deep in the ground with a stairway down to an aisle that leads straight through with double deck leads on either side. Usually room for about twenty-five men. No man's land is a large field filled with beautiful green grass and flowers and masses of barbed wire entanglement. The most disagreeable things are rats, high explosive shells, machine gun bullets and gas.

Not very long ago a German aeroplane was flying over our trenches with two men in it. It was struck by a shell from one of our anti-aircraft guns. The tank was bursted, [allowing] the gasoline to leak out and catch on fire. In an instant the whole machine was on fire. It looked like a solid blaze of fire going through the air. It was still several thousand feet in the air when one of the Germans jumped out. Of course the machine came down and the other man was burned to death.

There is lots more I could tell you, but I shall wait until next time, or until I get home.

We surely appreciate what the Red Cross is doing. It is lots of help to us in many ways.

Write me often and tell me everything.
Your son and brother,

Sgt. Mitchell J. Seale

SAMUEL KAYE JR., FRANCE, TO SAMUEL KAYE SR., UNDATED (DAUGHTERS OF THE
AMERICAN REVOLUTION, SHUK-HO-TA-TOM-A-HA CHAPTER, LOWNDES COUNTY
WORLD WAR I SCRAPBOOK)

Columbus, Mississippi, native Samuel Kaye Jr. (1894–1939) was a student at the Citizens Training Camp at Fort Logan H. Roots, Arkansas, when he registered for the draft in May 1917. After training at Mitchell Field, Texas, he served overseas from November 14, 1917, to May 31, 1919, receiving the Distinguished Service Cross and the Bronze Oak Leaf. He returned to Columbus and worked at an automobile dealership.

Dear Father:
I have had the most interesting trip today. We made an early patrol this morning and as that was the only time we were scheduled to fly, six of us decided it was a good time to have a look at the front from the ground. We got a car and left about nine o'clock headed for Fère-en-Tardenois which is a little town north of Château-Thierry that was just taken from the Germans last night.
  I had no idea that war was quite so destructive. The little villages that we passed through were literally shot to pieces. The buildings over here are all made of stone and in this case where there was once a house, there is now only a pile of rocks and plaster. Big trees along the road were cut in two by a single shell, and trees in the wood were burnt to death by gas. The ground was simply a mass of shell holes. The Allies have been advancing so fast that they haven't had time to bury all of the dead, and lots of places, the ground especially in the wood, was covered with dead Germans and horses.
  At last we came to the end, or rather as far as we could go, and there had lunch on the ground, camouflaged under some trees. It reminded me very much of the time I landed so close to the lines, for again I had the pleasure of hearing our big shells pass over head going into Germany, and when you see our wounded coming back from the first line trenches, that is one of sweetest noises in the world. One can hear them so plain as they pass through the air, that he instinctively turns to look, and of course can't see a thing. I don't mean the noise the gun makes when it is being fired, that it is an entirely different sound and more deafening. Well, for about an hour after dinner we explored the wood, saw some of the big guns in action, and took over a lot of shells and junk that the boche didn't have time to take with him. Up to now

Samuel Kaye Jr. (left), ca. 1918 (ancestry.com)

all of the noise we had heard came from our guns and shells, but pretty soon we heard shells coming, not going, and it took a lot of interest out of the place for us. We could hear the whizzing sound coming, then about a hundred feet in the air a white puff of smoke would appear with a bang! It was shrapnel that burst in the air, and scattered before striking the earth. In the mean time we had loaded the car down with boche helmets, bayonets, shells, and pistols, and were not quite ready to leave. However, we didn't get away, I am sorry to say, before a German aviator came over and shot down one of our observation balloons.[1] That made us feel like we were not on the job. In the morning we fly over this same territory at a very low altitude and I hope he tries it again.

Please excuse pencil, we don't have all the little conveniences here that one gets in Paris. With much love to all and hoping this finds you in good health, I am your affectionate son,

Sam

1. Each balloon was protected by a pair of machine guns on the ground, and the observers carried automatic shoulder rifles with them in the baskets. On clear days, it was possible to see for over twelve miles. Swinging aloft far above at the end of a cable, these balloons supported trained observers who, by means of powerful field glasses and telephones, gave the range and direction to batteries. These in turn put enemy batteries out of action and broke up infantry formations preparing for attack ("Balloon in War Does Great Work," 3)

WILLIAM RODGER GARCIA, FRANCE, TO NORA GARCIA, JUNE 27, 1918 (*BAY ST. LOUIS SEA COAST ECHO*, AUGUST 10, 1918)

Mississippi native William Rodger Garcia (1899–1944) remained in the army through at least 1920, when he was stationed at Camp Dix, New Jersey. By 1930, he had moved to New Orleans and was working as a bookkeeper (*Official US Bulletin*, March 14, 1919, 13).

Dear Mother:
I received your letter this date, and was "sure" glad to hear from you. It found me well; in pretty good health.
 I just got back from the front. Had a little hell while I was in the battle, but got out without a scratch. All I got was a broken thumb, which I don't think will be any more good to me. I got in some hot ground, where shells fell fast and hot. I never saw so much nerve in all my life as I saw then. The boys went "over the top," singing "Where Do We Go from Here, Boys?"[1]
 I was right with the boys. It was fun to see the Huns run. Those that did not run, stopped and begged for mercy. I got my share of Huns!
 Well, mother, you can take one American and he can lick a dozen Germans. They can't fight; they are just a bluff, that's all.
 Well, mother, I'm lucky to get back without a scratch. I have had machine guns to shoot at me, shells to fall within two feet of me. I have been nearly buried with the dirt from the shells. I have been in gas so strong that it choked me nearly to death. I could not put on my mask, so I went through without it.
 I have been shot at from aeroplanes. They tried to get us by dropping bombs. They came so near me I had to pinch myself to see if I was alive. This is all for the present. I feel that I am going to pull through all right, mother. Don't worry. It will come out all right.
Your son,

Wm Rod Garcia

PS Mother, did you get the little flower I sent you in my last letter? Let me know in your next letter.

1. Written by Percy Wenrich and Howard Johnson, "Where Do We Go from Here?" became popular just after the United States entered the war. A 1917 recording is available at http://www.firstworldwar.com/audio/wheredowegofromhere.htm (accessed January 1, 2015).

ROSCOE HOLMES BASS, FRANCE, TO H. T. BASS, JULY 2, 1918 (*HATTIESBURG AMERICAN, AUGUST 15, 1918*)

Roscoe Holmes Bass (1897–1983) was a native of Collins, Mississippi, who served in the military from May 28, 1917, to April 30, 1919. After the war, he moved to Washington, DC, and worked for the government before becoming an automobile salesman. He is buried at Arlington National Cemetery. This letter was written for Bass by Lieutenant Hal I. Green.

> *My Dear Brother:*
> *Perhaps you have wondered why I haven't written to you for some time, but no doubt you know the "marines" were in the advanced lines and doing hard work there.*
> *You no doubt were surprised to see my name in the "casualty" list; but don't worry, because my wounds were only slight. My body was burned and my eyes affected quite a bit by "mustard gas." This happened on June 13, during our engagement at "Belleau woods," and I've been in the hospital since that date; but I expect to be out and able to walk around in a few days.*
> *This is a pretty place, near a large town called Clermont-Ferrand. It is in the mountains and is quite like Hot Springs, Ark. It is quite a fashionable summer resort for the French—mineral waters, etc., here. There are beautiful parks, etc., here, but I have not been able to see any of the town yet, being still confined to bed; but I'll soon be up now. The nights are cool and pleasant and the days sunny and warm. They have concerts and bands here to serenade us. There are about nine hundred wounded men here. There will be big doings on the 4th. I don't know yet whether I can go.*
> *Your brother,*
>
> *Roscoe*

IN MID-JULY, THE GERMANS MOUNTED WHAT WOULD BE THEIR LAST great offensive of the war, again attacking Château-Thierry in what became known as the Second Battle of the Marne. After fierce fighting from July 15 to August 5 resulted in 168,000 German casualties and 120,000 Allied troops killed or wounded, the Germans withdrew to the lines they had occupied before April 1918, and the stalemate resumed (*Battles: The Second Battle of the Marne*).

HERBERT L. WEYMAN, 166TH INFANTRY REGIMENT, FRANCE, TO MOTHER, JULY 1918 (DAUGHTERS OF THE AMERICAN REVOLUTION, SHUK-HO-TA-TOM-A-HA CHAPTER, LOWNDES COUNTY WORLD WAR I SCRAPBOOK)

Herbert L. Weyman of Caledonia, Mississippi (1889?–), enlisted in the Regular Army on June 5, 1911, and was discharged on June 4, 1914. He served again in World War I and was wounded in the Second Battle of the Marne on July 15, 1918 ("Lowndes Boy in Casualty List" [clipping], October 10, 1918, Daughters of the American Revolution, Shuk-Ho-Ta-Tom-A-Ha Chapter, Lowndes County World War I Scrapbook).

Dear Mother:
I hope you are not worrying about me. Perhaps you didn't see the casualty list in the paper or it may be that the governor has wired you that I was wounded. My wounds are not serious and I expect to be up and at the Huns almost as soon as you get this. A high explosive shell burst near me and a piece cut my left wrist and another entered my thigh, but I'm not hurt much. Anyway, the French and Americans stopped the Germans, I'm very proud to say, and I'm proud of my wounds, too.

The Red Cross has certainly done good work and it has been appreciated by everyone. When we were brought back from the firing line it was very hot. Most of us had lost quite a bit of blood, so we were very thirsty. The Red Cross were there with cool lemonade and orangeade. You can't imagine our surprise and it was such a pleasant one, for lemonade and orangeade is indeed a treat to us over here. As I was saying, we were so surprised that most of us could only mutter our thanks, like school boys. You'll never know just how delicious and refreshing that lemonade was. It raised our spirits a thousand fold.

Now we began to experience new difficulties. We had been in the thick of the fight for some days and had but very little to smoke. If you want to see an American soldier's face brighten, give him a cigarette when he is coming in on stretchers. The Red Cross gave us each a package of cigarettes. This raised our spirits another thousand fold. I own our morale was low for we were disabled just when the fight was most interesting. We had the Boche in a trap, which was impossible for them to escape, and we wanted to be there at the finish. We wanted to capture all of the Boche in that trap without assistance from the French. That night the Boche dropped bombs all around our hospital, but did little damage. Our guns brought down two planes in flames. The next morning we wanted to shave, but we had no razor, no soap or brush.

The Red Cross saw our needs and again came to the rescue with the razor. The most of the men lost everything they had. As for myself, I haven't even a helmet, that being lost before I reached the hospital in the ambulance. That's just a few of the things the Red Cross is doing for our men. I know you are giving to the Red Cross, for you told me of it last December. I am going to give some, too. Of the little I send you each month to save for me I wish you would give the Red Cross ten dollars a month for the next six months.

Tuesday I saw a paper for the first time in almost a month, and I think the Red Cross are going to make another drive. If this little information will help the Red Cross to raise the required amount I'll be glad.

Don't worry about me, mother, for I'm getting on nicely and am just as proud of my wounds as I can be. I can now wear a service stripe and wound stripe.
With love from
Your son,

Herbert

J. D. WHITE, COMPANY A, 28TH INFANTRY, FRANCE, TO SISTER, JULY 23, 1918 (NATCHEZ DEMOCRAT, SEPTEMBER 1, 1918)

My Dear Sister:
At last I can write you again and try to tell you of my experiences in the last four weeks. Just think, I have been wounded for the first time, and I am here to tell you I am proud of it, too. Before this you will have read of the great drive which we have made and the results of it.

The Germans did not expect an attack, and to date we have taken twenty-three thousand prisoners, over seven hundred cannon and many thousands of machine guns, together with loads of ammunition. It is the largest drive since the beginning of the war, and is a complete success for us.

I was near some machine guns when we went over the top and they played havoc with our boys. It was a splendid sight to see them charging the Boche lines, with those guns spraying shot like rain among us.

It was on the second day of the battle, and we were advancing as fast as our artillery could follow us, when the order came to crawl thru a wheat field, and by the time we got through the Boche machine guns spotted us, and then the show commenced. We jumped up and charged over four hundred yards to them, and when we started the Boche artillery began playing on us. There we were with machine guns and artillery both playing on us, and we kept on going. A shell burst in the air close to me, and my leg felt like some one had kicked it. I looked around at the calf just as it went dead on me, and tumbled heels over appetite with my life-juice flying. A piece of the shell had taken a piece out of the calf of my right leg leaving a hole I could stick my finger joint in.

I bound it up with a first aid bandage, which all of us carry and walked two miles back to an ambulance. Meanwhile the boys had passed on, and I could see when they got to the Germans no mercy was shown.

It was a sight which shall live forever in my memory to see my regiment charge them Dutchmen, and I am proud that I have shown that an American was not afraid to fight and shed his blood for the ones at home. I am now in a French hospital, hoping to recover soon, and can promise you that never before as now were we so confident of victory, and this battle marks the beginning of the end. Address me the same to Your true brother,

Private J. D. White, Company A, 28th Infantry, American EF, France

My war No. is 56 738 if you write to my regiment or the War Dept. at any time for news of me.

WILLIS K. FORD TO MOTHER, JULY 24, 1918 (*HATTIESBURG AMERICAN*, AUGUST 20, 1918)

Dear Mother:
Guess you thought I was dead by this time, but am not. I have had several narrow escapes since I wrote last, but am still here. I am in the hospital now; was knocked out and covered up with dirt, but managed to kill two Boches before this happened. I thought I could stand a lot, but, seeing all the dead and wounded, and hearing the ceaseless firing of guns I can't stand any more.

I don't think "Kaiser Bill" can hold out much longer.

It just runs me crazy to hear the roar of the guns now, where, up until the last battle, it did not worry me at all. I am nervous and can hardly write. Guess I will go back somewhere in a few days. Keep in good spirits, for I am still OK, for a miss of getting killed is just as good as a mile. Tell dad and all the folks hello for me. With love to all, from your soldier son,

Private Willis K. Ford

REGINALD EDGAR SPIVEY JR., FRANCE, TO FAMILY, AUGUST 5, 1918 (*GREENVILLE DAILY DEMOCRAT-TIMES*, OCTOBER 15, 1918)

Reginald Edgar Spivey Jr. (1893–1967), a native of Canton, Mississippi, was working there as a deputy chancery clerk when he registered for the draft in June 1917. After the war, he became an attorney, practicing in Canton and New Orleans.

Dear Mama, Papa and All:
This message is a real message, a message which can only be conveyed from one heart to another. It is not a story of the war, the battle, but the message from me to each of you, after having lived, day and night for nineteen days in the very midst of the fiercest struggle the war has yet seen—nineteen days with the booming of the guns, the nerve-racking whine of the projectiles and the crash of the bombs over in your ears, nineteen days of breathing and eating the damnable gases which have shocked the civilized world, nineteen days of struggling, toiling, praying with very little food and very little sleep; nineteen days of hell, a message from out such surroundings, I say, from me just to you.

I shall not attempt to tell you the story of the battle, my own vocabulary is for too limited to even suggest to you just what I say—just what I lived. For four long years the most noted journalists of the world have been trying to picture the horrors, the glory, the wonder of that very hell on earth, and they haven't even awakened your imagination to the realization of even the smallest part of that which, upon our entrance upon the field of battle, was suddenly thrust upon us. In fact, when the languages of the world were being coined the words, the phrases, the sentences which would express to you that which I have lived for the past nineteen days were not conceived, and if I could express to you what lives in my mind, my heart, my soul today, no human mind has the power to picture it, to realize just what it is. Come here and see, and live through a period of time, under which conditions is the only possible way to realize, to know war.

The papers have been full of the achievements of "my" division, but just where we were, and what we did, I am not allowed to tell. Just remember, I was where the Hun struck the hardest, where he met his greatest surprise, and where he first started to run. I was in the direct path of the pride of the German army, and even though it be so very small, yet I, along with all the others, did my little part in causing the great German offensive to be turned into the greatest of allied victories. Read the papers and see what happened, what America did, and some day I'll tell you all about the part I played.

On July 9 the 10th Field Artillery went into action and for five days everything was quiet. We did very little firing, and were not fired upon, and we began to feel that war was a very tame affair. But we were doomed to a great disappointment, and it was not long in reaching us. On Sunday night, July 14, everything was unusually quiet and there seemed to be no war. At just ten minutes after twelve o'clock on the morning of July 15 that quietness suddenly came to an end, and in front of us the whole world seemed to "blaze forth" at the same time. As stated in the papers, the Germans opened up such a terrific fire of high explosives, shrapnel, bombs and gases as to make the walking into a machine gun and rifle fire seem like a holiday excursion. For about eighteen hours they kept up the fire, never slackening the pace. The country for ten miles back was completely covered; every building was demolished, the woods were cleared as clean as if a gang of wood choppers had been at work. They dropped shells about every ten meters, and each shell is supposed to cover thirty-five meters.

The 10th Field Artillery stood directly in the path of the oncoming Germans; a gang of raw recruits who had never been tested; all through the night and the next day that inferno of shell and blood and death continued, until late that afternoon it seemed that they would never stop coming; but, at last, they turned, and their fire ceased; it was then, after the smoke had cleared away, after nature had destroyed the gases, that that former gang of recruits were found still standing in the path of the Huns. They were veterans then, veterans baptized in their own blood and glorious in the fact that they never yielded an inch.

Then the chase began, and for the next eighteen days we chased the Kaiser's best, chased them over fifteen miles and still had them going, when we were relieved in order that we might get a little sleep and rest up. I never slept over four hours per night and many nights did not sleep at all. Never slept from Sunday night until Wednesday night, and then I was out in one of the hardest rainstorms I ever saw—wet to the skin. I slept about four hours and never even caught a cold. One meal a day was a luxury.

But every one was happy, happy in the thought that they were fighting, and fighting a winning fight for God, country and home. The spirit of the American soldier is the most wonderful sight of all. To daunt him is an impossibility; you cannot work him too hard; and with his faith in God he fears nothing; with death and destruction on all sides of him, and he can laugh at it all. Laugh because he knows that he is right, and that whatever the cost, the reward is worth it. He has made his peace with God, and is here to deliver the goods. He is not doing his "bit," but every day, every hour, he is doing his "all."

"The bravest battle that was ever fought,
Shall I tell you where and when?
On the maps of the world, you'll find it not;
T'was fought by the mothers of men.
Nay, not with cannon or battle shot,
With sword or nobler pen,
Nay, not with eloquent word or thought,
From the mouths of wonderful men.
But deep in the walled up woman's heart,
Of women that would not yield,
But bravely, silently bore her part,
Lo! there is the battlefield.[1]

The above conveys to you my only trouble, my only worry. I know that each of you is worrying about me, and my prayer today is that you cease your worrying. I am taking my chance, 'tis true, but it is so small a chance, and if I happen to be called, then what a call it would be, think of the victory, the personal victory that would be won.

I know you have fought your silent battles, from babyhood to the grave, and that you hate to see me go out, after all your years of toiling, of struggling with me, to take my chance upon the field of battle. But, dear ones, my prayer is, give me a thousand deaths upon the field of France, but God deliver me from the coward's heart which would make me stay at home. You have filled my veins with blood which will not allow me to do less than my best; you have filled my soul with a spirit which will not allow me to stay behind, and see others play the game. Yes, blood and spirit which cause me to glory in that God-given privilege of helping destroy the greatest menace to God and to man the world has ever known. So, on I go, with God as my guide and home my destination. Some day I will come back to you, but it will only be after my duty has been done. It may be hard on you, but no greater life can be lived, no grander death died.

All that I am looking for is peace and the end of war, and then home. When I come back to you I want no bell ringing, band playing welcome. The American army wants no honors for every honor that is showered upon us who return we realize that the price is our brothers who have gone to their eternal sleep beneath the sod of France. Let us come back, and fall in step, and live our lives, along with you, in such a way as to make the blood of America, which has been shed all over France, not have been shed in vain. We want to live our lives in memory those we leave "over here" and we shall demand that the principles for which they died live forever.

Just a few more words and I shall have finished. I must, in my first account of the war, make an attempt to impress upon you, and beg that you scatter the same all over the land, the vital importance of an absolute backing of the army at home. We know you are with us, but here and there a man is found who is against us; he is gathering personal benefits and we are paying the price. Every time a man does one little thing against the furthering of the war, the American boy's life is the price. If you had seen what I have lived you would, along with every soul in all the land, give up everything you have, and live in the woods, if necessary, to enable the army to drive this war to an early end. The man who puts self above his country, who thinks of profit and gain rather than service is worse than the blackest spy in the German army. It is up to you who are with us, body and soul, to clean out that class of reptiles in America just as if they were a den of rattlesnakes. We know that you are with us, and realize that your fight is the hardest, but all together, without a hitch, we can soon bring an end to it all.

I would like to keep on writing, to tell you of the wonderful spirit of the French people, to tell you what a sad picture is being presented to us every day as we see the old women and children returning to their homes, only to find them in ashes, and with tears in their eyes, yet smiles upon their lips, they murmur their "Merci" to America. Wonderful, indeed, are the sights which I have seen.

We will, in about two weeks, go into a quiet sector, and the chances are we will have very little to do for some time.

Do not worry about me, and if anything should happen you will receive a cablegram within two days.

Love to all.

Edgar

1. Spivey is quoting the first half of a poem, "The Bravest Battle," by Joaquin Miller (1837–1913).

HERMANN MOYSE SR., BLOIS, FRANCE, TO FAMILY, AUGUST 16, 1918 (*NATCHEZ DEMOCRAT*, SEPTEMBER 3, 1918)

Hermann Moyse Sr. (1891–1985) was a native of St. Gabriel, Louisiana, who practiced law in Baton Rouge before enlisting in the US Army's First Officers Training Camp in 1917. His wartime actions earned him the Distinguished Service Cross and the French Croix de Guerre with Palm. This letter is now part of the Hermann Moyse Sr. World War I Collection, Louisiana State University Libraries, Baton Rouge.

Dear Folks:

Of course I got mine, but things could have been so much worse that the only thing that bothers me now is the fact that I know you folks are worrying yourselves sick about me. Please try not to, for by the time this reaches you I will be up and about, with God's will, and then will have a nice period of convalescence.

In the first place, my wounds are not serious. The first bullet to get me was from a machine gun, which landed between the third and fourth toes of my left foot, necessitating their amputation the following day, August 1. That naturally slackened me up and while I was just getting through with the first aid a German sniper caught me, the bullet going through my left side, very fortunately missing my heart. The third hit is a mere scratch, the bullet merely grazing the left arm. There was no operation necessary on my side or arm and everything is going on nicely.

The doctors class the wounds as very clean ones and see no reason under the sun why there should be any complications. I imagine that the government will classify the wounds as severe, but I think the fact that I am writing this letter without the necessity of assistance from anyone, even to hold the paper, should be proof that I am telling the truth.

I can't say that being wounded is fun, but there are so many others who have so much more serious wounds and pains that it would be wrong for me to complain. Please look at it the same way. Oh, folks, if you could see what the Huns in their rule of terrorism have done to this country, you would willingly sacrifice, not merely worldly goods, but life itself in order that our own America may be forever spared such a visitation, for Germans victorious would have meant an America ruined. Don't let our own little griefs and pains make us blind to the truth.

The attention we received was wonderful, from the first aid through the examination hospital to one of the base hospitals, that at Blois, where I now am. The doctors are as skillful and patient as though they were treating million dollar cases, and no trained nurses in a stylish sanitarium could be more solicitous and attentive than are the faithful nurses we have here. Those women came over to work and they do it, and food is excellent—fresh eggs, milk, soup, custards; in fact, anything one could desire. I have a good, soft bed with plenty of clean linens, get washed every day and am treated as much like a baby as though I were back at 931 Main Street with mama and grandma as nurses.

Some of these days I shall write you all about the big drama in which I played my small part, but today I want to add only a few more lines. If a man had to choose the conditions under which he would like to be wounded I believe he would choose just such an occasion as that on which I received mine. It was in the great counter-drive against the Huns. I was in charge of my own men. We led the charge for the attacking forces and advanced in the face of the fire of bullets two kilometers, accomplishing as much as was expected of the platoon before we were stopped and doing our bit in making the subsequent further advance possible.

I forgot to say that I have had no temperature and my pulse is fine. Sent a cable the day after I was hurt my first opportunity and another today. Address my letters for the time being: "First Lieutenant Hermann Moyse, USNG, Section 1, American Base Hospital No. 43, APO 726, American Expeditionary Forces, France."

Please don't worry and remember that there is a Superior Being above us who remembers and protects us all.
With much love,
Yours,

Hermann

HUGH A. WILEY, BATTERY D, 17TH FIELD ARTILLERY, 2ND DIVISION, FRANCE, TO MOTHER, AUGUST 12, 1918 (*GREENVILLE DAILY DEMOCRAT-TIMES*, SEPTEMBER 25, 1918)

Hugh A. Wiley (1893–1958) was a Greenville, Mississippi, auto salesman and mechanic when he registered for the draft in June 1917. After serving overseas, he lived in Jackson and Greenville, where he operated an auto repair shop.

> *Dear Mama:*
> *Just received a roll of* Commercial Appeals *from you this morning, which are the first of all you have sent. Words are faint to express the pleasure I had in reading them—even to all the want ads.*
>   *About two weeks ago I had a letter from each of you and Mary—certainly enjoyed both of them. At the time of writing you did not know I had rejoined my battery. Will not go into particulars as I have written you four times telling why. Shall only say that I asked to go back when the Germans thought they were on the way to Paris—the engineers that I was attached to were a good many miles from the front with no prospects of getting nearer for months. I caught up with my battery between Meaux and Château-Thierry. Guess you have seen a good deal about both places and what the Americans did there. My regiment had only a few killed there. Our battery lost more men than any other in our regiment and we only lost eighteen men, but that was due to good luck. The Germans certainly fought hard for they hated to miss their trip to Paris. My division got a citation from General Pershing and one from the French Generals for the work we did there.*
>   *Well, I guess we deserved it, for when we went into position the first of the battle, it was an open field with nothing at all to hide the big guns. The Germans were advancing very fast.*
>   *My regiment which is heavy artillery had orders to hold at all costs and the light guns and infantry had orders to advance. Guess you know the result—they were stopped and our boys advanced 1½ miles the first day, and have been going forward ever since, a little at a time. We stayed on that sector a good deal longer than we anticipated, and about the 11th or 12th of July were relieved by another American division.*
>   *Thought then we were on our way to Paris for July 14th celebration.*[1] *We pulled back of the lines and stayed there until after the 14th. The report then got around that we were on the way to a rest camp, as "ours"*

had been at the front for six months. Just about dark one night bugles blew "assembly"—all ran up and received orders to saddle up full pack, which is marching order. Started about nine P.M. all thinking we were going on that long looked for rest. We marched all night without stopping and until two P.M. next day without breakfast or dinner. At two P.M. stopped, watered and fed the horses and had some hot coffee—lay down and slept for an hour—fed and watered the horses again. By that time the cooks had opened some monkey meat[2] and hard tack. It was then time to saddle up again. Started as soon as it was dark enough to conceal us from Boche airplanes, traveled all night, but were all convinced by then that we were not on the way to a rest camp, for we were pushing the horses for all they were worth.

About noon the next day we pulled the guns into position in the Soissons sector, about twelve hours before the drive was to start. We had a fine position on top of a high hill overlooking a good many thousands of acres of level fields. We were behind the marines and our doughboys—the Moroccans and Algerians on one side and the French on the other.

My battery was not only in the thick of it, but was where we could see everything that took place. It was a scene that is beyond me to describe, but one that can never be forgotten by those who witnessed it. We soon had them on the run, pushing them back so far that we could not reach them with the heavies, and had a hard time moving fast enough to catch up. It was open warfare for several days, and the ground over which we advanced for several days was covered thick with the German dead. In the advance two Boche planes circled over us and dropped two bombs on us killing six boys in our battery, giving the rest a pretty good scare, for an aero bomb is not like any of the other shells—you can't tell where it will hit. Suppose you have learned that the shells make a humming noise; anyone who has been at the front long can tell which way they are going and about how fast. The only thing to do when we hear one coming is to lie with the body just as close to the ground as a fellow can get, and believe me, there is always strong competition to see who can lie the closest when the Boche begins to send over the 210's.

Our captain got promoted for the good work he did at Château-Thierry, directing the battery fire. We were all sorry to lose him, but glad of his good luck. Our colonel was made a Brigadier General, and is in charge of our division (2nd).

Am in the best of health, but still dieting for fear of trouble again.

Just as I was closing this, seven Boche planes came over and shrapnel balls fell like hail, so close that we picked them up as fast as they hit the ground. No one was hurt, although one only missed the sergeant about three inches.

Sure have one sore ear—a field mouse, mink or something bit me the other night while I was asleep on the ground, wrapped in my blanket under a tree that is, wrapped up except an ear. We can't strike a light so it got away before I could see what it was.

Best love to Tom and Mary and all friends. Tell them all to write. Your loving son,

Hugh

PS Our division got a citation from Gen. Pershing and one from the French Generals after Château-Thierry, and our brigade of artillery was especially mentioned in it.

1. July 14 is the French national holiday, Bastille Day, commemorating the beginning of the French Revolution in 1789.
2. *Monkey meat* was canned beef from Madagascar (Mead, *Doughboys*, 195).

JAMES GERVYS LUSK, FRANCE, TO BILL HUMPHREYS, AUGUST 1918 (*GREENVILLE DAILY DEMOCRAT-TIMES*, AUGUST 28, 1918)

Dear Bill:
It has been some time since I have heard from you. I am now in a base hospital slightly wounded and am getting along fine. My only regret is that I must leave. That means that I lose my Div., and my platoon, the one I have been with for a year. It is rather hard and unjust; in a way, to learn every man's name and habits to a dot and work hard trying to teach him how to fight then have to leave them. Of course we realize it is for the benefit of our army and am willing to give up anything for the cause, "even our platoon." The reason for it is, when we are evacuated to a base, not knowing how long we will be there would mean for the company to be short of officers who are needed. Everyone here is growling over the fact of losing his platoon. There are about 150 lieutenants here in this base and one major. The Major said the only thing he hated was

losing his battalion, a Second Lieutenant said that's nothing, I am going to lose my platoon. This is a lieutenant's war after the battle starts. He is the big guy. Communications are broken and it is up to them to carry on—and we do.

My experience since here in France has been a wonderful one and a hard one. I have been over the top four times, in three battles, two of which were as hard as Verdun in '14. I have had pictures burned into my memory that I shall never forget. Some were horrible and some were pleasant. There was one that I think of every night when idle and am thinking of various things. The last battle I was in I passed a chap sitting on top of the parapet who had been mangled as soon as he popped it. He was in an awful condition. His clothing was drenched with blood. I and the Red Cross man stopped to see what we could do for him, but he refused to let us dress him. Well in fact he knew he would die. He gave me his mother's address and picture, asking me to write her and tell her he died game and gave 'em h—— for a while. Unfortunately I lost it and wonder if his mother knows how game the little fellow was. He was about seventeen years of age.

One would think seeing hundreds of men lying around dead in every condition possible, that it would lower the morale of the men, but it only makes them more determined to kill the Hun. Boy, this war is a little bit harder than hanging around the KK.

The funny part of our last battle was that it was supposed to be a surprise to the enemy—now speaking of surprises, it was more of a surprise to us than Fritz. We had captured C[censored] and had two months of hard fighting. They pulled us out and we could see a nice long rest in sight that failed us. We rode all night and all day in trucks and when we began to see the roads crammed with trucks, guns and soldiers our hearts flew up in our mouths. We thought the Huns were making another push but after a short rest and a little cold eats the Major kindly informed us of the fact that the American army would attack the German army in the morning. Well it surprised us and also surprised Fritz. I must say, I was a little uneasy as I hadn't time to think the thing over. We had seventeen or eighteen kilometers to go before reaching the line. As we fell in it grew dark and began to thunder, lightning and rain. The roads being crowded made hiking hard but we arrived there on time, plenty of pep and ready to fight. The soldiers pronounce when riding kilem-eters, walking kilo-meters. We didn't have much time before zero hour so we had to hustle but everything was OK *in plenty of time. Man, I could see Greenville just as plain and almost knew I would never see it again. I felt as though some kind hearted gent had hung a piece of crepe on my nose and another somebody was following behind me with a wooden cross, in fact I didn't feel at home. I had to hand out a little of that soft stuff to myself saying, come on Lusk, old boy, everything is lovely. I said if I only had the duck by the neck that set the time up in France I'd choke him. Oh boy, zero ho[ur], all the big guns, little and big opened up and the battle was on and I was well on my way to the German trenches before I realized what had happened. We dug in to them killing them left and right. I looked around and they were in the trench pulling this old komerad stuff. We only took prisoners that we couldn't reach. The others started on a long distance run with Berlin as the stopping point. The field was thick with dead Huns and we rejoiced every time we saw one. It doesn't seem like killing a human at all, well in fact, they are not. I killed my first Fritz in this fight, but he fairly scared the wits out of me for a while, it was another one of those surprise attacks. He jumped out and began to shoot at me with a luger pistol, how he missed me I can't tell but I got my "hip iron" out, got mad, scared and dangerous and hit the old boy three times. I now possess his pistol, field glasses, helmet and other souvenirs.*

There was a negro soldier bringing in a Bosche prisoner with the rank of Major. He made the Major carry his full field pack on his back, took the monocle out of the German's eye, placed it in his own and started down to headquarters.

Bill, the American private is the best soldier in the world. We should be proud to be one.

Ring up mama and tell her to send my mail to Co. B. 2nd MG 1st Brig. Until I let her know. Write soon, as ever.

Lusk

ERSKINE P. ODENEAL, FRANCE, AUGUST 5–19, 1918 (EXCERPTS) (*GREENVILLE DAILY DEMOCRAT-TIMES*, NOVEMBER 22, 1918)

Reared in Jackson, Mississippi, Erskine P. Odeneal (1872–1934) became an ophthalmologist, practicing in Greenville and Biloxi prior to the war. After serving overseas, he returned to medicine in Mississippi City (*Jackson Daily Clarion-Ledger*, August 4, 1934, 5).

We have very good news now from a part of the front, news that will be old when you get this letter. The [?] officers that we see regard it as the greatest success since the first battle of the Marne. We have been near the outskirts of the entire offensive, and it looks like now that we will be nearer still. All our wounded have come from the section that has the hardest fighting and the heaviest losses. A great number of our southern boys have made a great reputation with the French. We hear the French all through the country are celebrating—I hope it is not too soon.

August 8, after being moved: The [?] moved out of this place four days ago. The last ten miles of our trip was through country that they have occupied for the past three months. I never, even from the various magazine and newspaper articles and pictures that I had seen, during the past four years, expected to see such utter devastation and desolation. In one town four miles below here there is not a single habitable home, in what must have been a beautiful place of several thousand inhabitants. This town is about all destroyed. They had to leave [?] too suddenly to finish it up. The main highway, runs at the foot of a hill. Just on the other side of the road there is a large French and American escadrille. I don't know how many thousand pass here daily in trucks (the railroad that did run here being partially destroyed), but there is a world of movement and [?] day and night. Airplanes are coming and going all the time. The road is just a stream of trucks, lorries and ambulances bringing up men, supplies and ammunitions and bringing back the wounded.

As I have said several times before, this war could not run three months without gasoline.

The dead have not been buried around here yet—they have not had time. The fields are all torn up with shell holes. Every crest of the hills is filled with machine gun emplacements, [?], dugouts or bombproofs. In all of them were spoons, cans, letters, books, a world of empty and used cartridges, many empty and [?] shells, articles of clothing, a [few] machine guns, rifles, helmets, etc., etc.—a few contained [?] Germans. The letter I am enclosing you I found in a machine pit with his (a German's) cooking utensils, gun, helmet, etc., scattered around. He was shot through the head, doubled up in a corner. [I] put some of his letters and his luger in his helmet, covered him up with entrenching spade and stuck his helmet with contents, up on the spade so that the grave could be identified.

August 10: I have just finished supper, fighting flies for every mouthful. I keep one hand to "feed" with, and the other to fight them away. Now to writing with one hand and keeping the paperpad on my knee and fighting the flies with the other. Last night I counted forty planes overhead at one time. They maneuver [?] all sorts of stunts in com-[?] to make a landing. I understand that they have over two hundred [?] and American aviators in this [?]. Along the road there is a constant procession of men, motors and horses. Then will come two or more regiments of men on foot, then a bunch of [?] men, then fifteen or twenty big guns all going in and some coming out [?] rest period. Scattered among will be bands of men and women returning home for the first time in months, some have carts drawn by horses, oxen, or cows, but most of them push their own carts. Two or [?] old men and young women pulling and pushing, or packing big bundles, all they were able to save when they had to leave. One group had two [old] women pulling a small cart, a young girl pushing a baby car with two babies in it. A big dog [was attached] to this and was pulling.

An old man holding the hand of a small girl was bringing up the [rear]. They had to get out of the road for the troops to go by. I carried four cakes of chocolate that I [had] guarded for a rainy day, and a [pack] of cigarettes for the old [man].

They are all coming back—[to fix] up their ruined houses and to start a crop. One of the [?] has a good well. I went to the house: the furniture and [?] must have been handsome. [?] was not a usable thing in [?]. For instance, there was a mirror over the mantel. They [?] all the chinaware out of the [?] and closets and chunked them piece by piece at the mirror and windows in the rooms. In front of the [?] was a trunk full of broken [?]. Every room is the house was in the same condition. There was not a thing in that house of a dozen large rooms that could be used again.

August 11: We have a Red Cross tent with a captain in charge. He has a car and runs down to Paris every day or so. He asked us all to call at his tent and tell him how he could serve us. I told him about my mail and he promised to locate it. They can do anything they want to over here, so I have hope that he can get me a letter. He has papers, books, magazines, chocolate and tobacco for the enlisted men and patients—nothing sold, all given away. The RC is very popular with the boys. He gave me a Collier's of Dec. 15, 1917, today—I know I was glad to get any old papers, magazines or books to pass the time with.

I went to see the gun emplacement, of one of the "Big Berthas" that has been firing on Paris. The gun was gone; they had it in the woods at the end of a switch, but they did not have time to destroy the pit. It is immense—as large as the usual turntable pit in a railroad round house. A wonderful piece of machinery. The ball bearings on it weigh 150 pounds each! I have often wondered why the aviators could not locate those big guns. I don't, after seeing this one. All the way (around) they have holes in the ground, boxed and big enough for a tree fifteen or twenty feet high. They cut trees from the distant woods and place them in the boxes, water them to keep them fresh, and put new ones in when the leaves were brown; it was impossible to see the gun or switch from above.

We are all excitement over the good news from the front, coming back to us, also from the English front. The Hun prisoners coming back our way are all dead tired of war. They don't care any longer which side wins, just so it stops. No one permits himself to hope too strongly, but we cannot help but feel encouraged, over the daily victories; also over the fact that our men are full of enthusiasm and ginger, while the enemy is tired and discouraged. He had promised Paris by July 14, without fail. Now, the private, not officer, prisoner says he will never be as near to it again as he was on August 1. I thought when I first landed that he would be there—but I don't know.

August 12: Had only one case last night. A shell exploded in front of this boy. A piece about the size of a quarter and three times as thick passed through his eye, fractured the orbital plate and entered the brain. I removed the remains of the eye, repaired the upper and lower lids, and the foreign body was removed from the fractured plate. He should get well unless he has meningitis. We have a very powerful magnet that will remove anything in the brain that is steel; a fine X-ray plant that locates very definitely any foreign body. I believe we will be in our present location for a long time, as they are building streets, sidewalks, all through the camp. The eight EH (Evacuation Hospitals) have beds for seven hundred patients, with tents for the officers, nurses, operating rooms, kitchens, mess halls, etc. We will stay here for a long time if our friends "above" do not take a notion to make the nightly visits, as they did in our first location. We have a new moon now, so we will in a few nights know how they are going to treat us.

August 15: The Red Cross man located some stick candy somewhere, so I ate candy for the past two days—cut out "bully beef," and I feel much better today. If the Hun airmen would just stop trying to get us at night we would all sleep now. We can hear the barrage of the anti-aircraft guns going nearly all night. Can't sleep much when you don't know if they are broken through or not.

The people of this village and the next one to us are beginning to come back. Saw some half dozen women in the yards of the town yesterday. One of them opened a laundry two hours after she got in. From the way she charges she can rebuild her home in a month or two. We also found a small river near, and some of us went for a bath last evening. A bunch of French soldiers stood on the bridge and watched the performance. I have been through a good many ruined homes and chateaux since I came up here, but still have to see the first bath room. I guess that is the reason that toilet waters and extracts are so popular over here,

August 16: I am in the shade of my tent watching the stunts of a captain of airmen. Every time he makes a land he performs all kinds of tricks. He had a small Nieuport machine, and knows how to handle it. He has painted on the side of his fuselage a fox terrier pup and four dead rats stretched around it—the words "who said rats" under the picture. When he gets a fifth Hun plane to his credit he will become an "Ace." Told me the other day he would give five months' pay to be able to paint that fifth rat on his "ship." I am afraid he is too anxious and takes too many chances to get one. Every time a plane is hit by an enemy, just on that same spot, they paint a small German iron cross. This boy's ship must have fifty on it. I am trusting his care, he has told me so many tales of airmen combats—only twenty-two but old in experience. We got in over one hundred gassed men last night and today. They suffer very much, it is hard to treat them the first time. We evacuated all of them today at noon. They are taken in ambulances to [censored] and landed on hospital boats on a canal that runs to Paris. Just received word that four hundred more were coming this evening, so I will have a busy night. I operated on a case last night.

August 17: We had a bad night of it last night. The air swarmed with enemy planes. The sky was lit up with lights, rockets, and bursting shrapnel. The barrage of anti-aircraft guns—Archies—must have been effective, as none came down to bomb us. All of us sat around in our tin hats, waiting for it to stop, until near midnight. But even last night seems like a quiet Gulf Coast town to what our last four nights at [censored] were. The last night up there I was so dead tired that I slept through it all, with a helmet over my face and one over my abdomen.

We were able to do a lot of good work up here, saving a good many eyes, and a lot of trouble for the "eye men" at the base hospital, by seeing to these eye cases early and beginning treatment within twenty-four hours after the injuries. The most pathetic thing up here is the confidence and trust that the wounded have in the medical men. I never do any kind of operation before I tell them what I am going to do, or hope to accomplish. One boy, yesterday, when I told him that the "ray" had located a large foreign body in the eye and that while I was going to do my best for him, I thought the eye would have to come out—gave my hand a squeeze and said: "That's all right; I know you will do whatever is best for me." It is the case with all of them—no kicking or fuss. They are all so dead tired out that they only want to sleep, and a little water. There are so many at times that the surgeons can't get to them promptly. Some have to wait several hours for their time. Then it is the hard time—to go through the preparation ward and hear ask for just a little water. They get [it] in teaspoonful quantities, when they could get away with a bucketful, for the fever and hemorrhages gives them an intense thirst. But when we explain the reason for it—they are satisfied. We can tell from the sound of the guns when we will get a big number in. We will begin tonight about ten and keep it up all night, for all up in the north and northeast there has been a continuous, deafening roar for the past few hours.

August 18: Last night was cloudy—we did not have any Hun visitors. Today is cloudy—some rain—so we expect a quiet night. Not many patients today so I ran down to [censored] quite a large town and must have been pretty before the war; now it is all shot to pieces. Two fine old bridges, hundreds of years old, were a mass of ruins. The civil population are just returning to it. Today I saw many women and children wandering around the streets, looking at the ruins of their homes and trying to locate some of their looted furniture.

August 19: Do you remember the young man I wrote of who had "Who said rats?" painted on his airplane? He was shot down yesterday just above here, nothing left of him or his plane except a lot of charred remains. We have been expecting a lot of patients, but none have arrived so far. I think only about one hundred for the past two days, so we are not very busy. Capt. Johnson, of Biloxi, is down in E. Hospital No [censored] ten miles below us. He heard I was with this outfit and ran up to spend the evening with me. Enjoyed seeing and talking to him very much.

HENRY ROBERTS, COMPANY C, 335TH LABOR BATTALION, TO DR. F. L. SUMMERS, AUGUST 21, 1918 (*HATTIESBURG AMERICAN*, SEPTEMBER 14, 1918)

Henry Roberts (1890?–), a native of Alabama, worked as an "office boy" for Hattiesburg physician Frank L. Summers prior to the war. He was inducted into the US Army on May 2, 1918, and trained at Camp Pike, Arkansas, before serving overseas from July 26, 1918, to July 10, 1919.

> *Dr. F. L. Summers of Hattiesburg has received a letter from a negro, Henry Roberts, who worked for the doctor faithfully for nearly ten years and who is now serving with a labor battalion overseas.*
>
> *Dear Sir:*
> *I am safe in France near the front, and I am doing well and getting along well, enjoying life fine. So, I hope, when these few lines reach you they will find yourself well.*
> *Tell Dr. E. L. and Mr. W. L. that I am somewhere in France near the front, and not "afeerd," and will go anywhere my captain tells me to go. So, tell my brother, Tom, for me, that I am safe in France somewhere.*
> *Dr. Frank, we were thirteen days before we landed in France. Four thousand came on the ship, and we had a great time. I liked my trip. So, I will close.*
>
> *Priv. Henry Roberts*

ALEXANDER YERGER SCOTT, PARIS, FRANCE, TO "UNCLE DAN," AUGUST 25, 1918 (*VICKSBURG DAILY HERALD*, SEPTEMBER 28, 1918, WORLD WAR I SUBJECT FILE)

Alexander Yerger Scott (1870–1930) was a planter in his native town of Rosedale, Mississippi, when he joined the Red Cross to serve overseas in early 1918.

> *Dear Uncle Dan:*
> *I've expected a letter from some of you, but I've not had a word, so I do not know where you are or what you are doing. I expect that you are somewhere fishing, having a good time and will probably wind up in New York. I would enjoy it if I could be with you while there. This is of course a wonderful experience. I am in charge of the agricultural work*

for the Red Cross among the refugees, and I am in contact all the time with the most delightful French people so it proving a very delightful trip.

I am just back from an Inspection trip to Château-Thierry and its environs. The outside destruction there in the center of the town is not as great as I thought, but it has been great, and even though the French and Americans have been cleaning up for several weeks, the place is a sight. The bridge across the Marne was destroyed by the French. It was mined, and when filled with Germans blown up. The Frenchman who volunteered to do this work lost his life with the job. Such little acts of heroism as this are not unusual in the great war of heroic deeds and heroic men. I went to Vaux, near Château-Thierry, and there hardly a stone stood in place. It was completely demolished. Some people had come back and were digging around, propping a wall here and there, and trying to find a hole to live in 'till they could rebuild. We then went to Belleau Woods, where the marines made their greatest fight taking the woods, and I walked all through it into the German trenches and how in the world the Americans took that place I can't see, but the trees were literally mowed down by our shells. The bombardment before they attacked must have been terrific. They had to come across open fields of wheat with barbed wire entanglements everywhere. It was of course a wonderful feat of courage, bravery and determination. When you say "Belleau Woods" the French smile and says Americaine, and if you try to talk to him he will make the motion of taking off his coat, rolling up his sleeves, spitting on his hands and lunging with a bayonet, for France went wild over the way our boys charged and went to the bayonet, for France loves La Bayonette. They are great soldiers with it, and when the Americans took to it like a duck to water and sent the Boche running, it was glory for the Americans in Mr. Frenchman's mind. The Americans stopped the Germans here and then ran them, and they have been running ever since. I hope the spirit of Germany is broken, and I believe it is. They do not like to meet our boys, for our boys are real rough with Mr. Boche, and he remembers the American and the Australian wherever they happen to come in contact with them.

It's wonderful how these French people here endured, their courage and tenacity, and it's wonderful how they love the American. All France loves him. The Red Cross is doing a wonderful work here. I am enjoying mine. They have given me the rank of captain, and quite a job with it that I hope to hold down, and seem to be doing it all right at the *present. I will be glad though, when I can come back, for I am mighty anxious to get home and see the folks. I have been awfully home sick.*

Give my love to Dover and Mal when you write, and with love for all of you, I am,
Affectionately yours,

Alex Y. Scott

PS I see Harrison was elected. Good![1]

1. Byron Patton Harrison (1881–1941) defeated incumbent James K. Vardaman in the 1918 Mississippi election for the US Senate, largely as a result of Vardaman's opposition to the war.

DALTON C. ROBISON, COMPANY B, 38TH INFANTRY, TO FRIENDS, AUGUST 25, 1918 (*PONTOTOC SENTINEL*, OCTOBER 10, 1918)

Dalton C. Robison (1887–1927) was a farmer living in Pontotoc, Mississippi, before joining the army. From November 1917 to May 1918, he was attached to the 154th Infantry. After a two-month assignment at Camp Beauregard, he served overseas with the 3rd Infantry Division from June 1918 to April 1919. When the war was over, Robison moved to New Albany, Mississippi, and worked as a barber.

My Dear Friends:
It has been some time since I've written you but a fellow hasn't much time for writing here, as he is engaged most of the time in real warfare, but I shall relate at least to you some of my actual experiences.

If you will get your war map down and locate the village of [censored] which is on the west bank of the Marne River, you will find where I spent Sunday night of the 14th of July, when the great drive started, (and we are still driving).

If you had been there Monday morning the 15th, you could have seen the Germans being marched to the rear of our lines by companies, but I am glad for the sake of your life, you were not, for the shells were bursting thick all around us, but all day long we took prisoners. Just at sunset Monday evening, we had a big battle. I shot Germans until my rifle barrel was so hot I couldn't bear my hand on it; then came the order to "Fix bayonets!" "Prepare to rush!" I reached to the scabbard for my bayonet and it was gone. It had fallen out of the scabbard while I was crawling through the woods. So you see I was out of luck; but soon came the order that there was no rush, and I felt much better. Then dark came on and I was sent into "No Man's Land," as we call it, to spend the night. It was raining and the grass and bushes were wet, and I could crawl without making any noise at all. So I crawled within fifteen steps of the enemy lines, and lay there until just before day next morning. I could hear the Germans whispering to each other all through the night, and every few minutes, they sent a stream of bullets just above my head; it was luck for me, they were higher than I for they shot over me all the while. Just before day, they retreated and I went back to our lines. "Gee," but that was some night for me, as it was my first to spend in "No Man's Land," and I frankly confess, it was not my nerve that kept me there; it was what the soldier boys call —— (censored) if you will pardon the expression.

Now I know you are getting tired of this "preamble," so I shall not detain you longer.

I hope I may be favored with a letter soon, telling of all the happenings back at home.

Your friend,

Dalton C. Robison

....

WALTER ELZRA DOVE TO SISTER, AUGUST 28, 1918 (*MEADVILLE FRANKLIN ADVOCATE*, OCTOBER 3, 1918)

Dear Sister:
If you have been receiving all the letters I have written home in the past month you have certainly heard from me regularly. They must have come in bunches of four or five each time for I have written every few days to you or some of the home folks. I have had no news but have simply assured you that I am well.

Everything has been quiet for us during the past month and we hardly know that we are in the army. We have very little to do now but this can not last long as all of our men are now experienced in plane and motor repair work. I rather think they will send us to the front before long. We are very anxious to get up there and handle plan[e]s with the new American Liberty motor. We have been training artillery to fire by the wireless regulation of air planes ever since we have been here, and while it is important work we want to get up where we can see more real activity and hand the Huns some of their own medicine.

I think I have already told you that I am now Commanding Officer of this flight. A few days ago I was called upon to recommend a man for training in flying. I recommended three and am certain that they will take one of them pretty soon. I think I have recommended a man who will be as good as any they will have down there from the enlisted men. Until now the enlisted men have not been given an opportunity to fly and it is encouraging to them to see someone else trained besides officers. Most all of them want to fly and when they enlisted they thought they would be flying pretty soon. Until now they have been disappointed, but now I think the best men will be given an opportunity.

During the past few days we have been lots of influenza at the artillery camp and now it has started among my men but I think we have it pretty well under control and I do not expect any more cases.[1]

With love to all and assuring you that I am in the best of health, I am
Always your brother,

Walter

1. Beginning in the fall of 1918, a worldwide influenza pandemic struck. It ultimately infected one-fifth of the world's population and killed between twenty and forty million people—more than were killed in the war. In the military camps in the United States, one of every four men came down with the flu; one of every twenty-four developed pneumonia, and one of every sixty-seven died. According to estimates, forty-three thousand US servicemen died of the disease (Hallas, *Doughboy War*, 293; *Influenza Pandemic*).

....

VICTOR SYLVESTER ASHMORE, FRANCE, TO A. F. HERMAN, EDITOR, *PONTOTOC SENTINEL*, SEPTEMBER 1, 1918 (*PONTOTOC SENTINEL*, SEPTEMBER 26, 1918)

Editor, The Sentinel:
It has been several months since last I wrote to your valuable paper and many changes have taken place since then, too.

I have been in France over two months and in that length of time I have traveled many miles over this country and have seen several historical places of interest.

On arriving in France I was sent directly to the front line as the company I was assigned to was in support about one mile behind the front line trenches. Every night we had a grand display of fire works that far surpassed any that I had ever seen. A week after I reached the front our company was ordered to go and take over a certain part of the front line trenches, or relieve the ones who were holding it.

I am sure you all read about the big drive the Boche started on the 15th of July on a fifty mile front. Well, I was right there and I believe the Germans can raise more hell in a few hours than Satan can in a life time. They sent over a ten hour barrage with shells of every kind and size. Some hit so close to me I am wondering yet how I am alive.

The next day I was sent to headquarters and made company runner, which is the most dangerous job on the front line and the hardest. The duties that a runner has to perform is to carry important messages to the front line trenches from headquarters. I was exposed to the enemy many times each day and night, but I successfully delivered each message entrusted to me for a week, for I got slightly wounded on the 21st of July and was sent to a hospital where the wound soon healed, and now I am somewhere in France guarding Boche prisoners.

The war situation is looking very favorable at present. Any way some of the boys are writing their mothers to have the turkey cooked good and brown for Xmas, but if we do not eat dinner at home Christmas, it won't be many months thereafter.

I do not know where any of the boys are from Pontotoc County, as we were all separated after landing here.

I haven't received a letter since May so you may know I am anxious to get some news from Pontotoc County. With best regards to all,

Corp. Victor S. Ashmore

CLARENCE WYCH OSOINACH, ENGLAND, TO UNKNOWN, SEPTEMBER 10, 1918 (*BAY ST. LOUIS SEA COAST ECHO*, OCTOBER 5, 1918)

Clarence Wych Osoinach (1896–1952) was born and raised in Bay St. Louis, Mississippi. When he registered for the draft in May 1917, he was a student at the Citizens Training Camp at Fort Logan H. Roots, Arkansas. He subsequently served at Camp Pike, Arkansas, and at

Camp Dix, New Jersey, before being sent overseas. After the war, Osoinach worked as a salesman in a New Orleans department store.

Before starting my little narrative I will, if I may, give a little introduction.

It shall be this. After being very busy for several days during which time I sent several cards we left Camp Dix at a certain time. Had a most pleasant trip thru very historical country, which in itself was more than the ordinary, and finally arrived at the port of embarkation a city which is much admired. Our fare on the boat was good, and for a while no one was sick. But after a short time the weather got bad, and each day was a little worse. And each day a new chair was conspicuous on account of being empty. The weather got very rough and the boat pitched and rolled terrifically. Finally two days before we arrived in port the skies cleared and the wind calmed. All came on deck, and the miseries of the preceding days were forgotten.

At night and in the morning and during some of the days it was very cold. My trench coat felt fine, but even then the wind got thru crevices and bit and stung. When the waves were dashing over the bow of the boat, and the wind howled a dismal tune, and spray flew in clouds over and about us, I thought of the September storms that we have had at home, and I wondered if there had been one this year. Let me know when you write.

Arriving at a British port we took the train and came to the camp where I am writing. The docks were themselves wonderful. A train was there waiting for us and we got on it. The railroads were a great surprise to me. The engines are very small. Smaller in fact than the little engines which sometimes pull the pay trains at home. Later I saw some which were larger, but they were still very small compared to ours. The passenger coaches were as I had pictured them, having compartments that seat six to eight people depending on whether it is first, second or third class. They are very nice except that there are no conveniences such as water, lavatories, etc.

The trip naturally was slow as are all troop trains either here or at home. The scenery and the people were wonderful, but I will allude to that later. The big surprise came when I saw the freight cars. Surely thought there must be some mistake. Those little cars cannot carry their freight. But as they continued along the line in a continual string I decided they were the standard freight cars. The capacity was marked as ten tons and the little wheels were a rim of iron and iron spokes almost like truck wheels. In size they looked a little longer than the big five ton truck that we have at home. Peculiar as they look they surely must deliver the goods. The little coal cars were the same, and on the way we passed some sheep cars of which you no doubt have read. Quaint and curious.

There are no sign boards scattered over the country-side to mar the natural beauty. Every thing is spick and span. Not a piece of trash or flying paper anywhere. Every available foot of ground under cultivation. Passing thru the towns every back yard tho as small as a postage stamp had its little garden. Passing thru some of the towns we were elevated and could look down into the houses and yards and it was most impressive. The houses never seem to end. They are all brick and have slate roofs, and are built together as one house. Sometimes in the suburb they would continue for blocks without being separated as tho they had all been built at the same time.

But the most impressive thing of all was the reception we got as we passed thru the towns. It seemed as tho they knew we were coming and were out with flags, big and small, American and English, and waved and shouted. Our flag was seen on many a post and pole in many instances alone and in other with the British flag. The [French] tri-color was also conspicuous. From every house they thronged; on every street they could be seen running from every direction to see us. And young and old, (there were no males to be seen of eligible age) seemed drunk with joy. They yelled and waved and acted more like a base-ball crowd after the home team had scored the tying run than any crowd I have ever seen. Old women waved and the children ran and jumped and yelled. One old man came out of a bar room and held up a glass of beer, waved and then drank to our health. It was thrilling. I have seen the crowds at home. I have marched with bands playing, flags flying and crowds cheering, but never has it seemed so heart-felt, so sincere, so spontaneous as that exhibited by these people who have endured so much and who are facing so much more with the bravest possible front.

Have read several of the big London dailies and see that beer is to go,[1] that the draft age is to be raised,[2] and Boston has won two and Chicago one game.[3] When I left "Dix" Harrison had Vardaman beaten according to the papers, but as it was only the second day, the country vote may have changed the result. Let me know. These papers are another surprise. Some have four and some six pages and the sheets *are about the size of the Sovereign Visitor.⁴ But they are telling the good old tale of the German retreat and are very newsy what there is to them.*

You can't realize the way the people over here are working to win the war. The sugar allowance is one pound per month, and when the people buy tea or coffee, they have to bring their sugar with them. Other things are the same. But they say that they are better off since these regulations have gone into effect. The RR fare is five cents a mile and of course prices are up as they are at home. On the streets you see quite a few indigo blue suits with a red neck-tie which I take to be the convalescent uniform as lots of them are cripple, but besides these all the men in uniform are old men. The determination of the nation is wonderful, and there is no doubt as to the ultimate outcome. They simply grind their teeth and go on and wait results.

I wish that the people could see this country. Its economy, its thrift and cleanliness, and whole-heartedness would make some of the grumblers, the folks who quit because they cannot have things just as they want them realize their littleness. In the two days that I have been here I have seen the women driving autos and wagons, delivering messages, working in potteries and sawmills and junk yards. I have seen the girls in their brown uniform working in the factories craning their necks from the windows as we passed. I have seen women shoveling dirt and cement, and in one instance I saw them boiler-making, swinging sledges, and clamping rivets, stop for a minute and wave their tools as we passed. And in every instance there was the same cheery smile of determination, the same look of gratitude. It seems as tho they look upon us as coming directly to assist them—not that we are fighting against Germany on our own accord and for the preservation of the world and not England alone.

1. In December 1917, Congress passed the Eighteenth Amendment, prohibiting the manufacture, sale, and transportation of alcoholic beverages. On January 8, 1918, Mississippi became the first state to ratify the amendment. Thirty-five other states followed suit over the next year (including Louisiana on August 9, 1918), and the amendment went into effect on January 16, 1920.
2. The Selective Service Act of 1917 had required all men aged twenty-one to thirty to register for the draft. In August 1918, Congress amended the law to cover all men between ages eighteen and forty-five.
3. In June 1918, the US government issued the "Work or Fight" order, which mandated that nearly every activity in the country support the war effort. At the beginning of

September, officials canceled the remainder of the Major League Baseball regular season, and the first game of the World Series took place on September 5. The Boston Red Sox won the series, defeating the Chicago Cubs, four games to two.

4. The *Sovereign Visitor* was a popular monthly magazine published by the Woodmen of the World Life Insurance Association from 1891 to 1937.

ON SEPTEMBER 12–15, 1918, AMERICAN AND FRENCH FORCES UNDER GENeral Pershing's command attacked German troops at Saint-Mihiel, between Verdun and Nancy. The Germans had heavily fortified the area, preventing the Allies from shipping supplies and personnel by rail from Paris to the Eastern Front (*World War I: Sep 12, 1918*)

Just sixteen months earlier, Mississippian Fox Conner had persuaded General Pershing that Saint-Mihiel was where the Americans should make their big push and had designed the plan to do it (Brown, "Fox Conner," 208). Three officers present at Saint-Mihiel would become household names in the next world conflict: George Patton, Douglas MacArthur, and George Marshall (*War to End Wars*, 90).

The battle represented the AEF's first independent action of the war, and the German withdrawal raised the doughboys' morale and set the stage for the Meuse-Argonne Offensive, which began less than two weeks later about sixty miles away (*World War I: Sep 12, 1918*). The greatest American battle of the war, the Meuse-Argonne Offensive primarily sought to capture the railroad hub of Sedan, thereby cutting Germans' supply route and forcing their withdrawal from the occupied territory ("The Big Show: The Meuse-Argonne Offensive," *Doughboy Center*). The offensive lasted from September 26 until the armistice on November 11. During those forty-seven days, almost one-third of the Americans killed in the war lost their lives (Carroll, *War Letters*, 162).

....

HENRY FENNER KITCHENS, FRANCE, TO FAMILY, SEPTEMBER 28, 1918 (UNION COUNTY WORLD WAR I SCRAPBOOK, BOX 1)

Henry Fenner Kitchens (1894–1941) of New Albany was employed as a streetcar motorman prior to registering for the draft in June 1917. At the time of his induction into the army on May 16, 1918, he listed his occupation as farmer. He served with the Graves Registration Service (GRS), which was formed in August 1917 but did not deploy to Europe until October. During the war, the army could not transport human remains back to the United States, so casualties were buried in temporary graves near where they fell. After the cessation of hostilities, the bodies of all Americans killed in Germany, Luxembourg, and Russia were relocated to France or to the United States (Hirrel, *Beginnings of the Quartermaster Graves Registration Service*). Fenner Kitchens returned to New Albany after the war and became a barber and salesman (*New Albany Gazette*, December 8, 1941, 1).

> Dear Mamma and all:
> I have landed safely in France after a long voyage. I sure did get tired of the water before I got here. We didn't have much trouble coming over. I like France fine all except the water supply is short and I can't get a bath and what we do get is bad tasted. I guess I will have to act like a camel. The wine supply is plentiful over here, they say. I will be glad when I get to go to town. I guess it will be a long time for we are under quarantine for eighteen days on account of mumps. Some of the boys caught them on the ship. It seems that I am doomed to quarantines as I have been under ever since I have been in the army.
> We went out in the cemetery today to bury twelve soldiers and we have to bury eighteen tomorrow. The US cemetery is some pretty. Mamma you ought to see the pretty flowers they put on the graves. They are made of beads and celluloid.
> Well, I have seen a lot of German prisoners. They look mean. The Americans sure do treat prisoners nice. It is no wonder that the Germans want to give up to them. They feed them as much as they do us.
> The Sammies are doing some good fighting these days. I guess you have noticed that in the papers.
> Did my cotton and corn crop do any good? Write me a long letter because I can't get a letter often. I have not heard from home since I left Camp Johnson in Florida. I guess Earl had to register in the last draft.
> Mamma, I bet you would just laugh if you could just see me eating with these black African negroes. They think they are as good as the whites over here and they are flying pretty high with the low class of French women. They will all be ruined when they get back to the US, but the south will soon settle them down. I saw one walking down the street with his arm around the waist of one this morning.
> If you find anything scratched out you need not be surprised, because they read every letter we write. When you write me, write the address plain and spell it out—American Expeditionary Forces in France, 2915225.
> There are lots of American soldiers wounded here getting ready to go home. They all have a big tale to tell. We can't write anything about

what we see or hear. The women here are all doing men's work. I will write you all again soon.

Your son,

Seargt. H. F. Kitchens

THOMAS GLADNEY MCCANN, COMPANY A., 304TH INFANTRY, FRANCE, TO *CO-LUMBUS DISPATCH*, SEPTEMBER 29, 1918 (DAUGHTERS OF THE AMERICAN REVOLUTION, SHUK-HO-TA-TOM-A-HA CHAPTER, LOWNDES COUNTY WORLD WAR I SCRAPBOOK)

Thomas Gladney McCann (1894–1967) was living in Columbus, Mississippi, and working at an oil mill when he was inducted into the army on May 16, 1918. He returned to the mill as a superintendent when the war ended.

Dear Sir:

I have been thinking some time that I would write you a letter but have put it off, time after time, not knowing whether you had time to publish such as this but as we have a limit to our letters, and I can't write to all of my friends may be you can assist me by publishing these few words.

First I will tell you of my trip on the sea. Well, the first night we were lost, couldn't find our way out on top after we went down on second deck, but finally we learned the road, and the first night, of course, I pulled my shoes off as I had been accustomed to doing that, but the next morning I got up, couldn't find my shoes high or low, so I missed reveille and of course I got extra duty, but the rest of the trip my feet didn't get out of my hob nails, that's the name of our shoes. We had plenty of room. I guess we all slept in hammocks that could find hooks to hang them on, and the rest piled around on the floor. We were very crowded in the hammocks, as we had to sleep with a life saver, a canteen of water, and some hard tack for fear we were sunk during the night, but we never had to use them. But all we lacked was doing it for we had some excitement before landing and like I felt then I have never had that feeling before. Now I will start back with our eats; we had quite a variety of food, and our main meal was dinner; for dinner we could have cabbage, Irish potatoes, and peas; of course the potatoes had their cover on until it was boiled off and also had roast beef, but it had an odor like a nickel box of sardines and right out the port hole it went. Now for breakfast, we had bread and jam, and for supper we had a change—jam and bread. Now, this was what we had on the boat. The afternoon we landed in England we didn't have to hike, but just seven miles, and believe me, we were all dead on our feet, but when we finally reached the camp, they let us rest for two nights and one day, and then we had the pleasure of riding a third class English passenger train all the way across England and then we were packed in a boat like sardines without oil, just for one night, and then we unloaded next morning in France, and of course another hike for five miles took place. Didn't any of us mind the hike, but that pack was riding our back, did bear down for every step of the way. Well, they let us rest for a day and night, and then on a French train we suffered for three long days and nights. I'll tell you how they convey the soldiers in France—in box cars just half the size of the US boxes. On these cars they have stenciled forty hommes, which means forty men, or eight horses and besides the men there is forty packs which take up more room than the men; forty rifles, and here comes the light bread and corn ville, known in the states as corn beef. Now you can imagine the can being full. After that trip we were dumped off in a little village of about two hundred Frenchmen, and there we stayed for four weeks, and of course there was a drink shop there and if we didn't have some joy for a while I don't know who did. But, of course some of the boys had to get stewed, and the mayor closed the shop up, and swore he wouldn't let us have any more. But he found out the French were getting in more all the time, and he couldn't drink it all, so he issues an order, saying—boys drink all you can carry, if it is a barrel. But be sure you can carry a barrel. We started over again and we all got stewed, so did the major, but it didn't get closed up any more. From there we went up to the front and relieved the French soldiers. Of course we started marching just like regular guys. We got about six kilometers of where we were going and somehow Fritz found out we were coming, and over he came and dropped about six bombs right close by us; and by God, you talking about officers and privates mixing! You ought to have been there; we all went in dug-outs and remained until we were coaxed out; and when we got out you should have been there to hear one tell what the other did. I never had such a sensation in all my days. But we went on just the same, and now we don't mind Fritz at all; but somehow I can't help but feel funny sometimes.

Now, at little experience at the front. Fritz is a good fighter as long as he has the advantage of you; but let us just have the same pull as he has and all you can see is Fritz coming with both hands up and every step hollering "comrade"; that's the man Fritz is. But you talking about a yellow jacket's nest being dangerous, you had better not ever get into a Fritz machine gun nest, for he will sting you a hundred times in a second.

I know you all are tired of this, so I will tell you about the hospital and say good-bye.

Personal experience on the 20th of this month I was sent to the field hospital with influenza, stayed there one day and night and from there I was carried to the evacuation hospital in Red Cross Ambulance, and there they took this pack and gun that I have just finished telling you about me lugging all over England and France and tore it all to pieces and put it in the salvage pile, so that just left me with what I had on. Here I stayed two nights and one day, and from there I was transferred to a Base Hospital in a Red Cross train, and you talking about a fancy train you will have to come all the way to France to see one, for this is the prettiest in the world, both inside and out. Well, I reached the base in the A.M. about four o'clock. There they carried me to the bath house, stripped me, of course, and give me something I have been longing for ever since I left the states. After the bath they gave me a bed suit and carried me to a bed that had a real spring to it. It has been so long since I had seen one until I thought it was a thing of the past, and I sure have been enjoying it for the last few days and nights. I guess you all have heard that song, "I Don't Want to Get Well"; anyway if you haven't you should hear it for it is more truth in that song than poetry for the way you are treated by the nurses is too good to tell.[1]

Now in the conclusion I will say a few words to those who love their "booze," or I mean all the men. You should be here for you can get anything in the world you want to drink; and one good thing is that you feel so good the morning after the night before. Nothing like the old US feelings.

Here's hoping this will find you all well.

Write to me sometimes. I will be glad to hear from any of you all any old time.

Yours truly,

Thomas G. M'Cann

1. "I Don't Want to Get Well" was a 1917 song written by Harry Jentes, Harry Pease, and Howard Johnson. It tells the story of a wounded man nursed back to health by a beautiful woman. A 1918 recording is available at http://www.firstworldwar.com/audio/idontwanttogetwell.htm (accessed December 28, 2014).

GAYNOR [LAST NAME UNKNOWN] TO MOTHER, SEPTEMBER 30, 1918 (WORLD WAR I SCRAPBOOK [NATCHEZ], FOLDER 1)

My Darling Mama:
Your sweet letters of Aug. 20 and 26 came yesterday. You don't know how blue they made me because I can read between the lines what anxiety my poor little mama is going through for me. Did you receive the letter I wrote you dated Aug 5th. I spent about six or seven hours writing it, then I got an officer to censor it, after which I rewrote it. So you should have received a twenty-one page letter from me by this time with not a single line crossed out. I also wrote sister six pages and told her to swap letters with you. In this letter I told you all about the battle of July 14th [Second Battle of the Marne] or which rather began then. In that battle our commanding general issued us a memorandum previous to the battle which read: "The bombardment will be terrific; you will bear up under it without weakening." Believe me, he certainly knew what he was talking about.

Of course you have read of all the big battles the Americans have pulled off. Well, I have been in all of them except one. That was at Soissons, and it was before July 14th.

Of course, you have read of the big drive we pulled off on the 12th of this month in the Saint-Mihiel sector. Well, I am going to tell you as much about this as I can. But as I can not finish this letter today I will tell you of my religious affairs first, which is of most interest to you. A Catholic chaplain came to our battery today (the first I have had a chance to talk to since coming to France) and I went to confession to him. I feel proud of myself that it has given me so much relief and pleasure. I very, very seldom pass a day without saying the rosary and make acts of contrition several times a day. So without any presumption on my part I will tell you that if I am killed you may be consoled by the thought that I am rather well prepared. Well, I have to discontinue this until tomorrow.

October 1
This battle, so far as I was concerned was not near so hair-raising as the fight of July 14th. The shells were mostly all going out and few coming in. We all knew beforehand that a drive was coming off. For days ahead of time we were massing such great quantities of artillery,

ammunition, tanks and infantry, that I expected the concussion from the guns at the zero hour to almost knock me down. Well, it fell far short of this, anyhow. Don't judge from this that it was by any means a tame affair. As in all previous fights, the first part of the night was calm. During this time we were making preparations. At 12:30 we loaded our guns and stood by waiting for the zero hour to arrive. Believe me those are certainly some moments. To know that in a few moments you are to be in the midst of a big battle. Well, the zero hour arrived about 12:45. Well, all of our artillery opened at once. We kept up a terrific bombardment all night. At daylight we raised our fire to let the tanks and infantry go over the top.

I was talking to an infantryman later who told me that we "busted things up" so completely with our artillery that they did not have to do half the bloody fighting they expected.

After we got the order to cease firing, some of us beat it over to where a few hours before were the German trenches. In No Man's Land we ran upon a lot of skeletons of French and German soldiers that had been killed there a couple of years ago; neither side daring to go out and bury them. The skeletons were still dressed up in faded uniforms and had on shoes. One German skeleton's canteen was lying by him half sunk into the mud. I pulled it out, opened it and found it had some wine in it, which I started to drink to his health in his present abode. Although I did not wish him well, I changed my mind about the drinking part of it. Going on into the German trenches we found that they were much better than ours; some of the walls being concrete and having duck board floors, so you could stroll up and down the trenches in full dress with little chance of getting your clothes muddy. We spent several hours rambling from one dug out to another collecting German helmets, gas masks, etc., which we lugged around awhile, then threw away. In one dugout, which was a store room for officers, we ran upon a quantity of beer in kegs. Some of the fellows lost no time in tapping one of the unopened kegs, but I strolled off to return in an hour or two to drink a little myself, if they were not dead from poisoning. In the meantime some other fellow had found some gold tipped Turkish cigarettes in another officer's dugout which he passed around among the bunch in the beer dugout. Returning to the dugout, I found the bunch not only not dead, but full of life in the extreme, so I enjoyed a few drinks of beer freshly imported from the Rhine. In one dugout, which was being used as a kitchen we found the potatoes peeled and hash ready to be cooked for breakfast. We started to cook us a meal but decided we didn't have time. The first nine pages of this letter and the envelope in which I am inclosing it is written on paper I got out of a German dugout. I almost forgot to tell you that dead Germans were lying everywhere. Some with their heads and others with arms and legs blown off which was the result of our artillery fire.

Of course, all of the villages on the wake of the German retreat are in most part a mass of ruin. It is pitiful to the poor French women returning after being driven from their homes by the Germans four years ago; to find a pile of stones in place of the peaceful, comfortable home they left. In one place where we stopped for a short while one old man returned after being absent four years. The first thing he did was to go into his vineyard and dig up a little chest in which he had between five and ten thousand francs, in notes, gold, silver, and copper cents. He had one sack about the size of a one-thousand-dollar money sack full of one and two cent copper pieces. He said he had some cases of old wines buried too, but the marking stones for them had been removed, so it would take a little time to locate them. Perhaps he knew where they were but had better judgment than to excavate it in the presence of a bunch of soldiers. Anyhow, nobody volunteered to dig up the wine for fear they would have a joke pulled off on them somewhat like the two sons that were sent by their darling father to dig up the treasure in the vineyard.

Believe me, this war zone is the ninth circle of Purgatory. If Dante divided it thus—work, work, and more work. Hard manual labor, too. When we are not fighting we are bogging around in the rain and mud building dugouts. Do you remember the letters I wrote you in the States telling you of the strenuous training I was going through and how I thought it would kill me. Now I look back on those days as a child at play. Don't think from this that I am not in good health for I am 100 per cent stronger physically than when I left home. We may work and fight for thirty-six hours straight on "from ration" hard tack, corn beef and coffee—and without a wink of sleep, after which I lie down, sleep like a log for fourteen hours, and get up feeling fine.

Please send me Clifford's address. I may have a chance to meet him. My organization has changed names again. From now during the winter, I will be able to write you regularly.

Give my love to all and keep a bushel for my own sweet mama.
Your loving son,

Gaynor

WILLIAM ALEXANDER PERCY, [FRANCE?], TO LEROY PERCY, OCTOBER 4, 1918
(*GREENVILLE DAILY DEMOCRAT-TIMES*, NOVEMBER 7, 1918)

Dear Father:
I have been through hell and returned without a scar. Already it seems a lifetime distant. I cannot recall the sensation clearly, the sheer relief of getting away from it is so great that it will be impossible to give any vivid account of the experience. Here I've a room to myself, a bed, we've just finished a hot supper served on plates with knives and forks and spoons, and we are so happy to be alive that the nightmare we've just left seems unreal, a thing that could not actually have been experienced.

We were rushed up the night before the attack and at midnight the barrage commenced. Although it was a fearful din I was somehow disappointed in it. In fact, slept from sheer exhaustion through most of it on the concrete floor of our dugout. At dawn we attacked. I went to an OP (observation post) in the woods to watch, but the mist was so thick I could see nothing and my only sensation as the sun came up was listening to the wild canaries which suddenly and strangely moved to music that could be heard above the thunder of the guns. The general and I started forward in side cars, but the roads were so choked with traffic that we abandoned them and followed the assaulting lines on foot. Our first experience of battle was in a shattered hull of a town on the edge of our side of no man's land. Troops, wagons, guns, ambulances were surging through in inextricable confusion when suddenly a shell fell on the cross roads fifty yards ahead of us. An ambulance went up in a puff of cotton, horses and men fell; then another shell. One of our batteries on a slope at the cross-roads was replying, and as a third shell fell who should rush down from it, to grab my hand, sing out hello, and rush back, but Gus. I haven't seen him since.

We finally got out of town and into the torn and scarred region between the lines, when already the engineers were attempting to build back the roads. Our troops had swept at once into the woods and were going forward under the barrage with little opposition. We followed them and their wake was clear but for the rubble and refuse of battle—abandoned packs and guns, rarely a dead German, ammunition, helmets, tromblows for the V-bo, then trenches and shelters that had been "cleaned out," as the saying is, for throwing grenades into them. The enemy, holding the first few kilometers lightly, had evidently been surprised by the onslaught. We lunched in a German kitchen off of German food—tea, coffee, potatoes, cabbages, purple and white, and most surprising, good bread and fifty pounds of lump sugar. The day was clear and cool—picnic weather—and that first day was like a picnic. At leisure we examined the marvelous German system of defenses, dugouts, fifty and sixty feet deep, many of them concrete, often comfortable, sometimes even elegant, for one had a shower bath and another was papered with burlap. And the fine German equipment was scattered broadcast for the troops coming on in reserve to choose souvenirs from, knapsacks, warm socks, helmets (all camouflaged), big blankets, grenades and ammunition galon, shoes, underwear, personal property of all kinds, letters, pictures, books (I found a copy of Scott's Waverly), bottles of mineral water, canteens and pistols. All the resistance that first day was made by machine guns, which were cleaned up without much difficulty. It was rather a rollicking army that went forward those first six or seven kilometers. But that night it rained.

Next night as I rode forward in the darkness the roads over which all our food and supplies had to come were already becoming muddy, and the mud from that time on was one of the things we had to fight. Perhaps you'd like to know what I wore and carried into the affray. A helmet, a gas mask, your field glasses, a heavy cane, a case, a pistol, belt and canteen, a trench coat, a musette bag containing one loaf of bread, a can of corned beef, a pair of socks, a toothbrush (never used), a few letters, a compass, the Oxford book of verse, and a shaving set. It's easy to tell the simple things, but I can't catalogue sensations of the events or the next two or three days.

I once wrote mother not to pity the soldier. Well, now I think the infantryman is the most to be pitied person in the world. The sheer misery he endures is not approached by man in any other branch of the service. He not only fights, but he marches unending miles, carries all he has to eat or keep himself warm on his back. The artilleryman rides with his guns and sees little of the actual horror, and the airman is just a mad adventurer, but these doughboys! I don't see how they do it. If there were no such a thing as bullets and shells and bayonets, what they suffer in hunger and cold and exhaustion would earn them eternal reverence.

The second day was cold and rainy, I was detailed at a cross roads behind the assault echelons to direct the wounded and send back the stragglers. It developed into a big undertaking. The wounded themselves were tractable enough, many gas cases and some hit by shrapnel and machine gun bullets. But every litter had extra volunteers as carriers whom I had to send back and all the unheroic of the battle came my way, and the cowards and deserters and maligners. The drawn faces of these were even more awful than those of the wounded. Once a whole line broke and came tumbling back, led by an officer gone mad with shell shock. I ordered and pleaded and threatened and just as things were at their worst there was the sound of horsemen galloping to us up the road from the rear and it was our artillery coming up to support us, headed by Col. Luke Lea.[1]

That day was bad enough, but the next was worse. The generals went up to the front line to investigate and encourage the men. I followed on foot, and on reaching the forward dugout was told my general had gone forward, so without orders, I started out to find him. And as I wandered along wondering vaguely where he was the enemy's barrage suddenly opened up and I was caught in it. I had no duties of any kind, so I hopped into a shell hole for a minute and waited, then thinking that was poor business, went on. To be shelled when you are in the open is one of the most terrible of human experiences. You hear the rushing, tearing sound as the thing comes toward you, and then the huge explosion as it strikes, and, infinitely worse, you see its hideous work as men stagger, fall, struggle or lie quiet and unrecognizable. I was on a wide reverse slope, where there was no timber or shelter, and when the shells were falling ceaselessly in groups of three. Suddenly over the crest a company broke, and I saw their colonel single-handed trying to rally and direct them. So I joined him and took over the company, a fine young chap by the name of McSweeney (General [censored] aide) joining me.[2] It was vivid, wild experience, and I think I went through it calmly by refusing to recognize it was real. You couldn't see men smashed and killed around you and know each moment might annihilate you, and bear it except by walking in a sort of sleep, as you might read Dante's Inferno. The exhilaration of battle—there's no such thing, except perhaps in a charge. It's simply a matter of will power. As for being without fear, I met no such person under this barrage, though most played their part as if they were without it. When we had rallied the men and put them in shell holes, I went up to the crest and as our advance had ceased, sat down in a hole which a soldier had dug the night before, next to the hole of a French lieutenant. With slight intermissions the barrage continued for four hours. We sat there laughing and talking and wondering if the next one would get us. He had a wife and child and had seen four years of this hell; once he remarked, "Oh, we will never leave here," but he was coolness and politeness itself. Hits within twenty yards almost deafened us, but we both escaped without a scratch.

That night the two of us and some twenty more passed in a wide dugout listening to the shells and waiting the counter attack, which did not develop. That dugout I shall never forget. It was about ten feet wide and forty feet long. The two sides were of mud, drippy and shiny, likewise the floor. The roof was a few logs and a layer of elephant iron[3] which, far from furnishing protection from shell burst, did not even keep out the rain which all night long trickled through onto our faces and hands and down our backs. We sat shoulder to shoulder on the floor in two rows, our backs against the mud of the walls, our feet against the feet of the man opposite. Our candle made visible our weariness and discomfort. I've never seen such tired men. We'd all been a bit gassed and during the night four mustard shells fell at the door and forced us to climb into our masks (all but me, who was in charge and answering the telephones all night). The features of the men had sagged and run together with the fatigue; it was cold and they had no blankets; our only food for two days had been bread and corned beef, the horror of the impending destruction tortured them while it could not hold them from sleep. They slept prone in the mud or propped up against each other; clothes, helmets, hands, faces and hair all one color—mud. There was no complaining, little talking and no thinking. Fatigue, cold and hunger quickly made of us mere animals. It was a long night and outside the soldiers were lying under the rain and bitter wind, unfed, but holding.

The next morning the general and I went back to the elegant dugout of the artillery and Luke Lea served us a meal which was so good it almost brought tears to my eyes; no other meal will ever be as good. Coffee, broiled bacon, hot cakes and syrup. I may sometimes forget Luke's cordiality, but his breakfast never.

Well, we're out of it all now. Most of the mud is scraped off. I've washed my face again and brushed my teeth and slept in a bed. The hardships and miseries are almost forgotten and we're looking forward to several weeks of training and instructions in this pretty country, almost within sight of the cathedral and moated town you visited.

Nuff said. I'm alive and awfully glad to be alive. I've lived through unforgettable experiences, and I have nothing to regret. Will write again shortly. Best love to you and mother.
Your devoted son,

W. A. Percy
1st. Lt. Inf.

1. Luke Lea (1879–1945) was a US senator from Tennessee from 1911 to 1917. He volunteered to serve in the war and became an artillery officer.
2. Probably Captain John McSweeney Jr. (1890–1969), an aide-de-camp to General Charles S. Farnsworth who received the Silver Star for his actions in battle near Cierges, France, on September 29, 1918. After the war, McSweeney represented Ohio in the US Congress.
3. Elephant iron is semicylindrical sheets of corrugated steel used as roofing for military installations.

W. R. BARKSDALE STEVENS, US INFANTRY, FRANCE, TO C. Z. STEVENS, OCTOBER 6, 1918 (*HATTIESBURG AMERICAN*, NOVEMBER 8, 1918)

Hattiesburg, Mississippi, native W. R. Barksdale Stevens (1893–1956) received a bachelor's degree from the University of Mississippi in 1914. When he registered for the draft in May 1917, he was a student at the Citizens Training Camp at Fort Logan H. Roots, Arkansas. In 1919, he received a law degree from the University of Michigan. He subsequently became an attorney in Houston, Texas, and taught at the South Texas College of Law and the University of Houston Law School.

Dear Dad:
You can realize how much good physically the army had done me when I passed the physical examination for aviation service perfectly. You have to be sound in every respect to get by. The third day I was here I made a flight in one of the big new machines, and it was the experience of my life. It would be foolish to say that I took it as a matter of course because my knees shook and I was afraid to look out over the side. Finally I screwed up my courage and glanced over and saw the country rolling by under me. My confidence came by degrees and before the flight was over I was standing up in the machine making notes on the topography of the country.

As I wrote you, the general asked for volunteers for this work because of the great number lost on the front. I immediately volunteered because the mere fact that the work is dangerous should not deter the grandson of two Confederate Veterans. Besides the work is highly individualistic. You are not a cog in a machine. You are a highly specialized machine of a rare type. I am given a map of a certain sector and told to accomplish a definite mission. How I accomplish this is my own business. The pilot must go where I tell him and all he has to do is to handle the machine like a chauffeur running an automobile.

Several men have been killed since we arrived but the daily work goes ahead as smoothly as if nothing had happened. In fact all the fellows joke about their chances, which is a good viewpoint because he who treats death lightly will never fear the consequences of any mission.

Bulgaria's withdrawal from the war[1] *is but the beginning of the end, and the real climax may be expected any minute.*

When you get hold of Ben tell him to write me about his work. I am anxious to know his outcome in the Officer's Training Camp. I would like to see the "old married man" of the family. Tell Ben to select an artillery commission if possible. Then he may be sent to the great school Saumur in France. Have met several fellows from the last camp who were sent directly over here.

Am having an awfully hard time with my baggage, which was lost. The most expensive thing in France is a pair of shoes and boots.

If you get a chance to send me a Xmas package, get me one of those knee-length aviator's coats, leather, from Godchaux. Practically impossible to get them over here, and they are the only garment for our work. We have an American Express branch here.

Write all the news. Every item of trivial interest to you people at home is of tremendous significance to us who hear nothing but "parley-vous Francaise."

Write me at this address: W. R. B. Stevens, 1st Lt. US Inf., 2nd AIC, US Army, PO 717.

Lots of love to everyone at home.

Tell Doc that he shouldn't forget to write even though he is very busy looking after his garden and chickens.

Has Inman [Cook] ever left the States? Get his address from Aunt Annie and send it to me. Have run across several Mississippians in various French towns.

Your boy,

Barksdale

---

1. Bulgaria was a German ally in the war from October 14, 1915, until September 30, 1918, when a revolt among the soldiers in the Bulgarian Army forced the country to seek an armistice.

LEO D. HOLLOWAY, FRANCE, TO WIFE, OCTOBER 14, 1918 (UNION COUNTY WORLD
WAR I SCRAPBOOK, BOX 1)

After the war, Myrtle, Mississippi, native Leo D. Holloway (1889–1971), moved to Memphis and became a mail clerk and a lumber inspector for the National Hardwood Association (*New Albany Gazette*, September 23, 1971, 7).

I suppose you will have decided by this time that the Boche has got me, but if you could see how much ground I have covered in the past thirty days you would think I was very much alive. I can say that the Hun is a very good mover, as he is always hard to catch. Since I have been at the front I've scarcely had a chance to write, and when I did I could not get hold of paper, as we are kept busy trying to keep up with the Germans. Fortunately, some Boche got in such a hurry to leave he forgot to take this paper along, or else he had as much as he could very well carry.

I am about to become accustomed to the whizzing of shells, but must admit that the tune is quite lonesome. As to souvenirs, I have had the opportunity to get a piece of every kind of equipment the Germans use, but already have more stuff to carry than I can very well take care of, but before I return hope to make a small collection at least. I have a button in my pocket I cut off of the coat of a good (dead) German soldier I will send you when I get a chance. We cannot send this stuff as ordinary mail or I would enclose it in this letter.

Nothing you have seen, heard or read can express the desolation the Hun has left in his path. What once were thriving villages are now but masses of ruins all grown up in weeds and grass and have the semblance of ruins of some ancient and extinct race of people. No one but an eye witness can realize the somber appearance of "No Man's Land" as it appears, a mass of wire entanglements, all plowed and furrowed by months of constant shell fire. But, thank God, the vandal is retracing his steps, and let us hope the allied armies will soon be on the banks of the Rhine and the Kaiser will soon see from his palace at Potsdam the glow of the American camp fires.

I have now been at the front for about six weeks and every day have seen something of genuine interest and in some instances quite exciting times. I have also experienced some pretty severe hardships along with them, but if they think they can hurt me with rain, mud and cold or sleeping on the ground they have another guess coming.

A few days ago I was with a friend trying to observe some of the fighting from a safe place, at least at a point where no shells were falling, when a somewhat daring Boche aviator decided a certain American observation balloon was doing the Germans no good. His intentions were discovered and the balloon was rapidly brought down, although he kept after it, but came too close to the ground and of course suffered the consequences, as one of our machine guns mangled him. Our prudence was soon overcome by our curiosity to see a German plane, and just as we crossed a road Fritz also selected the same place for a little artillery practice and a shell dropped so close that for a time being it robbed it of any sense of humor. We were almost covered up with mud and gravel, otherwise no harm done, but we hustled off the road before the next one came.

Our regiment has been in action almost constantly and seen some real hard service. We were in the drive on the Saint-Mihiel sector and were in the fighting in the Argonne Forest. At Saint-Mihiel the Huns left in a hurry and I could have gotten most anything I wanted, but didn't care to be encumbered with extra equipment. In the Argonne we met with considerable resistance, but we gave them "h——," if you will allow the expression, for no other word in the English language can describe a heavy artillery barrage. So they moved, most of them; those that did not heaven alone can help. Our own regiment, however, has been very lucky, as our casualty list is slight, three men having been killed in action, but do not know just exactly how many were wounded.

I've never seen anything that looked better to me than the long columns of German prisoners marching to the rear, led by American MPs [military policemen], but am not so callous as to say that I enjoyed seeing them dead, as they are at least human, but each American boy I see dead, murdered by these Huns three thousand miles from home, makes me feel as though I should like to pull the string that would send them all to eternity.

I don't wish to be any prophet, but mark my word down—the Germans can't stand the pace these American boys have set and are soon going to holler "nuff" long and loud.

Little girl, I am longing to "sot" eyes on you again and now can almost taste the glad welcome that awaits me back in that dear old country. Let us hope that it won't be long. Don't get jealous—I have not seen more than a fleeting glance of a skirt in six weeks.
With lots of love, I am as ever.

Leo

GEORGE QUISENBERRY, FRANCE, TO EVERETT QUISENBERRY, OCTOBER 20, 1918
(*NATCHEZ DEMOCRAT*, NOVEMBER 17, 1918)

Dear Dad:
This probably will be pretty much of a Boche letter, as it is being written in a Boche shack, by the light of a Boche lantern, in a village that was Boche not long ago and in sound of the Boche guns. Our stove is Boche and the fire is made of wood that I am sure the Hun left here when he decided the climate wasn't very good for him.

We entered the village yesterday and thought at first there wasn't much left of it. Every house seemed pretty much shot to pieces, even the church was ruined and the altar statue of the Virgin Mary was almost demolished. So, last night, we slept in our trucks, while Fritz shot up all the neighboring terrain.

But today we got to investigating and found a "beautiful" little shack formerly occupied by a Boche "kommandantur," with tables, stoves, chairs, etc., with only three or four shell holes in it. So we moved in and tonight have a very happy home. If Heine will just forget the place and leave us in peace, we will have no kick over the hardships of the war. But I doubt it.

As you can guess, the village has been under Boche domination for some years was so far back that he thought it would never be captured. Boche signs are everywhere, marking all the streets and houses. There is even a Boche electric light plant, now a ruin, and a soldiers' library and camp theater. We have been busy salvaging all day and now have nearly anything one could desire. As my prize find, I have a new camp lantern that is one of the best I have ever seen. I prize it highly.

I was assigned, as it happened, to one of the companies of the old 3rd squadron—the 7th—that is a part of the 5th army corps. Already, I have spent some hours observing the Boche lines from our balloon but the weather is too rotten for much good visibility. It has been raining all day and the mud is about as slippery and disagreeable as one can imagine. But that is part of the luck of war and to be expected at this time of the year. It isn't nearly so cold as it was in the mountains and, all in all, I am quite cheerful.

The country, over which the advance has been made, is indescribable, shell holes, trenches, barbed wire and ruins everywhere. Many trees have had their branches shot off and some of the hill sides literally *are nothing but shell craters. The Boche thought his positions impregnable but the American doughboys, backed by good artillery, ploughed straight thru—I wish I could send you a bunch of pictures.*

Tonight is starting off rather quietly after the activity of last night. In which Fritz dropped a number of shells not far from us. We had one gas alarm but the gas didn't materialize. I am glad to say.

I wish you would send me several packages of Enders razor blades, put a package in each of your letters. I am about to run out and don't know where I can obtain any more.

Well, no more tonight, with love,

George Quisenberry

....

WILLIAM ALEXANDER PERCY, FRANCE, TO LEROY PERCY, OCTOBER 25, 1918 (*GREENVILLE DAILY DEMOCRAT-TIMES*, NOVEMBER 28, 1918)

Dear Father:
Since writing mother a few days ago of our trip through Paris, we have arrived in our new area which lies in the newly liberated country quite close to my stamping ground of last year. Before coming here I have been on three different fronts, but never before have I seen the nightmare land that you always hear about and that you imagine the whole line to be. To get into this reconquered zone, we had to pass through the old No Man's Land which for four years first our side and then the other would dash in waves of blood, vainly attempting to break through.
No description can give an idea of the desolation and horror of that landscape. It was once a flat grazing country, crowned with a lovely town which gave the salient its name. This town is now a heap of bricks and stones with two shattered towers left like decayed teeth to mark the spot where so much beauty perished. And this once green country around has become one of the plains of Dante's hell. For mile on mile as far as the eye reaches it is an upheaval of filth and decay. Not a square yard but has been gouged with shell holes, now full of green slime and grown up with weeds. The roads, mere channels of mud, lose themselves in the craters made by mines, or pursue a haunted course through spots shown on the maps as towns where no stone is left to show the passer-by men once lived. In the mad welter of shell holes and filth and mud emerge, like prehistoric animals from the slime of creation, the wrecks

of battles lost and won—shelters of elephant iron, for in the waterlogged land trenches could not be dug; concrete pill boxes torn apart fill the iron ribs shattered by gigantic explosions, tanks, fantastic and terrible, that had crawled to the roadside or into a shell hole to die (you could not believe they belonged to men till you looked inside and saw the skeletons still by the wheel and the guns); planes that crashed down doubtless into the midst of hurly-burly; shells of all sizes, exploded; duds and unused, helmets, coats, equipment, belts of ammunition, these were sown broadcast over the loblolly and in and around and across in inextricable confusion, pattern without plan, ran the barbed wire, a crown of thorns on the mangled landscape. Even more horrible were the trees, they appeared everywhere, singly and in clumps, in long lines, but always branchless, leafless, their barks torn away, rising white and distorted and twisted out of the mud like the skeleton fingers of creatures drawn down into the slough raking and tearing at the dismal sky. How people could live in such a place without going mad, I can't conceive, yet the English and Belgians did it for four years. And we Americans think we have fought!

That's all behind us now. Here there are green fields and gold leaves cling to the trees, the village where we are billeted has many red roofs though no window panes, the enemy retiring left piles of coal and kindling which comes in handy these chilly gray days. The natives are already crowding back to their poor little belongings, to tell of their four years of misery and their innumerable wrongs. We hear far off the great guns, but for a few days anyhow, we'll take no part with the forward units. I hope though we do help drive this cruel, faithless enemy back to his own land.

I'm without news from anywhere. My last letter was dated September 1st. Much love to you and mother. Write when you can. Your devoted son,

W. A. Percy

....

JOHN BREVARD MCCEARLEY, FRANCE, TO MOTHER, OCTOBER 1918 (*NATCHEZ DEMOCRAT*, DECEMBER 11, 1918)

John Brevard McCearley (1894–1935) was born in Natchez, Mississippi, and raised in Concordia Parish, Louisiana. He enlisted in the Regular Army at Jefferson Barracks, Missouri, on

January 18, 1910, and was discharged at Fort Bliss, Texas, on January 17, 1913. He reenlisted and served on the Mexican border before being called up to serve in France (*Natchez Democrat*, February 6, 1935, 2).

> Dear Mama:
> My last letter was written to you only a few days ago, but I am where it is never "so noisy, or lousey" tonight, and I have actually pulled off my shoes, so I will write again "the writing is good."
> I have had three days of hellish work since I wrote last, but it's satisfactory work, for the division I am in now, on the whole, is a wonderful outfit, and doing lots of the fine work you read about in the papers. My first trip "over the top" was a surprise to me, in one way, for our captain went over at head of the men and that is something which is not only not expected, but not thought of over here, but it's done in this outfit. By the way, he's a mighty well known man, though I'm sorry to say for we have seen the last of him, but when captains go "over the top," as their hides were of no more value than a lieutenant's, and faces a [?] of machine gun fire, the Huns may as well give up.
> We have gained lots of ground lately, and lost lots of men, too, but, of course, that is all in the game, and in taking one town last week, which the Germans thought could not be taken, I know we killed four Germans for every man we lost, and took a prisoner for almost every man in the company.
> This is a mighty interesting game after all, and you may be hungry, cold and tired and wet, and covered with "cooties" but it's worth all that when you go over the top with a mob of your men behind you "squalling" for blood, and going "over the top" is our strong point.
> I will write to the girls as soon as I have time. Wish they could have taken a picture of me and my "top sergeant" this morning, setting in eighteen inches of mud and water, picking "cooties" off of our shirts under fire. At first I dodged the shells, but now I'm used to them. They seem to play different tunes. The Germans give a pretty fair rendition of "Home Sweet Home," and ours play "Yankee Doodle."
> I never was able to see Andrew, but from what I hear, his regiment did fine work on the front, and is now behind the lines. You ought to hear from him soon.
> They surely did not send me over here to make a "parlor soldier" out of me. I've been to the front thirty-five days now and am not through yet, but I've got my share of Dutchmen, and "evened up" for some of our

American boys, if this war ends tomorrow. I shot a German captain through the head and jaw the other night, and he died in the hospital Saturday. It's unusual luck to get an officer, as they generally get out of the way, but we made a surprise attack. The "skunk" managed to say, "kumrade" even with a "45" in his jaw.

Never have heard if my liberty bond and allotment have reached you, and you say my box from Beauregard was lost, and I lost all of my clothes over here, so I seem to be in hard luck. My field glasses that cost $39.75 were shot to pieces two days ago, but I have a German pair, which are just as good.

Well, take it all in all, no matter what we lose, this is a great little war, and while I get "peeved" personally at times, I like it fine. The infantry catches "hell" on all sides, and we eat "hard tack" and jerked beef, while the fellows back of the line have regular rations, but no one else get "as close up" at a moving target, or to make a bayonet charge into a town full of Germans, and bomb them out of their holes, and when the war is over, I wouldn't like to say: "I wasn't [with]in ten miles of the front once," or "Oh, yes, I was within sound of the big guns."

The infantry and artillery are winning this war, and take it from me, it's almost won. The men behind the lines are doing their share, and we couldn't get along without them, but I just naturally came over here to fight, and I am mighty glad I got to do it.
With lots of love,

"Boy"

....

WALDO EMERSON JACKSON, FRANCE, TO MRS. B. L. KEITHLEY, OCTOBER 1918 (EXCERPTS) (*HATTIESBURG AMERICAN*, NOVEMBER 5, 1918)

Waldo Emerson Jackson (1892–1945) was born in Amite County, Mississippi, and raised in Hattiesburg. When he registered for the draft in June 1917, he was employed as a broker. He returned to Hattiesburg after the war, moved to Jackson for a time, and subsequently returned to Hattiesburg, where he worked as a civilian personnel relations supervisor at Camp Shelby (*Hattiesburg American*, September 24, 1945, 1).

My letters home have been rather infrequent due to the facilities in camp or camps. It seems that the arrival of our division here was a signal to move, move. Honestly since arriving here, I have not (with the exception of two months) been in one place over two weeks. About the time we begin to get settled, orders come to move.

I and my company are at present attached to one of the shock divisions, the best in France, so you can see the why and wherefore of the continuous move. First we are in the western part of France, going over the top after the Hun, next we are at the other side doing the same, with a few days rest in between—sometimes. Being with a shock division I have been in or near all of the big fighting of any consequence in which the Americans have participated, and you must know that we have seen and been in some very thrilling experiences, of which I would love to tell you, but here it is best to cut out the details.

Ere this reaches you, you will have read of the battle around Saint-Mihiel, and I will break no rules when I tell you of some of the successes we have had. At three minutes to one on the battle line the largest barrage I ever witnessed started with the roar of large cannon at the army's left and right of the fronts, which seemed to be a signal for all of them to open. At once the guns of every caliber opened fire, and from this time until six A.M. there was one continuous roar. It was a deafening noise, but a most beautiful sight, the flashes from the guns keeping the sky in illumination while the rockets and flares of different colors illuminated the surrounding country for miles. The Americans threw flares as signals for the artillery to lengthen or shorten the barrage, and the Germans do the same, of course. They are different colors which is a part of the system, and then the Huns throw up a rocket which illuminates No Man's Land in order to see the Americans as they advance. This is usually the case, but on this night I think the main thing was to see their roads leading the other way, for the hits on their trenches were almost direct, and the bombardment must have been terrific. I know the hits they made for I advanced over the captured territory the same day and was an eye witness to what the Americans can do with the guns they man.

The shells were landing pretty thick; no one appeared to pay much attention to them and all work was continuing as much as possible as usual. Mr. Hun decided to overdo the thing and put three HEs [high explosives] near the same spot at about the same time. Now I have always managed to get out of the way of one, but three coming at once is two too many, and a few splinters from one caught me, one just below the knee, and the other in the left shoulder, but thanks to good luck, Providence or something, they were very slight, and I will be out of the hospital very soon. Personally, I don't think I should have been sent here, but I guess they know more about it than I do, and if they are willing the "life of Riley" suits me for a while. The only thing is that our men are still going and I would like to be in on the fun.

INMAN ISHAM COOK, FIFTH ARTILLERY CORPS, FRANCE, TO MOTHER, OCTOBER 27, 1918 (*HATTIESBURG AMERICAN*, NOVEMBER 27, 1918)

Inman Isham Cook (1894–1981) attended Millsaps College and Mississippi A & M (now Mississippi State University). When he registered for the draft in May 1917, he was a student at the Citizens Training Camp at Fort Logan H. Roots, Arkansas. He returned to Hattiesburg after the war and worked as the assistant manager of McArthur Chevrolet and served on the school board (*Hattiesburg American*, July 31, 1981, 1).

My Dearest Mother:
I am writing you from a small village in France where we are billeted. Four of us have a large room with single beds (good feather beds, too), large fireplace, comfortable chairs, plenty of tables and everything to make things comfortable. Our room overlooks the garden which is filled with fresh vegetables and fruits, including the inevitable grapes. This is wine country, very famous for its light vintage. An elderly gentleman and his wife own the house and live here. Their son has been killed in the war. They have no other children. There are lots of pictures of Napoleon's time on the wall, also lots of fine hand-painted china. The furniture is very old and is mahogany and walnut. They have no bath in the house, but the lady brought out an old iron tub which we brushed the dust out of and scalded out good and we use it to bathe in. We bought some wood and have a good fire at night when it is chilly. My orderly was born in France and of course speaks the language very well, so he gets us everything we want, including fresh vegetables, meats, milk and fruit.
    The water here is not good. We boil it and can drink it then. The houses are all made of stone in the village and are very, very old. The church is over three hundred years old and there are other landmarks which date back further than that. The people raise sheep, goats, cattle, etc., and farm. They have corn and barley and raise all kinds of vegetables. The lady brings us in a cup of hot tea nearly every night, but has no sugar, so we give her some of our sugar to use in return for her tea.

We had a ride on a French railroad. The cars are small, have only four wheels to them and four compartments which accommodate forty people, ten to a compartment. The engines have no bells on them and remind me of the little dummies that haul logs in our country. The people have no automobiles, of course. They ride in two-wheeled carts when the carts are not loaded down with wood, vegetables, etc. I've seen only one four-wheeled wagon since I have been here. The roads are fine, made out of rock and they are kept in good shape. The farms are kept in good cultivation and when we look out over the landscape I don't wonder that there are fine artists in France.

The scenery is just like a painting, it is so regular and fine. The men are billeted in vacant houses and some in barns. We took our company down a few days ago and let them wash their clothes in the village creek. I gave my washing to an old lady, who charged me one franc, or about eighteen cents, for a week's wash.

This house is wired for electric lights but the old gentleman told me that just after the war broke out that the company went bankrupt and consequently they use candles for light, or some oil lamps. They have to get permits to get anything, from bread to soup. The people here are all old or very young. I have not seen a man or woman anywhere near my age. There are lots of old men, women and children, though. I never saw so many old people before it seems like. It looks like these people live to an older age than the American people, as I know half the people here are around seventy or eighty years old. They are brave, stalwart people, though, and are certainly bent on winning the war. They are very kind to us all and seem to appreciate our efforts and to try to do all they can to make us as comfortable as possible.

We have taken over one bakery here and [are] making our own bread. The loaves are round and have a large hole in the center, like a doughnut. I am missing Edna very much, of course, and will be glad to get back to the States and start a home.

We can't get anything to read here but the chaplain told us at church this morning that he was going to bring down a truck load of magazines, so I suppose we will have something to read soon. We get the New York Herald, which is published in Paris, every night at eight o'clock. It gives us all the war news, but no news from home. I haven't had a letter from anyone since I have been in France but am expecting mail at any time now. I hope you are all well and that Edna is with you Thanksgiving.

Lots of love to all. Affectionately,

"Inman"

GEORGE QUISENBERRY, FRANCE, TO EVERETT QUISENBERRY, OCTOBER 1918 (*NATCHEZ DEMOCRAT*, DECEMBER 1, 1918)

Dear Dad:
Written by candle light. We have just finished our customary nightly argument—the subject is always different, and now that the gang has quieted down a bit, I will try to write you some sort of letter. No telling what kind it will be.

We are still in the same place from which I wrote you last, living quite happily, despite the occasional shells the Huns try to drop on us, and his unsuccessful attempts at night to bomb us out. He has gotten a bit closer a few times with his shells, but that is about all—just enough so that we don't forget to carry us.

He has made me jump from the balloon twice (Oct. 23) since I last wrote you, but fortunately both my landings were nice ones and I was no more than shaken up and made a bit stiff for a couple of days.[1]

The jumps were made on the same day within one and one-half hours of each other. The first came when two Boche planes made a threatening dive at the bag and the two of us—a student observer and myself, were ordered to hop out. Which we did, from about six hundred feet, with startling rapidity. Our parachute became a bit entangled and I had to kick loose from the other one before it opened out well. I sailed on down with all the grace of a circus performer, barely missed a bunch of old barbed wire and lit with a wallop in an abandoned trench. I certainly got cracked one amidships then.

But the Boche had not fired the balloon. You know they shoot at it with incendiary bullets, the hydrogen igniting in from seven to ten seconds. Well, after getting new parachutes, we re-ascended to continue our observation work. The Boche came back, six of them, and one came suddenly from the clouds and opened fire, the balloon being about fifteen hundred or sixteen hundred feet. It was being hauled down and we got the order to jump at about one thousand feet. But we hopped again—the parachute opened safely—it is a grand and glorious feeling when you see them fill out and your fall is broken. I looked over and saw the old balloon burning merrily, all the time being hauled down to get below the observer so that none of the ignited fabric will fall upon you and burn the parachute. We both landed on the wrong side of the hill in a somewhat stiff breeze. The speed, of course caused us to fall down, and away we went, dragging out the hill behind the parachute, kicking long in the wind. I tried to get out my parachute knife to cut the ropes but the thing stuck, and I ploughed on through the mud, fortunately on my back. Here came a smooth wire fence. I scrouched myself into as small a size as possible, missed a post by inches and came under the wire with no more harm than a lot of dirt in my head. But I did get the knife out and cut loose, after having gone some fifty yards at a pretty good speed. The other fellow had the same experience minus the fence, but plus several shell holes that he was pulled over.

We were both pretty muddy and I had a couple of minor scratches on one hand.

All of which constitutes war time ballooning and is an expected part of the game. Some men have had to hop quite frequently, and nearly every one in our service at the front has had to do so. But two in such a short time is rather unusual, I am told. The parachute we use has been made on the most scientific principles and has been well-tested; in fact, in our army [one] has never failed to open. I am glad to say.

The Boche who burned us was one of a famous enemy squadron, the nose of his plane was painted red and most of the rest of it black. I never saw him, being engaged in the business of jumping from the basket. Our machine and anti-aircraft guns almost but did not quite get him. He got quite a hot reception from them.

Fritz is doing a bit of bombing several meters from us tonight and the artillery is making quite a lot of racket. I am getting so used to it that I believe I could sleep in a boiler factory. The morning barrages— they can generally be expected about dawn, never arouse me any more. It is a great war.

Continue to address me care Hq. SOS Balloon Section APO 717, as there is no telling where I may be.
With love to everybody,

George Quisenberry

1. On March 24, 1919, General Pershing presented Quisenberry with a Silver Star citation for "gallantry in action while serving with the Balloon Section, 1st Army, American Expeditionary Forces, in action near Gesnes, France, 23 October 1918, while on a mission to locate enemy batteries" ("Lieut. Quisenberry Receives Citation" [clipping], n.d., World War I Scrapbook [Natchez], Folder 1; http://projects.militarytimes.com/citations-medals-awards/recipient.php?recipientid=81187).

CLARENCE WYCH OSOINACH, FRANCE, TO CHARLES G. MOREAU, EDITOR, *BAY ST. LOUIS SEA COAST ECHO*, OCTOBER 30, 1918 (*BAY ST. LOUIS SEA COAST ECHO*, NOVEMBER 30, 1918)

My dear Mr. Moreau:
Anticipating that in the near future I will be able to write to you about my friends, the Huns and their country, thought I had better put the cart where it belonged, and not write you from Germany before I had dropped a few lines from France. Our little party, that "contemptible" little party, has seen about all the sights available in northeastern France, and are considering an extensive tour of Germany, first stopping at Metz.

I am greatly indebted to you today for relieving me of what was almost a case of the good old fashioned blues. At present I am the only officer with the company, and have had my hands pretty full, as you can imagine. On top of this, I was appointed on an investigating board, and spent most of the day yesterday working on some investigations. Had to be absent some time today, and when I got back found a number of matters that I had to attend to.

Lots of the administrative work is different over here from what we were used to in the States and consequently I have to rack my brain quite a bit on some of the matters that arise, as I am not with the rest of the regiment, but have my company detached.

When I was feeling as though I was the most misused human in France in comes the mail orderly and announces, "No mail." But he had one paper in his hand which he had not taken the trouble to look at as we receive so many, but the minute I saw it, over the right guard I went and scored a touchdown with The Echo in my hands. NUFF SED. I have been in the best possible humor since.

Before I put the good old sheet away for future reference. I knew the contents almost as well as I did Evangeline in the good old days when Bro. Hilarian used to peep out the corner of his eyes to see if I was studying.

The figures on election were the first that I have seen, although I heard the winners. And the locals all looked good to me.

It might interest you to know that I am going to call a meeting of the company tonight to organize a "newspaper." The circulation will be very limited due both to the scarcity of paper and to the fact that each copy

Whether at training camp or overseas, letters from home always boosted morale. (Camp Shelby Photograph Collection, Box 22, Folder 52, No. 2)

will have to be hammered off on the typewriter. If I am successful in organizing the staff, I will send you a copy of the first edition.

A little picture of the workings of a company in France might be of interest before I tell you of the trip here, and the travel since we have been here. First you must understand that anywhere we are must be home, either temporarily or permanently. We are billeted in the empty building of a town, next find us in a rest camp and later in pup tents. The orderly room must be made from any available scrap of lumber, and in France scraps are scarce. Three planks nailed together make an excellent chair or table. It is surprising how comfortable one can make himself with practically nothing if the necessity arises.

To get the trip over. After a ride of twenty-four hours through very interesting country we arrived at the port of embarkation, and immediately went aboard ship. The censorship regulations forbid mentioning the first week of the trip, not because it was the first week, but because to do so would disclose the port of embarkation. Will resume the narrative on the high seas, in convoy. We were caught in a storm which lasted five days, and which buffeted us around a bit and had all the landlubbers sick. One Friday evening it cleared, and the sea calmed and we all enjoyed the sun and a smooth run. But Saturday evening when we were all in the best of spirits and even the most woe begone of a few days before were again out and around, we had our first introduction to the Hun. A deep dull boom, a slight quiver of the ship and everyone knew a sub was at work. It hit the ship, made port OK and no one was hurt. Then came the thrilling part—the fight with a sub. Wish I could tell you about it, but again I would be violating the censorship by telling the manner in which the convoys are protected, so can only say that we exterminated the bloody bloke. I have seen clippings of the incident from some of the American papers that have been sent in letters to men of the company so no doubt you noticed it at the time.

We landed in England and received a rousing reception, saw some historical places, among which was one of the famous English cathedrals, rested in a so-called English Rest Camp, and in a few days resumed our journey. Across the channel sans incident, landed in France and went to another English Rest Camp. I drew the job of unloading the ship, and kept my company down until eleven P.M. on the job. Next morning took in a little of France or rather of the outskirts of this particular city, and in the evening marched out to take the train for parts unknown. Passing through the town our company was in the lead and I was at the head of it. When we got into the center of the city the population had turned out to see us. As we neared them a good-looking girl (get the "good-looking?") ran out and gave me a boutonniere, much to the amusement of the company, but in a few more minutes they were all a mass of flowers.

After a ride of sixty hours we finally arrived at our destination. The ride was made in side-door Pullman cars for the men and day coaches for the officers. From our stop it was a matter of five miles to the town where we were to be billeted. Then we marched into town, it was nothing but a mass of flags. And in every door was the owner of the house with glasses and wine. In England there were more American flags to be seen than British, but in France they cannot get the American flags, but surely make up for the reception they gave you.

We have changed stations several times since then, and in every place it is the same. They seem not to be able to express all the gratitude they feel. As one French officer told me, "We owe much—without you we could not much more have done."

Speaking of the cost of living you should see the prices here. Condensed milk costs sixty cents a can. Choice meat eighty cents per lb, cheese one dollar per lb and everything else in proportion.

I would like to write more, but I simply have to get some of my work done tonight. Will drop you a line again before long.
Sincerely yours,

Clarence

W. R. CASTLE JR., DIRECTOR, AMERICAN RED CROSS BUREAU OF COMMUNICATIONS, TO THEODORE WENSEL, NOVEMBER 1, 1918 (WORKS PROGRESS ADMINISTRATION, HISTORICAL RESEARCH MATERIAL: ADAMS COUNTY)

Emma Eugenie Wensel Venn was born in Natchez, Mississippi, on September 30, 1884, and died of influenza on October 26, 1918, in France, where she was serving as a Red Cross worker ("Appendix," 160).

My dear Mr. Wensel:
I do not know whether you have yet heard the very sad news that your sister, Mrs. Emma E. Venn, succumbed to pneumonia in France. I am sorry to say that she died on Saturday morning, October 26, while at the hospital in the line of duty as an American Red Cross Searcher.

As you probably know, influenza, followed, as it is here so often, by pneumonia, has been playing havoc among our troops in France. Your sister evidently got the disease in trying to carry out her noble humanitarian work of helping to care for the soldiers who were ill.

She herself received the best possible medical attention, and everything was done for her, both to save her life and prevent her from suffering.

I hope you will always feel, sad as you must inevitably be for your personal loss, that she died as truly as any soldier in the pursuance of a noble duty.

We shall receive further details by mail, and shall, of course, send you any word that may come to us. You have the very sincere sympathy of the American Red Cross, which has lost a faithful worker.
Sincerely yours,

W. R. Castle, Jr.
Director

The grave of Emma Gene Wensel Venn at Natchez City Cemetery (findagrave.com)

HARRIS DICKSON TO JOE MITCHELL CHAPPLE, EDITOR, *NATIONAL MAGAZINE*, NOVEMBER 2, 1918 (HARRIS DICKSON PAPERS, BOX 2)

My dear Chapple:
Glad as I am to get a letter from you, it always puzzles me to give data about myself. Do you remember that cheerful old idiot in Flora Dora who was always saying "allow my my photograph?"

I am as you know a Southerner from generations of Southerners, and have always lived in the South spending however a great deal time in Northern cities and in other countries. This I believe is necessary in order that a man may know somewhat of his own country.

Whatever of my work may be approximately worth while deals with the South and Southern conditions. This has always been absolutely true, as I never allowed myself to be tempted to sacrifice the facts in order to give any apparent dramatic effect.

In this country where there are so many negroes the black man naturally enters into every phase of life, tinging and moulding to a very large degree the lives of the whites around him. In order to imagine the Southern man's attitude on any social or political question, you must always figure on this black factor. The question interested me so much that a few years ago I went down into middle Africa in order to see what the negro was like at home. And there I found amongst the British exactly the same ideas that obtain among thoughtful white men in my own country.

For the last two or three years however, I have been so completely occupied by the necessity of winning this war, as to have lost sight of my old friend the negro. It may be pertinent here to remark that the negro is standing loyally by his country, and by his white friends. Up to the present moment there can be no complaint whatever as to what our negroes are doing, both in the matter of sending their men to the army, and of giving from their small means for all war purposes. You may remember what I said at Birmingham. That was the truth.

In July 1917 I went to France with the 7th Field Artillery, and was fortunate enough to have myself attached as a correspondent to that regiment. My purpose was not so much to get at the big military maneuvers, but more to find out the personal psychological attitude of our lads in France. Looking at this from the coldest and more dispassionate point of view I firmly believe that we have in France to-day an army that is at least equal to the best. This has been a very remarkable out-come, particularly remarkable to those men who have studied the military history of this country, and know what a series of blunders has been caused by lack of discipline amongst our troops, and because of the vicious system of volunteer enlistments for short terms.

While nothing much was said about it at the time, many of us who went to France with the first contingent felt a sense of uneasiness as to how our Southern lads would take to rigid training, which was necessary to make them into modern soldiers. Although I have been away from France now for a year, I believe I know the present point of view of our higher officers. I knew their point of view a year ago, and subsequent events have left room for but one opinion, namely, that we have as efficient a force as any nation has ever put into any field.

I feel quite sure that this is your own opinion, into which opinion there enters no atom of American enthusiasm. I gained this same idea from French and British officers.

This letter hastily dictated can not be used as written. You are free however, to use any of the material or ideas that it contains, but you must put it in proper language, and look after the spelling.

I am sending you herein a recent photograph. If you would prefer one in uniform, I will fire it along.

With warm regards and hoping that some day I may [see] you sitting in the other end of a boat watching a line for the wary trout, I am, Most sincerely your friend,

[Harris Dickson]

GEORGE QUISENBERRY, FRANCE, TO EVERETT QUISENBERRY, NOVEMBER 6, 1918 (*NATCHEZ DEMOCRAT*, DECEMBER 5, 1918)

Dear Dad:
Your good letter of October 8th reached me late today, reaching our present location only a few days after the Germans got out. It was mighty good service, and letter pleased me much. It was a good one. I haven't read the enclosures from Maxine yet, as they are written in pencil and we haven't enough light, a single candle. I will hold them as an additional dessert for tomorrow.

We have been chasing Boche until figuratively our tongues are hanging out. I didn't suppose any body would move so fast but you wouldn't have blamed them a bit if you had seen or heard our artillery preparation and barrage. It was so intense that it sounded like a continuous roar for hours. We have passed miles and miles of territory where the shell holes were laid like checkerboards every five or ten feet. Trees, shacks, everything was down and in the underbrush it was hard to find even a bush that hadn't been scarred. Prisoners said they had no idea there could be such preparation.

The thing has been surprisingly successful and really I believe, went beyond expectations. We are now in territory that has not been fought over—the doughboys went so fast that our barrages played out and although the artillery played leap frog in advancing, the guns couldn't keep up. Back in the old positions there were all the devastations and destruction of years of war. Here there is very little, thus far. We are in a village that is scarcely knocked about any. We are temporarily in a peasant's house that has good furniture in it, an old grandfather's clock that runs and chimes as merrily as all you please. The village church has only one shell hole in it and the organ was not hurt. Some doughboy was playing it all afternoon—rag time and everything else. Can you imagine that—suddenly hearing American rag from a French church, with our artillery banging away just over the next hill and Boche day *bombers in the air trying to locate us. I think that is one the best things that I have run across yet. The doughboy kept on playing, although we had an alert to stand to shelter and the planes dropped a few bombs not far away.*

Spoke about a single hole in the church. Surprisingly enough the burst was right near a statue of the Virgin Mary and it was not at all harmed. I have noticed that same thing at several places—the church itself may be badly broken up, but the statues such as that seem generally to have come through safely. It's quite an oddity.

The advance was surprisingly fast; they had to put the doughboys in trucks at one place north of [censored] in an effort to keep up. Infantry in motor cars! Unheard of. We had to change our destination forward four times, the line kept going ahead of us so fast. The infantry came into this town with a yell, I am told, with Fritz streaking for cover.

We even got into towns where there were French refugees who had lived under German domination for four years. Things were so fast that they couldn't get out of the fighting zone. Perhaps you think they weren't glad to be "captured." A big bunch of them came in yesterday, pitiful looking creatures, with a few clothes and a little bedding made up into all kinds of bundles. The army distributed them out some rations, about the only real meals they had had for some time. They were happy, grinning all over themselves, and doing nothing but talking about the Americans.

The prisoners were numerous, many of them kids. Most of them came back grinning merrily; they were not a bit sorry to be captured by the Americans, as they figure it means the end of the war for them. Most of their resistance was rear guard machine gun action.

I wish I could describe the appearance of the battlefield to you—devastation, mud, shell craters, abandoned equipment of all kinds, more mud, piles of ammunition, fox holes and other quickly dug shelters, and tired, muddy, dirty men, some of them almost dead for sleep, but pushing on upheld by the magic cry "Fritz is on the run." Then the traffic behind, trucks full of provisions, ammunition, lines of guns, with traffic so heavy that the roads were never clear. Military police vainly trying to separate it and send it along the proper routes. Signal corps and telephone men throwing hasty lines behind the advancing troops. Mud-grimed engineers working on the roads and trails. Hastily set-up mess kitchens; ambulances going backward and forward; doughboys along the road eating "corn willie" and hard tack or plodding wearily along. A wonderful, wonderful kaleidoscope that can never be forgotten. It is a hard job to move an army forward, particularly over territory that has been fought over.

Naturally, there was a lot of rain and everything was a sea of mud in a short time. I have quit trying to keep clean. My shoes and leggings would make a well-trained valet gasp with horror and my rain coat, hasn't had a brush for days. There are really just two things I am really longing for now—one is a bath and clean clothing and the other is a breakfast of eggs. The first is nearly impossible and the other is a fond, fond dream!

I am living now in a house that has a big "Gott strafe" [God punish] England sign on it. It is No. 24 Hindenburg Street and the commanding general is in a big house, the wall of which is decorated with the German coat of arms and a "Gott Mit Uns" [God with us], inscription on it. We have been a little too busy to remove them. But the Boche thought he would never lose this. But he reckoned without the American doughboy.

Well Dad, it has gotten a bit late and I must close. I didn't intend to string this out so long and I have no idea what the censor will do to it. But it kept on going and I didn't stop it.

Continue to address me: Hq. SOS Air Service Balloon Station, APO 717 as formerly.

With love to you all, your son.

George

ELLIS BOWMAN COOPER SR., FRANCE TO G. L. HAWKINS, NOVEMBER 10, 1918 (EXCERPTS) (*HATTIESBURG AMERICAN*, DECEMBER 14, 1918)

Ellis Bowman Cooper Sr. (1886–1951) received a bachelor of laws degree from the University of Mississippi in 1908 (*Historical Catalogue*, 312). When he registered for the draft in June 1917, he was a practicing attorney in Jackson. After the war, he resumed his law practice in Laurel.

Knowing how interested you are in this war, I thought I would write you a little of the actual war and not what the newspapers tell you of.

I started one Sunday morning for the front in a Pierce-Arrow. But it wasn't of the type you have. It was a truck of three-tons capacity. Being on the brigade staff we got a little transportation, and this was the means of getting there. Over there, the ambition is to get over here, and once here it is to get to the front.

The roads were beautiful for a part of the distance. It wasn't long before we began to pass trains and truck after truck, each loaded to the rim with shells, or food. And those delightful shells containing mustard gas predominated. Presently the roads began to get worse and shell-swept hills were found on each side. This was from ten to twelve kilometers from the front and the line marking the greatest advance of the Germans in this sector. They didn't get very far here, because there was a city which blocked their path, and the city is now practically demolished because of the intensity of that fight.

As we moved forward the towns and villages were only partly destroyed. Planes had done this; but as we drew closer the only way to recognize a town would be by a sign or the word of a soldier behind there. Every single building gone, no stone left untouched. The completeness of the devastation was bewildering. It surpassed even the pictures you see.

The hills were dotted with dug-outs and lined with shell holes. The forests were destroyed. It looked as if some monster wielding a giant scythe had swept through them with irregular strokes. The ground was only a mass of shell holes, varying in size from four feet in diameter to twenty-five feet in diameter. How any living thing, even a snake or bug, could live in that perfect hell, I can't imagine. It is inconceivable and beyond comprehension. Trees in the forest that cost us so much, and the work was that of our artillery. You would at once recognize its name, because it has figured in the news so much.

It was getting dark and we moved in a stream of traffic that would bewilder the New York traffic police. A halt of five minutes would affect the traffic five miles back. Truck after truck, shell after shell! Engineers constantly at work. One group told me they laid stone along an entire road and went back the next morning to find it as they found it before a stone was laid. Were it not for the stone from destroyed villages no way to remedy this trouble with the roads could be found.

It was dark and out over the distant hills it looked like the furious play of lightning. It was the flash of the big guns. You could not hear their reports, but their flashes lighted the whole heavens.

After a while we moved into the place to which we were going and the roar of the guns was deafening. Still we were some distance from that enchanted land we call the "front."

I've got a comfortable Boche dug-out, about which I wrote little George, and they shelled us from a hill which had already cost thousands of lives, and which we finally took. I had no trouble sleeping, for I have long since become a fatalist, in so far as injury in this war is concerned. If you wasn't you'd lose your energy dodging shells.

But I have seen it all now. The above is simply the prelude, a path to show that war had passed there. Dead Man's Hill, with its burden of skeletons and unnamed graves, was in our rear.

Confronting us was the pride of the German army, so said: divisions of pure Prussians of the cruel type of the Kaiser. It was a source of gratification to know that they deemed it necessary, and there they are, hidden in the undergrowth of a hill, an undergrowth far better than barbed wire.

That morning I went out to get the lay of the land and it took me to the real front, and, in reality, a chamber of horrors. As we walked along we saw the dead, heaps on heaps. Our own and the Germans. Out in that awful weather, for a slow, drizzling rain falls all of the time. This particular spot is one of the bloodiest on the entire front. The houses are gone now, and there is no sign of life except the soldiers. But if blood were seed this spot would grow an army next year. I went on further and there were the doughboys in their little holes, facing the Prussian brutes. There are no trenches now. We haven't time. The shell holes and the little trenches about the size of a man—they look like, and frequently are graves—are all they have. Wrapped in the blanket with the drizzling sky as a roof, these boys are all night along with a constant rain of shells, machine gun fire and gas upon them. Any minute may be the last. They don't know; and they don't care.

But you may safely take off your hat to any doughboy who is now in the trenches or who has been here. A "show" is pulled off, the artillery opens up and drenches the enemy with shell, and the doughboys move forward. All they have to fight now is the machine gun. They don't fight otherwise, and it is good to see how far away they are being pushed.

The litter bearers soon follow; then the ambulances, and, far to the rear, giant trams. All are for the wounded. Then the burial squads search for friend and foe, and the last act for a great many is closed. A little stick, with that little disk we wear around our necks marks the end.

I wish I could tell it as I saw it and the thousands of incidents that hurt because of their pathos.

I hope to be back soon, a little wiser but hardly any better. But I hope we get an everlasting peace. I would hate to think little George would ever be thrown into anything like this.

In a town I visited I saw the telescopes used by his majesty, the crown prince, in watching the battle around Verdun. The house was about the size of yours. In its center, from roof to cellar, a reinforced concrete room had been constructed. It was about four feet square. The telescopes extended from the floor out of the roof, where a periscope was fixed. He could with safety sit there and watch proceedings. His room was in this house, and it also had been concreted and reinforced. That is how he fought his battles and won his iron crosses. The poor devils under him paid the price.

- 4 -

ALL QUIET ON THE WESTERN FRONT

JAMES GERVYS LUSK, PARIS, FRANCE, TO MOTHER, NOVEMBER 11, 1918 (*GREEN-VILLE DAILY DEMOCRAT-TIMES*, DECEMBER 9, 1918)

Dear Mama:

The war is over and I have lived through it, but I never expected to.

Gen. Foch sent word to Paris today to remove all sand bags, turn on all lights; that Big Bertha (the gun that fired on Paris) had run away with the Kaiser.

I was sitting up in bed at eleven o'clock this A.M., *all of a sudden the defense guns of Paris began to fire, whistles blew and bells rang. All of the convalescent officers went up town. I was the only one left, I think. The Col. Dr. came through and said he thought I was well enough to go up, so I wrapped up good and he carried me up in his car.*[1] *Mama, I saw the sight of my life. My battles and war experiences watching big guns fire and other things can't be compared with it. It was the most complete demonstration of a happy celebration I have ever seen. It was not a parade nor a celebration that we are used to, but it was the disorganized population of Paris, women, men, children, and soldiers from all allied countries. Thousands and thousands swarmed the streets and sidewalks,—blocked all traffic; the street cars couldn't run. When trucks came by they would force the drivers to stop and as many as could load on, would. They would get on top of taxicabs and pay nothing. The cries of "Fini le guerre" [The war is finished], "Fini le Boche" [The Boche are finished], "Viva l'Amerique" [Long live America], were heard on every side. They were mad with joy. The stores of merchants who failed to close and take part in the celebration were entered, their stock pushed* on the floor; or just as they felt like doing. Men and women were kissing on the streets; some were crying. I have never seen such mobs in my life. They picked up our men and carried them down the streets on their shoulders. The girls would run up to Americans, hug and kiss them and no one paid any attention to it; I never was so embarrassed in my life. One jumped up in the car, hugged and kissed the Col. and I, saying "thank you, thank you." I sure wished I was well. My side has been blistered and she hurt it some, but you know I didn't mind a little thing like that. American flags flew everywhere.

The Place de l'Opera is a place where five streets converge and in peace time has more traffic than any other place in the world. At one end of it is the Opera House, the steps of which will hold about a thousand people. All of this place was packed and the whole crowd sang the "Marseillaise," their national anthem.

The police stood on the corners in bunches of ten and twelve, and laughed as they tore up what they wanted to. They dared not interfere.

Well, after our little affair, the Col. decided to drive on; I tried to persuade him to stay, telling him there would be more along after a while. He didn't seem to like it a bit. I know the old gent was just fooling himself, he surely wasn't fooling me.

After five years of this horrible war, and their capital threatened twice, 2,500,000 French killed—not casualties, but killed—don't you think they have a right to celebrate?

Mama, it makes me feel so bad when I think of these good old Americans that we must leave in France. But they haven't died for nothing, thank God! And I got my share of the boche, and avenged the death of some of my dear friends that I have seen go down in battle like true American heroes. We all have done some things to the boche that might seem dishonorable to the average citizen, but the boche deserves all of what we gave him.

Mama, after seeing so much killing and dead men, you become hardened to it and take it as a business proposition. To see dead men never bothers you and to stay in the same shell hole with one over night where he has crawled for protection, you think nothing of it. No, [while] this is a little raw letter to write to you, but as it is over I want you to know why people celebrate as they have in Paris today. After the sons of France have had five years of it; after Lt. Slaton of Texas, one of my friends was killed at Soissons, I and many others swore to kill all the Huns we could. Now such as this has occurred in every army *organization. I wish we could take all the prisoners in France and push them in the ocean.*

I guess the boche that are still left will use their popular slogan—"It took the world to do it." The first one that ever opens his mouth to me will require careful attention of some of our prominent doctors, and I know some of these Huns who are going to try it when everything is over. Whether it took the world to do it or not, we certainly have made a cute job of it, and one that won't wear off in a couple of weeks.

Maybe you think your son isn't glad that it is all over, but I am tickled to death. To think that I don't have to sleep in a cracker box under the ground and wade in muddy trenches up to my knees this winter just makes me as happy as if I had good sense. You know I just love to stand in a trench and watch the snow fall as thick as everything and in great big flakes until it fills the trench, then you call out a working party to throw it out, which takes all night. Stand around in this until your feet are wet and you are wet to the skin and freezing. And the men laugh when you get them out for an all night job of this kind. Then you retire to your cracker box and on the way there some one has spilt the wash water on the duck boards and this has turned into ice. Up you go—git up rubbing. Then it's an hour before you say anything that can be printed. You proceed to your room—ha, ha. When you enter you find the snow has broken through the wall paper and has covered your mattress less bed and some one has turned the steam heat off that Uncle Sam has so generously installed for your sleeping accommodation. Well, you lie down to get an hour's sleep before stand to. All of a sudden the end of your thirty dollar per month room is knocked off. You jump up and feel yourself to see if you are all there, then you realize the fact that the darn old square head wants a prisoner and is rising to raid and from the looks he is going to pull it on your sector. The barrage is on and is tearing h—— out of everything. You slip and slide running up and down the trench to see if all hands are on the guns. Then you say to yourself, "if he gets away with it and captures one of my men, won't the colonel give me h—— in the morning." All the high officials will be down and investigate and they decide to send you home. Then old Fritz shifted it to another sector only to keep you guessing where and when he is going to pull it. You stand there and say a short prayer, hoping he doesn't shift it back. Then he comes over further down. You feel sorry for those chaps, but glad you didn't have the responsibility. All is over and from the bombardment you need a burying party—three dead and five wounded.

Now at this last paragraph my fever went down, and when I say at the start I just love to watch the snow. That is the way some poet might look at such a night. This is trench warfare in winter time. Good night.

Gervis [sic]

1. Lusk received the Distinguished Service Cross and the French Croix de Guerre with Palm for his actions as Montrebeau Woods on October 4, 1918, when he led troops in capturing two enemy machine gun emplacements and was wounded in combat. In *Lanterns on the Levee*, fellow Greenvillian William Alexander Percy wrote, "Gervys Lusk left home a wastrel and returned a hero; he left with a black eye and came back with a D.S.C." (225).

....

VAN ANDREW CAVETT SR., AT SEA, TO FATHER, NOVEMBER 23, 1918 (*JACKSON DAILY CLARION-LEDGER*, DECEMBER 22, 1918)

After the war, Jackson native Van Andrew Cavett Sr. (1900–1963) returned to Mississippi and became a teacher in Sledge and a school superintendent in Coahoma.

Dearest Daddy:
At last there is no more censorship on our mail, for as you know there is no more, "German High Sea Fleet." That, at least, is one thing that will go down in history, and I can very proudly say that I was certainly right there. I expect that you have read various accounts of it (the surrender), but I will try to give it to you just as any one would see it from the inside.
 Last Saturday in one of the worst fogs ever seen, the German Admiral came into the Firth of Forth on the Royal Oak, *better known as the "Kings and Beatties Destroyer," and immediately went aboard the* Queen Elizabeth, *the flag ship of the Grand Fleet. What happened aboard is not known. But it was arranged that fifteen A No. 1 ships should surrender on the 21st day of November. The morning of the 21st all hands were called at three* A.M., *as we were to go out about one hundred miles to meet and escort them in to the Firth of Forth, where they were to anchor and to lower their colors. At 9:10* A.M. *we first met them and all hands were at the battle stations with ammunition up and in the guns, so if there was to be any treachery on the part of the Huns we would be prepared. But they showed no signs of any hostility and as soon as secure all men were on the top side with kodaks, etc.*
 It was certainly one of the most humiliating scenes that I ever saw, but when you think of what they have done you have no pity for them.

They anchored just about a mile from where we were and the men and officers were sent back to Germany on a transport the same day.

It has now been one year, less two days, since we steamed out of Lynn Haven Roads for foreign service. So you see I am entitled to wear two gold Service Stripes, that is one more than the soldiers out of our family will have.

If you will get a large map of the British Isles you will see in the most northern part, "Orkney Isle." Well, that is the place where we were all of last winter. It is without a doubt the most dismal place in the world. Nothing to see but small mountains covered with snow, and it gets so rough there at times that we had to get up steam to keep from going on the rocks. No liberty of any kind, as there is but one place there, so you see I have seen the British Isles from the most northern part to the most southern part.

All last winter our job was to convoy the merchant ships from here to Norway and Sweden, and to go out with the mine layers so that if the Germans did come out we would be there. Let me tell you something, some think that the men in the Navy get away with it; but they do not; for while we were out we stood watch twenty hours on and four hours off, as many as three days, and no more than we would get in port than we would have to take on about 1,200 tons of coal. We burn 360 tons a day at full steam so you can readily see that it was no picnic; and I for one am certainly glad it is over with. The USS *Florida* leaves today for the States, and I guess that it is our time next. Anyway they have the plans for a ten thousand dollar ball at the Astor Hotel as soon as we arrive in Brooklyn.

I expect that I had better close, as I expect to see you soon. Then I will be able to tell you more than I can write.
Love to all,

Van

PS We just came out of quarantine for influenza for four weeks, and I just got my pictures yesterday, but they were absolutely no good, so will wait now until I see the Home Land again.

The candy arrived and certainly was appreciated, but it is a little steep at $1.50 per, so give mine to Patsy, as she says she certainly does enjoy that you gave her.

LIEUTENANT COMMANDER K. J. POWERS, USS *SIOUX*, LA PALLICE, FRANCE, TO ANNIE L. COTTON, DECEMBER 17, 1918 (EARL DOUGLAS COTTON PAPERS, FOLDER 2)

Earl Douglas Cotton was the first Jackson serviceman killed in the war.

My dear Mrs. Cotton,

It is with deep regret that I find it necessary to inform you regarding the death of your son Earl. Though the [loss] is without a doubt, felt keenly, it is without question a comfort to you to know that he died for his country and at his post of duty.

On the night of December 7th, we had the misfortune of running into a heavy storm. At 2:30 A.M. the following morning the ship was hit by a heavy sea that demolished the radio room. Earl was on watch at the time, and the crash of the sea against the radio room crushed him against the operator's table.

He first attempted to send an SOS message thinking the ship to be in a sinking condition. Upon finding his efforts to be futile, he started for the bridge to inform me of his useless attempt, but could not get any further then the pay-office on the starboard of the vessel.

All possible aid was rendered him under the trying conditions that we were undergoing as the sick bay and dispensary was destroyed at the same time as the radio room. He died at 5:59 A.M. December 8th. Apparently he suffered but little, passing away peacefully. His remains and effects are still on board and will be forwarded immediately upon our return to the states.

Earl was a boy well liked and respected by both officers and men of my ship. It was a great pleasure to have a young man of his type under my command. I cannot speak too highly of his character. His very valuable service and patriotic spirit is an honor of which I am sure you are justly proud, and that [?] I am sure be a great comfort and help to you in bearing his [?].

Assuring you of my own most sincere sympathy, I am,
Respectfully yours,

K. J. Power[s]
Lt. Comd. USNRF
Commanding, USS Sioux

WILLIAM ERNEST BUTLER, COMPANY D, HEADQUARTERS BATTALION, FRANCE, TO
BESSIE HOOD, JANUARY 1919 (WILLIAM ERNEST BUTLER AND FAMILY PAPERS, BOX 1)

William Ernest Butler (1896–1975) was born in Utah but moved to Mississippi as a child. He grew up in Greenville and worked as a clerk prior to registering for the draft in June 1917. He served in Europe but did not see combat, and after his discharge in 1919, he returned to Greenville and worked as a clerk and cabinetmaker (Collection Description and Notes, William Ernest Butler and Family Papers, Box 1).

> Dearest Mother:
> I want to thank you again for the lovely X-mas package, my last letter was written hurriedly, I am stationed at present in the old city of Bourges; you once mentioned it in one of your letters. We have a very large force of clerical men to fill the various offices. There are men here from every Division of the AEF. My work is of a very interesting nature, chiefly of verifying reports to Washington of men whom are either dead or missing in action. There are various ways of tracing these men thru files especially prepared for this operation. I have traced down several cases where the parents had been notified of their son's death when thru thorough tracing it was found that the boy was not dead only wounded in Hospital, etc. There was a meeting in our Section last night, our Captain gave us a very interesting talk and mentioned several very interesting cases where different men were either brought to life or found dead and the process of the search was explained in such a manner that no one could help enjoying it. He also brought out how our own parents would feel if certain cases had been our own. This of course placed a different atmosphere on the work. We realized we were working on human lives instead of trying to make the day go by. No mistakes can be made because every case means probably the happiness of a mother or wife at home, in some cases the death of one at home. Everything depends on the correctness of our work. It may be several months before we will be able to return to the States, every thing depends on the tracing or the "Sub-Paragraph" section. The sooner we clean up all these cases the sooner we go home.
> How are the "little folks"? I certainly do wish I could see them. I have not seen Capt. Beams since I left [Soings?]. I was told he was stationed here but upon arriving here found that he was not here. I suppose the

"flu" is just about extinguished over there now, is it not? [We?] write when you can.
Devotedly,

Ernest
Co. D, Hqrs. Battalion
APO 902 AEF France

I have not heard from you since leaving Saint-Florent[-sur-Cher] Nov 20th, 1918. I expect to receive a "bunch" of mail in the near future.

E

ANSE CARROLL KELLY, SAINT-DIZIER, FRANCE, TO FAMILY, JANUARY 8, 1919 (*HATTIESBURG AMERICAN*, FEBRUARY 11, 1919)

A native of Walnut Grove, Mississippi, Anse Carroll Kelly (1894–1981) was a motor car operator who enlisted in the Mississippi National Guard on May 7, 1917. He was discharged on July 7, 1919, and subsequently became a mechanic in Jackson and Hattiesburg. His brother, William Lacy Kelly (b. September 13, 1887), enlisted on August 11, 1917, and fought with Battery F, 319th Field Artillery, until he was wounded on October 22, 1918. He died at Walter Reed General Hospital in Washington, D.C., on July 23, 1919.

Dearest Mother, Sis and Dad:
I am back in Saint-Dizier again. I came in this morning. I was down to see Lacy last Sunday and Monday. He is getting along fine. His eyes are all right now, in fact, he can read now. His spirits are very high and there is no cause for worry on your part. His legs are nearly well and soon he will be back in the States. I wrote to you about him getting his legs crushed by the train. They were crushed on December 8, 1918, when the ambulance he was in was struck by a train and he was pinned underneath and both of his legs were crushed. Then he was taken on to the hospital where they were amputated. Before this accident occurred we received a letter from Lacy and he was feeling fine. This letter was dated December 6, before he was hurt. His wound across the eyes occurred in the fighting on two battlefronts, Saint-Mihiel and the Argonne Woods, and in his letter he asked me if I could come to see him, so I got permission to visit him. Lacy will be able to wear cork legs all right,

although both of his legs were taken off above the knees. The government will furnish the cork legs when he gets back to the States and he will not be turned loose until he can walk good with them. It is pretty tough, but it can't be helped. He is a lucky boy to be alive and well. The whole hospital is proud of him and all admire him for his pluck. He was given three transfusions of blood from comrades in the hospital before they operated on him, and they say this saved his life. I am proud of him, you bet. He is as game as they make them. His division has been decorated for bravery and efficiency in action. He'll come home a proud boy, so don't worry about him. The hospital is near Baume, France. The lieutenant doctor that operated on him is a fine doctor and his home is in Alabama, so you understand why he took such an interest in Lacy. The reason we were not notified was because he would not give them his address.

I will write you again in a few days.

Corporal Anse Kelly

ROBERT C. MOLISON, BASE HOSPITAL NO. 131, FRANCE, TO ROBBIE KITCHENS, JANUARY 18, 1919 (UNION COUNTY WORLD WAR I SCRAPBOOK, BOX 1)

Lewis Wesley Kitchens was born in New Albany, Mississippi, on April 29, 1887. After training in Memphis, Tennessee, at the Memphis Hospital Medical College and the College of Physicians and Surgeons, he became a doctor, practicing in New Albany and Strayhorn, Mississippi. He entered the service in April 1918 and went overseas in early October. He died of pneumonia on November 1, 1918, at a British hospital in Calais, France.

Dear Mrs. Kitchens:
I am just in receipt of your letter relative to the death of Lieut. L. W. Kitchens and will answer same at once. I had written you about two months ago about the death of my true friend, Lt. Kitchens, but surmise you had not yet received it at the time you wrote me. The mail service has been so slow and irregular that much of our mail has been lost. I will enclose a postal from Capt. Jackson. It shows the Chateau which the British had converted into a hospital. Just back of the Chateau is the little cemetery in which they laid the body of Lieut. Kitchens. I want to return through Cherloury and visit the grave of my friend whom I found at Jefferson Barracks last May. Much regret was expressed by

the officers of No. 131 when we learned of Lieut. Kitchens' death. He was a favorite with each one of us. I had much reason to cherish his friendship and helping hand, because of "my asthma" he would take my clothes roll together with his own and give me a chance to keep up with the rest. So much were we together they called us the 131 [twins]. I will always remember the modest unassuming officer from Mississippi and will ever regard his true friendship as one of the bright spots in my life's journey. Sometime ago I had written to the hospital authorities, but have not yet received my answer to my communication. One of the officers, "Capt. Bissel," who was in the hospital suffering from influenza when Lieut. Kitchens died, came on here about three weeks ago and since has been returned to the US to regain his health.

I am truly glad that you take the loss of your husband with such noble fortitude, and especially so because we had promised one to the other to visit the family which might be called upon to mourn, and I surely will come your way on my return. The sympathy of our unit was with you and the little babes in the hour of your grief and loss. I received your letter at mess this noon and many expressions of kind feeling toward you and the memory of Lieut. Kitchens.

I know from the talks which I often had with him it is as he wished you might do, should anything happen to him.

I wanted so much to stay with him, but our orders were imperative and I to leave him and go on to the front with my unit. Truly this terrible war has left many desolate homes and aching hearts which time alone can repair.

I will write you again on receiving answer from the hospital when I can go more into details relative to the matter as mentioned in your letter. Meanwhile, I wish again to carry to you my sincere sympathy and ask that you write me any time when I may be able to assist you in any manner whatever.

With best wishes, I beg to remain,
Your sincere friend,

Robert C. Molison
Capt. MCUS

LONNIE WILL LINCOLN, FRANCE, TO BERTON A. LINCOLN, N.D. (DAUGHTERS OF THE AMERICAN REVOLUTION, SHUK-HO-TA-TOM-A-HA CHAPTER, LOWNDES COUNTY WORLD WAR I SCRAPBOOK)

Lonnie Will Lincoln (1888–1977) was born in Columbus, Mississippi, and educated at Mississippi A & M (now Mississippi State University). He moved to St. Louis before the war and worked as a traveling shoe salesman before enlisting in the Mississippi National Guard and serving in the infantry. He later returned to St. Louis and resumed his sales career.

Mr. B. A. Lincoln, of this city [Columbus], is in receipt of the following letter from his brother, Lieut. Lonnie W. Lincoln, who was a member of the tank corps in France:

Have just gotten back from Xammes and will write you of my visit. I left Brest the night of the 8th and got to Thiaucourt the afternoon of the 10th. There are no railroads running through there now and I caught a truck out of Nancy part of the way and another truck the remainder. Xammes is only a mile and a half from Thiaucourt and I walked over there that afternoon.

I had no trouble in locating Atwell's grave and found it in excellent condition.[1] The little cemetery contains about forty American soldiers and is laid out in three rows and each numbered. Also on a lead plate on the head cross is the name, rank, and organization of each, also date of death.

As you no doubt know they are at present moving all bodies into three or four large cemeteries and the men killed in the Saint-Mihiel fighting are being put in the Saint-Mihiel Cemetery, which is on the hill just out of Thiaucourt and in sight [of] Xammes. This one will contain four thousand graves, is in the form of a square and in the center will be a flag pole with the American flag. The officers are being grouped around the center and all graves will be marked the same way; a large white cross at the head and standing about four feet high with the name, rank, organization and date of death plainly in black. It is right in the heart of all that fighting and it is fitting that these brave fellows should rest so near the place where they gave their lives.

The cemetery will be kept up by the national cemeteries in the States and consequently will receive the best of care and attention. The officer in charge of the work told me they would have it completed in about six weeks and that all the bodies would be moved from the cemetery in Xammes by that time.

I was unable to tell just which woods Atwell was killed in, but I walked over a great part of the field and went to Berry. Thiaucourt is in the valley, but Xammes and Berry are on the ridge which is broad, slightly rolling and very open. All the villages are in bad shape. A few civilians are returning and beginning to work the fields, but very few so far. They have no homes to go to. The country presents a very quiet and peaceful appearance now which made it all the more impressive as I stood and looked over the field after supper. The German dugouts, barbed wire and shell-wrecked villages show what they went through. The boche had line after line of entanglements but it did not do them much good when the Americans started.

The new cemetery is on the road between Thiaucourt and Berry and is probably five hundred yards from Thiaucourt. The largest of these is at Romains in the Argonne and will contain thirty thousand graves.

Returning I came through Saint-Mihiel and stopped off at Verdun. While I do not think there is a single house there that was not hit and plenty are completely wrecked, it is not the mass of ruins I expected to find. I went into the citadel, which is the underground place where the soldiers stayed, and which enabled the city to hold out as it did. It held twenty-five thousand troops and was completely equipped with quarters, kitchens, ammunition rooms, electric lights, etc. It was commenced in 1705, I was told.

I also went out to Fort Vaux, which, with Fort Douaument and two others were captured and held for four months by the Germans.

There are about thirteen forts around Verdun and they were connected with each other and the city by tunnels. They are anywhere from five to ten miles from the city and occupy commanding positions. I also went to Dead Man's Hill. All the country around there and the forts are now nothing but shell craters and the remains of trenches and dugouts. It is estimated that one million men were actually killed in the four years of fighting there, about six hundred thousand boche and four hundred thousand French.

All of the front is still strewn with the remnants of shells and equipment of both sides. I wanted to go by Reims, but did not have the time. I passed through Château-Thierry, but did not go there. There are practically no American troops anywhere along the old front now. They are gradually bringing them nearer the ports with the exception of the army of occupation.

1. Lonnie Will Lincoln's brother, Captain Atwell Lincoln (b. October 1877), was killed on September 27, 1918, while commanding a machine-gun company in the 354th Infantry during the St. Mihiel campaign. The brother to whom this letter was written, Berton A. Lincoln (1880–1940), also served in World War I.

HENRY FENNER KITCHENS, FRANCE, TO FAMILY, MAY 30, 1919 (UNION COUNTY WORLD WAR I SCRAPBOOK, BOX 1)

Dear Mamma and All:
I guess you would like to know what we did over here Decoration Day.[1]
First, we fixed the cemeteries up nice and decorated them with flags. I have some Kodak pictures of the performance.

The French [carillons?] led the parade, after the band, which was about fifty strong; then the little girls with flowers came, I suppose there must have been about a thousand, then the French Cavalry, all mounted on white horses with flags flying; the American Red Cross nurses came next, dressed in blue with black hats; then, the firing squad, the ones that shoot over the dead soldiers; I believe the troops came next, I would judge about twenty thousand. I never saw so many soldiers together before in my life. They were lined up outside the cemetery. My little bunch was lined up inside to wait on the Red Cross nurses, carry flowers for them, two truck loads of them that the Red Cross brought not counting what they brought in their hands, and what the French brought. The band played several nice pieces, the "Star Spangled Banner," etc., and we also had some nice speeches by some American officers.

When they got through with the performance at the American cemetery, they crossed over into the French cemetery and decorated their graves. I got through my part and got in ahead of the parade and came back to camp. I would have given anything to have gotten to go over in France where Wesley [Kitchens] was buried, for I am sure lots of pretty flowers were put on his grave.

Well, we are almost through with our work here. I don't know where we go from here, but we will leave sometime next week.

It is almost supper time, so guess I will go fall in the mess line and get a little "beans and beef stew." I am sure getting tired of the army cooking.

I bet the new road over there is looking fine.

I got Lucile's letter yesterday and was glad to hear from her. Write often.

Your son,

Sgt. H. Fenner Kitchens

1. Beginning in 1868, Decoration Day was celebrated each May to honor the US Civil War dead. After World War I, the holiday came to commemorate all of those killed in war, and it is now known as Memorial Day.

EPILOGUE

WORLD WAR I WAS UNLIKE ANY OTHER WAR, ERADICATING AN ENTIRE generation of European men and devastating the landscape of France and Belgium for decades to come. More than 4,000,000 American men served, and more than 100,000 of them died, including 704 from Mississippi. For European countries, the casualties were far greater. More than 8,000,000 men were killed, and countless others were injured, with many of them suffering physical and psychological wounds that plagued them for the rest of their lives.[1]

The war changed the map of Europe, as new nations emerged from the ruins. It also brought massive technological changes, particularly in the area of weaponry—the machine gun and the artillery shell, tanks, poison gas, and airplanes all entered world arsenals, enabling humans to kill each other faster and in greater numbers than ever before. The American Expeditionary Force was the first modern US Army, not only in terms of weapons but also in terms of the supply system. Most of the generals who oversaw the US conduct of the World War II cut their teeth in this earlier conflict.[2]

Medical advances sought to counteract some of the damage wrought by these military developments—for example, new techniques in plastic surgery helped thousands of disfigured soldiers, and the evolving field of psychology/psychiatry sought ways to combat shell shock, a term that originated during the war.[3]

In economic terms as well, World War I was horribly expensive. To help finance the war effort, the European Allies not only sold colonial landholdings but borrowed heavily, thereby stimulating the US economy, increasing employment, and bringing great profits to some individuals and companies. Wartime industrial growth changed the face of the American workforce, as labor shortages meant that both women and African Americans found employment in fields that had previously been closed to them. And at the end of the war, European economies were devastated, a situation that had consequences not only across the Atlantic, as the United States became the new world economic leader, but also across time, setting the stage for the rise of the German Nazi Party and ultimately World War II.[4]

Southerners who served in the armed forces found their horizons expanded, with new opportunities for education, health care, travel, and exposure to other cultures. Though most of the men and women whose letters are included here returned to their Mississippi hometowns, many other veterans, both black and white, migrated north and west in search of a better life. Thus, just as was the case across the globe, the war changed Mississippi forever.

NOTES

1. Smith, *Path of Fire*; Bailey, *American Pageant*, 745; *WWI Casualty and Death Tables*; *War to End Wars*, 135; Cox, *Mississippi Almanac*, 13.
2. *War to End Wars*, 54, 55–56; Stamps and Esposito, *Short Military History*, 340; Russ Stayanoff, "Major General Fox Conner: Soldier, Mentor, Enigma: Operations Chief (G-3) of the AEF," *Doughboy Center*.
3. Welsh, *USA in World War I*, 136.
4. "FC128: The Results of World War 1."

BIBLIOGRAPHY

COLLECTIONS AT THE MISSISSIPPI DEPARTMENT OF ARCHIVES AND HISTORY, JACKSON

Bernays, Mary, Photograph Collection—PI/WW/1981.0030
Bolivar County War Roster—Z/0207.000
Butler, William Ernest, and Family Papers—Z/2025.000
Camp Shelby Photograph Collection—PI/WW/1982.0088
Conner, Fox, Subject File
Cotton, Earl Douglas, Papers—Z/0389.000
Crawford, Walter Wesley, M.D., Papers—Z/2158.000
Daughters of the American Revolution, Belvidere Chapter (Greenville, Miss.), Washington County World War I Scrapbook—Z/1889.000 (microfilm roll 36580)
Daughters of the American Revolution, Shuk-Ho-Ta-Tom-A-Ha Chapter (Columbus, Miss.), Lowndes County World War I Scrapbook—Z/1887.000 (microfilm roll 36578)
Dickson, Harris, Papers—Z/0124.000
Dickson, Harris, Subject File
Ferrell Family Papers—Z/2268.000
Gill-Price Family Papers—Z/1758.000
Griffith, B. W., and Rondo A. Westbrook Papers—Z/1287.000
Heidelberg, Roger, Collection, Accretion—Z/1768.002
Holmes County War Roster—Z/0167.000
Howorth, Joseph Marion, Collection—Z/0957.000
Howry Family Papers—Z/1875.000
Lampton Family Papers—Z/1753.000
Lea Family World War I Letters—Z/2060.000
Mississippi, Governor, (1916–1920: Bilbo), World War I Correspondence and Papers, Series 878
Mississippi, State Board of Health, Death Certificates. Series 2144
Mississippi, Veterans Affairs Board, World War One Statement of Service Cards. Series 1731
Percy Family Papers—Z/0209.003
Percy, William Alexander, Subject File

Pullen-Carson Family Papers—Z/1431.000
Quekemeyer, John George, Papers, Accretion—Z/2148.000
Stubblefield, Bernard B., Papers—Z/1279.000
Union County (Miss.) World War I Scrapbook—Z/0172.000
US Selective Service System. *World War I Draft Registration Cards, 1917–1918: Mississippi.* Microfilm. Washington, DC: National Archives and Records Administration, 1990.
Vardaman, James K., Letters—Z/1798.000
Wall, J. Percy, Papers—Z/1272.000
Wall, James Percy, Subject File
Watt, J. H., Collection—Z/1483.000
Works Progress Administration, Historical Research Material: Adams County, Series 447, Box 10635
Works Progress Administration, Historical Research Material: Forrest County, Series 447, Box 10689
Works Progress Administration, Historical Research Material: Hancock County, Series 447, Box 10697
World War I Scrapbook—Z/1660.000
World War I Subject File
Wynn-Dockery Scrapbook—Z/0189.000 (microfilm roll 36001)

NEWSPAPERS

Bay St. Louis Sea Coast Echo
Columbus Dispatch
Greenville Daily Democrat-Times
Greenville Delta Democrat-Times
Greenville Weekly Democrat-Times
Hattiesburg American
Jackson Clarion-Ledger
Jackson Daily Clarion-Ledger
Meadville Franklin Advocate
Ocean Springs Jackson County Times
Natchez Democrat
New Albany Gazette
Pascagoula Democrat-Star
Pontotoc Progress
Pontotoc Sentinel
Woodville Wilk-Amite Record

PUBLISHED WORKS

American Expeditionary Force: Doughboys in World War I. http://www.usaww1.com/American-Expeditionary-Force/. Accessed November 29, 2014.

Americans at War in Foreign Forces. http://www.americansatwarinforeignforces.com/canadian-expeditionary-forces--american-legion.html. Accessed November 29, 2014.

"Appendix: Report of the Publicity Director War Relief Service Committee of the National Society of the Daughters of the American Revolution to the Twenty-Eighth Continental Congress, April 14–19, 1919." In *Twenty-Second Report of the National Society of the Daughters of the American Revolution, March 1, 1918, to March 1, 1919*, 151–61. Washington, DC: US Government Printing Office, 1921.

Babb, Sara M. F. "Washerwomen: Greenville, S.C., Sets a Pace for Others to Follow on the Sanitation Highway, and Is Conserving Health and Life." *Red Cross Magazine* 10, no. 2 (February 1915): 88–92.

Bailey, Thomas A. *The American Pageant: A History of the Republic.* Boston: Heath, 1961.

"Balloon in War Does Great Work." *Ocean Springs Jackson County Times*, September 21, 1918, 3.

Banks, Raymond H. *Births 1872–1900 of Men with Ties to Mississippi as Found in the Civilian Registration Cards.* Salt Lake City: Banks, 2000.

Battles: The Battle of Belleau Wood, 1918. http://www.firstworldwar.com/battles/belleau.htm. Accessed January 1, 2015.

Battles: The Second Battle of the Marne, 1918. http://www.firstworldwar.com/battles/marne2.htm. Accessed January 1, 2015.

Biennial Report of the Adjutant General of the State of Mississippi for the Years 1918–1919. Jackson, Miss.: Tucker, 1919.

Biggs, Donald F. "Review of the World War and Other History Making Events of 1917." *Pontotoc Sentinel*, January 10, 1918, 3.

Brown, Charles H. "Fox Conner: A General's General." *Journal of Mississippi History* 49 (August 1987): 203–16.

Brown, Charles H., and John Ray Skates. "Fox Conner: A General's General." *Mississippi History Now*, June 2010. http://mshistorynow.mdah.state.ms.us/articles/346/fox-conner-a-general-s-general. Accessed December 1, 2014.

Bryan, Jami. *Fighting for Respect: African-American Soldiers in WWI.* http://www.militaryhistoryonline.com/wwi/articles/fightingforrespect.aspx. Accessed November 29, 2014.

Busbee, Westley F. *Mississippi: a History.* Wheeling, Ill.: Harlan Davidson, 2005.

Carroll, Andrew. *War Letters: Extraordinary Correspondence from American Wars.* New York: Simon and Schuster, 2008.

Cox, James L. *Mississippi Almanac: The Ultimate Reference on the State of Mississippi.* Yazoo City, Miss.: Computer Search and Research, 1997.

Daughters of the American Revolution. Ish-te-ho-to-pah Chapter. *Cemeteries of Union County, Mississippi.* New Albany, Miss.: Ish-te-ho-to-pah Chapter, DAR, 1980.

Dictionary of American Naval Fighting Ships. Vols. 1, 6, 7. Washington, DC: Naval History Division, Department of the Navy, 1959–81.

The Doughboy Center: The Story of the American Expeditionary Forces. http://www.worldwar1.com/dbc/dbc2.htm. Accessed November 29, 2014.

"Edward Hines, Jr." *Edward Hines, Jr. VA Hospital.* http://www.hines.va.gov/about/about_hines.asp. Accessed December 7, 2014.

Eisenhower, John S. D. *Yanks: The Epic Story of the American Army in World War I*. New York: Free Press, 2001.

Everman, Grace G., and Lavinia D. Fort. *History of St. James' Church*. Greenville, Miss.: Office Supply, 1946.

"FC128: The Results of World War 1." *The Flow of History*. www.flowofhistory.com/units/etc/19/FC128. Accessed November 29, 2014.

Fickle, James E. *Mississippi Forests and Forestry*. Jackson: University Press of Mississippi, 2001.

Hallas, James H., ed. *Doughboy War: The American Expeditionary Force in World War I*. Boulder, Colo.: Rienner, 2000.

Hirrel, Leo P. *The Beginnings of the Quartermaster Graves Registration Service*. http://www.army.mil/article/128693/The_beginnings_of_the_Quartermaster_Graves_Registration_Service/. Accessed November 29, 2014.

Historical Catalogue of the University of Mississippi, 1849-1909. Nashville: Marshall and Bruce, 1910.

Horne, Charles F., ed. *Source Records of the Great War*. Vol. 5. Indianapolis: American Legion, 1931.

The Influenza Pandemic of 1918. https://virus.stanford.edu/uda/. Accessed December 28, 2014.

Journal of the House of Representatives of the State of Mississippi at an Extraordinary Session Thereof in the City of Jackson, Commencing Tuesday, September 25, 1917 Ending Friday October 12, 1917. Jackson, Miss.: Tucker, 1917.

Keegan, John. *The First World War*. New York: Knopf, 1999.

McLemore, Richard Aubrey, ed. *History of Mississippi*. Hattiesburg: University and College Press of Mississippi, 1973.

Mead, Gary. *The Doughboys: America and the First World War*. New York: Overlook, 2000.

Mitchell, William. *Memoirs of World War I: "From Start to Finish of Our Greatest War."* 1922; New York: Random House, 1960.

Morrisey, Carla R. *The Influenza Epidemic*. http://www.history.navy.mil/library/online/influenza%20epid%201918.htm. Accessed November 29, 2014.

Morton, Kate. *House of Riverton*. New York: Atria, 2008.

Nicholson, Christopher. "To Advance a Race: A Historical Analysis of the Intersection of Personal Belief, Industrial Philanthropy and Black Liberal Arts Higher Education in Fayette McKenzie's Presidency at Fisk University, 1915-1925." Ph.D. diss., Loyola University Chicago, 2011.

"Nursing News and Announcements." *American Journal of Nursing*, February 1, 1918, 416-34.

Ocean Springs Genealogical Society. *Surnames from Biloxi, Mississippi Newspapers: 1920-1960*. Ocean Springs, Miss.: Ocean Springs Genealogical Society, 1994.

Payne, Caledonia Jackson, comp. *Old Greenville Cemetery, 1880-1982*. Leland, Miss.: Payne, 1983.

Percy, William Alexander. *Lanterns on the Levee: Recollections of a Planter's Son*. New York: Knopf, 1941.

Pontotoc County Historical Society. *Cemeteries of Pontotoc County, Mississippi.* Jackson, Miss.: Express, 1999.
"*Requiem*": *Jackson County Cemetery Records.* 3 vols. Pascagoula, Miss.: Jackson County Genealogical Society, n.d.
Rowland, Dunbar. *Mississippi: Comprising Sketches of Counties, Towns, Events, Institutions, and Persons, Arranged in Cyclopedic Form.* Vol. 3. Atlanta: Southern Historical, 1907.
Smith, Thomas. *Path of Fire: The Meuse-Argonne Offensive of 1918.* www.firstworldwar.com/features/pathoffire.htm. Accessed November 29, 2014.
La Société des Quarante Hommes et Huit Chevaux, Palmetto Grand Voiture du South Carolina. *Merci Box Car Memorial Book.* 2nd ed. Lamar, SC: La Société, 1984.
South Mississippi Genealogical Society. *Forrest County, Mississippi Tombstone Inscriptions.* Hattiesburg: South Mississippi Genealogical Society, 1986.
Stamps, T. Dodson, and Vincent J. Esposito, eds. *A Short Military History of World War I.* West Point, N.Y.: US Military Academy, 1954.
Stokesbury, James L. *A Short History of World War I.* New York: Morrow, 1981.
"Story of War Is Told by Pershing," *Meadville Franklin Advocate,* December 12, 1918, 2.
Sullivan, Charles L., and Bourbon Hughes, comp. *Valor Remembered: War Dead of the State of Mississippi.* Perkinston: Mississippi Gulf Coast Community College Press, 1996.
Teaching with Documents: The Zimmermann Telegram. http://www.archives.gov/education/lessons/zimmermann/. Accessed December 1, 2014.
This Fabulous Century: Sixty Years of American Life. Vol. 11, 1910–1920. New York: Time-Life Books, 1969.
Thoumin, Richard. *The First World War.* New York: Putnam's, 1963.
Toland, John. *No Man's Land: 1918—The Last Year of the Great War.* Garden City, NY: Doubleday, 1980.
"Transporting the Troops." *Letters Home from the War.* http://www.u.arizona.edu/~rstaley/wwessay.htm#Transport. Accessed November 20, 2014.
"A Tribute to Caro Blymyer Dawes." *Evanston Women's History Project.* May 29, 2013. http://evanstonwomen.org/2013/05/29/a-tribute-to-caro-blymyer-dawes/. Accessed December 7, 2014.
Tuchman, Barbara. *The Guns of August.* New York: Macmillan, 1962.
US Adjutant General's Office. *Congressional Medal of Honor, the Distinguished Service Cross, and the Distinguished Service Medal Issued by the War Department.* Washington, DC: US Government Printing Office, 1920.
The War to End Wars, 1914–1918. Pleasantville, NY: Reader's Digest Association, 2000.
Welsh, Douglas. *The USA in World War I.* New York: Galahad, 1982.
Wentworth, Harold, and Stuart Berg Flexner. *Dictionary of American Slang.* 2nd supp. ed. New York: Crowell, 1975.
Who Declared War and When. http://www.firstworldwar.com/features/declarationsofwar.htm. Accessed November 29, 2014.
William Sharp on the German Retreat. http://firstworldwar.com/source/hline_sharp.htm. Accessed November 29, 2014.

World War I: Sep 12, 1918: U.S. Launches Saint-Mihiel Offensive. http://www.history.com/this-day-in-history/us-launches-saint-mihiel-offensive. Accessed December 28, 2014.

WWI Casualty and Death Tables. http://www.pbs.org/greatwar/resources/casdeath_pop.html. Accessed December 29, 2014.

"YMCA with the A.E.F." *Letters Home from the War.* http://www.u.arizona.edu/~rstaley/wwessay.htm#YMCA. Accessed November 29, 2014.

INDEX

Page numbers in *italics* indicate an illustration.

African Americans, 8, 21–22, 88, 152, 168, 197–98. *See also* Brister, Harrison; Lee, Jesse J.; Pickett, Andrew M.; Roberts, Henry
Air warfare, 7, 126–29, 134, 136, 149–50, 154–56, 179, 182; balloons, 136, 182–83, 191–92; training, 18, 19n, 20, 161–62
American Expeditionary Force (AEF), 7, 98, 144–45, 176, 178, 198, 203; artillery, 79, 135, 143, 148–49, 172–73, 188; cemeteries, 213, 215–17; education, 27, 68, 85; engineers, 14–15, 94–95, 175, 200, 202; food, 26, 64, 82–83, 85, 111, 174, 178, 187, 189–90, 200, 218; parades, 15, 165, 195, 217; quarters, 80, 82, 85, 112, 185, 189, 194, 201, 207; training, 8, 14, 15, 32, 42, 46, 48–49, 63, 83–84, 97, 198; uniforms, 23, 27, 176. *See also specific camp names*
American Red Cross, 17, 25n, 30, 56, 58, 61, 84, 86, 96, 103, 134, 139–40, 151, 154–55, 158–59, 171, 196–97, 217
Ames, Theodore J., 45
Amiens, 78n
Anderson, Sarah Catherine, 56
Antigone, 110
Armstrong, David, 88
Arnold, Seguine Allen (Beppo), 80, 132
Ashland, Mississippi, 31
Ashmore, Victor Sylvester, 38, 39, 99, 162

Babb, Sara M., 61, 104
Bailey, Benjamin M., 89
Ballard, Russell, 27
Baltic, 6
Barbed wire, 4
Bass, Roscoe, 138
Bay St. Louis, Mississippi, 17, 32, 36, 41, 137, 163, 193
Belleau Woods, 130, 138, 159
Big Berthas, 117, 155
Bilbo, Governor Theodore, 22, 48
Biloxi, Mississippi, 152
Boes, John Morris, 110
Bontemps, Clement, 37, 37n
Brandon, Mississippi, 18
Brevard, Jean, 52
Brister, Harrison, 120
Britain: description of towns, 100, 108, 165; monetary rate, 100; people, 100, 108–9, 165–66; transportation, 112, 164–65
British Expeditionary Forces: artillery, 69, 72–73; medical facilities, 72–76, 86; race relations, 77; training, 32, 69, 72–75
Buck, William J., 11, 22
Butler, William Ernest, 211

Caledonia, Mississippi, 139
Camp Beauregard, Louisiana, 30, 38, 41, 48–49, 56, 160

Camp Funston, Kansas, 22, 24
Camp Hill, Virginia, 65
Camp Pike, Arkansas, 25–26, 158, 163
Camp Shelby, Mississippi, 32, 35, 57, 63, 64, 187, 194; construction of, 33–34, 36
Camp Stewart, Texas, 14
Camp Wheeler, Georgia, 45
Canadian Expeditionary Forces, 12–13, 122–25, 130–33
Cantigny, 120, 127
Canton, Mississippi, 142
Capdepon, Henry Paul, 36
Carr, Richard Thorp, 101
Castle, W. R., 196
Casualties, 6, 102, 138–41, 146–47, 150–51, 163, 167–68, 188, 205–6, 211–13
Catholic sisters, 61–62
Cavett, Van Andrew, 208
Central Powers, 3, 81
Chamberlain, Lucy, 58
Chapple, Joe Mitchell, 197
Chateau-Thierry, 130, 133, 138, 148–51
Clark, Reuben T., 102
Cleveland, Mississippi, 106
Coahoma, Mississippi, 208
Collins, Mississippi, 138
Columbus, Mississippi, 22, 65, 95, 135, 169, 215
Conner, Lieutenant Colonel Fox, 6–7, 167
Convoy system, 51–52, 99, 101, 110, 115, 209
Cook, Inman, 180, 189
Cooper, Chris H., 18
Cooper, Ellis Bowman, 201
Costley, L., 67
Cotton, Earl Douglas, 20, 43, 210

Daughters of the American Revolution, Belvidere Chapter, 85
Davidson, Philip G., 90, 117
Decoration Day, 217, 218n
DeKay, Robert H., 54
Dickson, Harris, 121, 197
Dillard, Earl, 64
Diseases. *See* Medical care

Dove, Walter Earl, 128, 129, 161
Draft boards, 8, 22
Draft quotas, 22

East Indian soldiers, 77

Ferrell, William Maury, 31
Fitz-Hugh, William Henry, 25
Florida, 209
Foch, Marshal Ferdinand, 11, 205
Foote, Thomas, 107
Ford, Willis K., 141
Fort Logan H. Roots, Arkansas, 125n, 135, 163, 179, 189
Fort Monroe, Virginia, 66
Fountain, J. Q., 17
France: devastation of, 5–6, 71, 126, 135, 153, 157, 159, 174, 181, 183–85, 199–200, 202, 216; houses/hotels, 86, 93, 154, 189–90, 199; monetary exchange, 81–82, 103–4, 195; people, 86, 93, 95, 112, 123, 129, 145, 154–57, 189–90, 200; transportation, 112–13, 113n, 170, 189–90

Garcia, William Rodger, 137
Gas warfare: attacks, 13n, 138, 142–43, 156, 178; equipment, 12, 32; training, 12, 32, 79
Gaynor (last name unknown), 172
George, J. W., 11
German: air warfare, 72, 76, 127–29, 134, 156, 182, 191–92; artillery, 73, 78n, 117, 124–25, 125n, 136, 143, 149, 155, 163, 172, 182, 188; naval fleet, 4, 122, 208; ships seized, 110, 115; strategy, 8
Goolsby, Henry J., 93
Graves Registration Service, 167–68, 215–16
Greenville, Mississippi, 25, 56, 58, 61, 69, 80, 85, 88, 90, 97, 104, 106, 117, 122, 130, 142, 148, 152, 174, 184, 205, 211
Gurd, George E., 12

Haig, Field Marshal Douglas, 70
Hall, Casey, 26
Hamburg, Mississippi, 128

INDEX

Hancock, 53
Harrison, Bryon Patton, 160n, 165
Hattiesburg, Mississippi, 32, 107, 137, 141, 158, 179, 187, 189, 201, 212
Hesperian, 12
Hines, Edward, 81
Hodges, Major General H. C., 48
Holbrook, Colonel L. R., 121
Holloway, Leo, 181
Home front activities, 16–18, 29–30, 45n, 48, 66, 85, 89–90, 109, 121, 145, 165, 166n3

Insurance, 50, 87

Jackson, Mississippi, 20, 25, 70, 102, 122, 148, 187, 201, 208, 210, 212
Jackson, Waldo Emerson, 187
Jamestown, Virginia, 114
Jayne, Lowry, 57

Kaye, Sam, 96, 135–36, *136*
Kelly, Anse Carroll, 212
Kelly, William Lacy, 212–13
Kelly Field, Texas, 18–19
Kentucky, 114
Kiln, Mississippi, 41
Kinberger (first name unknown), 21
Kitchens, Henry Fenner, 167, 217
Kitchens, Lewis Wesley, 213–14, 217
Kittermaster, Dougal, 12
Kossuth, Mississippi, 38

LaFollette, Senator Robert, 98n
Laurel, Mississippi, 201
Lea, Luke, 177, 179n1
Lee, A. E., 45, 110
Lee, Jesse J., 88
Leppert, W. J., 17
Lincoln, Atwell, 215, 217n
Lincoln, Lonnie Will, 215
Louisville, Mississippi, 93
Lusitania, 4
Lusk, James Gervys, 69, 150, 205, 208n

Mail/censorship, 65, 83, 104, 107, 128, 132, 168, 172, 193–94, *194*
Marne, Second Battle (1918), 138–43, 146–47, 151–52, 160–61, 163, 172–73
Marshall, Captain George C., 167
Mauldings, 101
McArthur, Colonel Douglas, 167
McCann, Thomas Gladney, 169
McCearley, John Brevard, 185
McCutcheon, Joe, 27
McWhirter, Robert Jeff, 63
Meadville, Mississippi, 51, 67, 120, 128, 161
Medical care, 26, 31, 33, 96; equipment, 25, 203; hospitals, 12, 72–73, 86, 96, 147, 155, 157, 213; influenza, 162, 162n, 171, 196, 209; quarantine, 26, 41, 168, 209
Metcalf, Mrs., 85
Meuse-Argonne offensive, 167, 182, 216
Mexico, 4–5
Military bands, 45–47, 217
Mitchell, Herron, 55
Mitchell Field, Texas, 135
Molison, Robert C., 213
Monkey meat, 149, 150n
Motano, 79
Mount, Emanuel Brandon, 106
Moyse, Herman, 146
Myrtle, Mississippi, 181

Nance, Aderton and Margaret, 88
Natchez, Mississippi, 28, 30, 49, 52, 90, 102, 111, 126, 140, 146, 172, 183, 185, 191, 196, 199
National army, 23, 24n
Nebraska, 53
New Albany, Mississippi, 61, 113, 160, 167, 181, 213
Nicaise, William Randolph, 41
No Man's Land, 124–25, 131, 134, 161, 173, 181, 184, 188
Norfolk Training Station, Virginia, 40, 113–15
Nurses, 102, 147, 217; drills, 59–62; quarters, 58–59, 104–5; singing, 59–61; uniforms, 56, 59

Ocean Springs, Mississippi, 45, 92, 110
Odeneal, Erskine Patrick, 152
Orion, 52
Osoinach, Clarence Wych, 163, 193

Paris, France, 103–4, 117, 130, 205–6
Parris Island, South Carolina, 36, 54
Pascagoula, Mississippi, 79
Patton, Captain George, 167
Pennsylvania, 79
Percy, Senator Leroy, 92, 174, 184
Percy, William Alexander, 97, 174, 184, 208n
Perrie, Frederick W., 28
Pershing, Major General John J., 6–7, 7, 79, 93, 117, 127, 167, 192n
Pickett, Andrew M., 67
Pontotoc, Mississippi, 14, 23, 26, 38, 40, 54, 63, 93, 99, 101, 133, 160
Powers, Lieutenant Commander K. J., 210
President Lincoln, 110, 111n, 115
Price, Frank R., 14, 23
Price, Ralph, 19
Prisoners: German, 152, 155, 168, 182, 200; US, 38–39, 48–49

Queen Elizabeth, 208
Quisenberry, George, 126, 183, 191–92n, 199

Randle, J. R., 22
Recreation, 18, 46, 63–66, 68, 85–87, 106–7, 110, 130–31, 190, 193–94, 199
Religious opportunities, 19, 30, 77, 84, 90, 172
Remondet, Herbert J., 49
Roberts, Henry, 158
Robison, Dalton C., 160
Rosedale, Mississippi, 158
Rosenberger, Robert E., 32
Royal Oak, 208
Rupp, Robert Walter, 92

Saint-Mihiel, 167, 172, 182, 188, 215
Schweizer, Carl Walz, 85

Scott, Alexander Yerger, 158
Seale, James H., 51
Seale, Mitchell J., 133
Selective Service Act, 7–8, 21, 166n2
Services of Supply (SOS), 117–18, 200
Sharp, Ambassador William, 5
Sioux, 43, 210
Slackers, 11, 50
Sledge, Mississippi, 208
Smith, L. Pink, 90
Soissons, 141, 149
Songs/singing, 10, 16, 18–19, 59–61, 64, 67–68, 85, 137, 171n, 206
Spivey, Reginald Edgar, 142
Springfield, Mississippi, 63
Statistics, 8, 22, 138, 162n, 206, 216, 219
Sterzenback, August, 111
Stevens, W. R. Barksdale, 179
Stewart, Nolan, 25
Strauss, William S., 65
Submarine warfare, 4–6, 53, 92–93, 110, 115–16, 195
Sudduth, Henry Perry, 40
Summers, Frank L., 158
Surrender: land forces, 205–6; naval, 208–9
Susquehanna, 115

Tinnin, Finley Watson, 30
Torjusen, Cornelius O., 79
Trench warfare, 37, 69–70, 74–75, 126, 134, 173, 176–77, 207–8
Troop transport, 21–22, 51–52, 99, 101–2, 106–8, 110, 115, 120, 158, 164, 169–70, 194, 200
Tylertown, Mississippi, 120

U-boats. *See* Submarine warfare
US Congress: declaration of war, 6; Selective Service Act, 7
US Marine Corps, 36, 138; training, 37, 54–55
US Naval Reserve Force, 54n

US Navy, 7, 209; burial at sea, 107; casualties, 210; coal transport, 44, 52–53; food, 21, 41, 43, 45; rescue efforts, 28–29; supplies, 40, 43–45, 53, 114; training, 21, 40–41, 114–15; warfare, 20, 209

Vacuum, 6
Vardaman, Senator James K., 98n, 160n, 165
Venn, Emma Eugenia, 196, *197*
Verdun, 216
Vicksburg, Mississippi, 121, 158
Vulcan, 28

Wall, James Percy, 70, 86
Walnut Grove, Mississippi, 212
Waters, James Earl, 95
Waveland, Mississippi, 33
Weather, 27, 29, 34–35, 64, 94, 114, 164, 183

Wells, Preston, 27
Wensel, Theodore, 196
Weyman, Herbert L., 139
White, J. D., 140
Whiz bang, 124, 131, 136
Wiley, Hugh A., 148
Wilhelm, Crown Prince, 204
Wilson, President Woodrow, 4–6, 45n
Wolfson, Philip, 26
Women: role of, 103, 108–9, 156, 166, 168
Wood, William Henry, 113
Woods, Morse, 64
Wynn, Thaddeus Kinman, 122, 130
Wynn, William T., 123, 125n

YMCA, 30, 35, 66, 85, 91–92, 102–3, 118

Zimmerman note. *See* Mexico

www.ingramcontent.com/pod-product-compliance
Lightning Source LLC
Chambersburg PA
CBHW030619230426
43661CB00053B/2069